Shakespeare and the
Grammar of Forgiveness

Shakespeare and the Grammar of Forgiveness

Sarah Beckwith

Cornell University Press

Ithaca and London

First published 2011 by Cornell University Press
First printing, Cornell Paperbacks, 2012

Library of Congress Cataloging-in-Publication Data

Beckwith, Sarah, 1959–
    Shakespeare and the grammar of forgiveness / Sarah Beckwith.
        p. cm.
    Includes bibliographical references and index.
    ISBN 978-0-8014-4978-9 (cloth : alk. paper)
    ISBN 978-0-8014-7835-2 (paper : alk. paper)
  1. Shakespeare, William, 1564–1616 —Tragicomedies. 2. Forgiveness
in literature. 3. Penance in literature. I. Title.
    PR2981.5.B43 2011
    822.3'3—dc22   2010047912

Cornell University Press strives to use environmentally responsible
suppliers and materials to the fullest extent possible in the publishing of
its books. Such materials include vegetable-based, low-VOC inks and
acid-free papers that are recycled, totally chlorine-free, or partly composed
of nonwood fibers. For further information, visit our website at www.
cornellpress.cornell.edu.

For Bart

There is a saying that to understand is to forgive but that is an error, so Papa used to say. You must forgive in order to understand. Until you forgive you defend yourself against the possibility of understanding. Her father had said this more than once, in sermons, with appropriate texts, but the real text was Jack, and those to whom he spoke were himself and the row of Boughtons in the front pew, and then, of course, the congregation. If you forgive, he would say, you may indeed not understand, but you will be ready to understand, and that is the posture of grace.

Marilynne Robinson, Home

Contents

ACKNOWLEDGMENTS

I would like to thank the actors and performers who have lent their bodies, souls, and minds to Shakespeare's figures in the complex forms of the late romances I have seen while I was writing this book. Their readings and sense of accountability charted subtle and haunting paths into these rich and difficult plays. I thank my new friends and colleagues in theater studies whose dedication to theater is inspiring and humbling.

Richard Fleming in his magical seminar on Wittgenstein's *Philosophical Investigations,* and Nancy Bauer, Tim Gould, and Sandra Laugier helped me to richer understandings of the work of J. L. Austin, Ludwig Wittgenstein, and Stanley Cavell, in their visits to the Ordinary Language Philosophy Working Group I convened at Duke with Toril Moi in 2007–2009.

An early version of chapter 3 appeared as "Medieval Penance, Reformation Repentance and *Measure for Measure*" in *Reading the Medieval in Early Modern England,* edited by Gordon McMullan and David Matthews (Cambridge: Cambridge University Press, 2007), 193–204, and is reprinted with permission from Cambridge University Press. Chapter 6 appeared as

"Shakespeare's Resurrections" in *Shakespeare and the Middle Ages,* edited by Curtis Perry and John Watkins (Oxford: Oxford University Press, 2009), 45–67, and is reprinted by kind permission of Oxford University Press.

I would like to thank David Aers, Toril Moi, Marianne Novy, Miri Rubin, Stanley Hauerwas, and two anonymous readers for their invaluable reading of the entire manuscript. Thanks also to Heather Hirschfeld, Jim Knowles, Julie Paulson, Beth Robertson, and James Simpson for reading sections of the manuscript, to Will Revere for indispensable help with the bibliography, and to Sarah McLaughlin for help at the copyediting stage. David Aers has read every chapter in progress and spent many hours in true generosity reading and sharing ideas with me over the years of our friendship, for which I am deeply grateful. Toril Moi has also been a constant companion in conversation as we evolved our books on Ibsen and Shakespeare whose work we love, and explored the extraordinary resources of Stanley Cavell's astonishingly deep and suggestive writings. Stanley Cavell's thinking is all-pervasive in this book, especially his work in *The Claim of Reason, Must We Mean What We Say?* and *A Pitch of Philosophy.* With his excellent ear and incredible generosity, he also whispered crucial words of encouragement along the way for which I cannot thank him enough.

Several friends and colleagues helped the work along by inviting me to participate in conferences, give talks, share Shakespeare, and test out my ideas in front of different audiences. Thanks to Larry Rhu at the University of South Carolina, Ralph Berry at Florida State University, Toril Moi at Duke, Chris Chism at Rutgers, James Simpson and Christina Wald at Harvard, Dale Martin at Yale, Ken Graham at the University of Waterloo, Jim Rhodes at Southern Connecticut State University, my hosts at the University of Chicago where I gave the Yves Simon lecture, Clare Lees and Gordon McMullan at King's College London, Ryan McDermott and Elizabeth Fowler at the University of Virginia, Jennifer Wald and Mike Witmore at the University of Pittsburgh, Mike Witmore and Will West at Northwestern, and Lincoln Faller, Mike Schoenfeldt, Julia Hell, Cathy Sanok, and Karla Taylor at the University of Michigan in Ann Arbor.

My thanks also go to Danny Herwitz and my lively, fascinating colleagues at the Institute for the Humanities at the University of Michigan where I held the Nicholas Frehling fellowship in the spring of 2005. Thanks to Regina Schwartz, John Watkins, Heather Hirschfeld, and

Elizabeth Fowler for providing the occasion for stimulating sessions at the Shakespeare Association of America and the Renaissance Society of America, where I tried out some thoughts in this book.

I also want to thank the chairs of the English department at Duke University, Maureen Quilligan and Ian Baucom, for support during the time I wrote this book, particularly Maureen, who has always taken the most (characteristically) generous and encouraging attitude to my Shakespearean explorations, even when she thought I might be doing better things with my time. Thanks also to deans William Chafe and George McLendon, who allowed me leave to draft and complete this book. I thank the wise and intuitive Peter Potter at Cornell University Press for helping this manuscript reach its audience, and to Kay Scheuer, Kate Mertes, and Candace Akins for their efficiency, kindness, and skillfulness.

I still hope that one day I will write a book that my family will enjoy reading. I may not have done so here, but I thank them all for their loving interest and for being the fascinating, strong people they are. To Simon and Val: I wish you more pleasure and joy as you finish the Shakespeare marathon, whenever that might be.

I dedicate this book in love and friendship to my amazing husband, Bart Ehrman. The Ehrman universe is a world of extraordinary focus and intensity, and quite alarming productivity. But in this world he still found the time to listen to my intuitions until they became thoughts, and then he read every page I wrote with his wonderful blend of precision and common sense. Though he has sworn off any more performances of *Othello,* I am grateful to him for his companionship at the many plays we have seen together. It is true that he has seen more Shakespeare than I have seen football games. This lack of reciprocity in our marriage is unlikely to be rectified. I offer to him the words of Montaigne to his friend La Boétie: "If you press me to tell why I love(d) him, I feel that it cannot be expressed, except by answering: Because it was he, because it was I."

Abbreviations

The following abbreviations occur throughout the book.

EETS   *Early English Text Society.* Oxford University Press.

LW   *Luther's Works*, ed. Harold J. Grimm. General editors, Jaroslav Pelikan and Helmut T. Lehman. 55 vols. Philadelphia: Muehlenberg and Fortress, and St. Louis: Concordia, 1955–1986.

MED   *Middle English Dictionary,* ed. Hans Kurath. Ann Arbor: University of Michigan Press, 1953–2001.

OED   *The Oxford English Dictionary,* 2nd ed. Oxford University Press, 1989, and updates.

ST   *Summa Theologica.* Complete English edition. 5 vols. Trans. and ed. the English Dominican Province. Notre Dame, IN: Ave Maria Press, 1984.

Unless otherwise noted, all Shakespeare quotations are from *The Riverside Shakespeare,* 2nd ed., ed. G. Blakemore Evans. Boston: Houghton Mifflin, 1997.

In Middle English quotations the thorn has been modernized to *th*.

Shakespeare and the Grammar of Forgiveness

Introduction

PROMISING, FORGIVING

Grammar tells us what kind of object anything is.
LUDWIG WITTGENSTEIN, *Philosophical Investigations*

This is a book about the grammar of forgiveness in Shakespeare's late, post-tragic plays, *Pericles, Cymbeline, The Winter's Tale,* and *The Tempest.* In it I explore the conditions of possibility of this grammar, its historical contours in the abandoned sacrament of penance, and the changes to it entailed in the revolution of ritual theory and practice we know as the English Reformation. I draw out the implications and consequences of this grammar in the new post-tragic forms of theater that Shakespeare develops in these astonishing experimental plays.

Each of these plays ends with a public spectacle, event, or ceremony, one in which private fantasy, isolation, grief, self-immolation, or despair is overcome, and the protagonists return to what is common and shared as the ground of their relations and as a place where their expressions of themselves can have a local habitation and a name. They heal the terrible, world- and soul-destroying split between a self that "passeth show" and a face and body that can only betray a mind too lonely and inaccessible to be expressed. In this way the plays pioneer a theater of embodiment; they return the protagonists to themselves and to each other all at once. They affirm the priority of peace before violence, of the social before the individual, of trust before doubt. But they do this after the tragedies, which have diagnosed the relentless costs of imagining that language can be a private property of the mind. The protagonists of those plays define a world from their single perspective—and lose it and everyone they love.

Hannah Arendt has said: "without being forgiven, released from the consequences of what we have done, our capacity to act would, as it were, be confined to one single deed from which we would never recover."[1] Shakespearean tragedy is a world without such possibilities, where its central protagonists are utterly exposed to the consequences of their own passions and actions. Forgiving holds out the possibility of redemption from the predicament of irreversibility.[2] That is why in the creation of a post-tragic theater Shakespeare turns with a renewed intensity to the structures, histories, and practices of penitence and repentance, and their available languages, languages of forgiveness and acknowledgment. To this extent *Pericles, Cymbeline, The Winter's Tale,* and *The Tempest* are all reworkings of *King Lear.*[3]

The medieval home of the language of acknowledgment is the sacrament of penance, and the earliest usages of the word "acknowe" are intimately bound up with the histories of this sacrament, especially in the act of confession. (The first definition given for confession in the *OED* is "to acknowledge"; the second "to make oneself known.") What acknowledgment comes to be in the late plays is bound up with the investigation there of the languages of penitence. The late romances explore the vulnerabilities, exposures, and commitments of forgiving and being forgiven in new forms of theater charged with finding the pathways and possibilities of forgiveness in the absence of auricular confession and priestly absolution. For just over three hundred years the language of forgiveness had been adjudicated by priests in the cure of souls and linked to a compulsory annual confession to a local parish priest at Easter. Forgiveness was declared on God's behalf by his authorized officers. The priest's absolution declared the sinner relieved of the *"culpa"* and the *"poena"* of sin.[4] But the reformations in Europe began, almost accidentally, as David Steinmetz suggests, as a debate about the word for "penitence."[5] Penance was to be not so much a set of actions (the *agite poenitentiam* of the Vulgate) but repentance, translating *metanoia,* the turning or returning of the whole mind and soul and life to God. "There is therefore, none other use of these outward ceremonies, but *as far forth as we are stirred up by them,* and (they) do serve the glory of God" (my italics), says the Elizabethan homily on "Repentance and True Reconciliation unto God."[6] All life, says, Luther, is a baptism declaring that we are not initiated once and for all but rather that we are always beginning.[7] What ensued was not the tidy replacement of one doctrine or practice by another, but a long conversation and conflict about the conventions of forgiveness. This book traces the fortunes of the component parts of the sacrament of penance—contrition, confession, and absolution in the Church of England's liturgy and theology (Catholic and Reformed), and in Shakespeare's late plays.

In Shakespeare's theater there are almost countless instances of the word "confession" and its cognates, yet only three instances in the entire corpus of the word "absolution," even though both terms were once an intrinsic part of the sacrament of penance. Consider some of the following uses of "confession":

> "Dear daughter, I confess that I am old" (Lear to Regan, *King Lear,* 2.4.154)
>
> "Therefore confess thee freely of thy sin" (Othello to Desdemona, *Othello,* 5.2.53)
>
> "I will hereupon confess I am in love" (Armado, *Love's Labors Lost,* 1.2.57)
>
> "I confess nothing, nor I deny nothing" (Beatrice in *Much Ado about Nothing,* 4.1.273)
>
> "…scarce confesses / That his blood flows" (Angelo in *Measure for Measure.* 1.3.50–51)

To hear these words in these circumstances (to take a bare few examples) is to be exposed to: Lear's ironizing of the rites of confession in the face of Regan's demands for amends; the grim usurpations of the role of confessor trying to enforce the admittance of truths Othello can hardly bear to hear; the inevitable coming to awareness of truths the rest of us had known long ago, and long awaited, all the more delicious in being uttered by the one who has, in denying them, denied his nature; the jocular denial of a woman outed in her emergent, despite-herself love; the wedding of a mind to its own fierce purity here seen as a denial of a human capacity to feel. In short, to confess is to begin to chart paths to self-knowledge, commitments made to different futures, and claims, callings out in the light of these avowals, and admittances which risk and require response, and in kind. Consider, by contrast, the three instances of absolution.

The first instance is the jocular black humor by which Cardinal Wolsey's execution of Buckingham is referred to as an absolution with an axe in *Henry VIII*. The second is in the same play when Katherine of Aragon interrupts the same Cardinal's Latin to declare "the willing'st sin I ever yet committed/May be absolved in English" (3.1.48–49), thereby depriving him of his Latinate authority and restoring the task of absolution to the common vernacular. The third instance is in *Romeo and Juliet* when Juliet asks her nurse to tell her mother that she's going to Friar Laurence's cell to confess and be absolved of the sin of having displeased her father (3.5.231–33). And here it is a ruse to put them off the scent of her real mission to the friar to find a remedy for the consummation of her forbidden love for Romeo. So the putative confession and absolution are a disguise to ward off discovery. In Shakespeare's corpus, then, absolution is either punishment, joke, or disguise. The post-tragic plays I examine here on the other hand chart the paths to forgiveness, paths that seem essential to the ability of the communities therein to find their feet with each other, to go on at all.[8]

The transformation of the languages of penance and repentance were at the very center of an unprecedented, astonishing revolution in the forms and conventions of speaking, hence of modes of human relating. Confessing, forgiving, absolving, initiating, swearing, blessing, baptizing, ordaining—these are a mere few of the speech acts so transformed in the English Reformation. We might say that it is not clear any longer how any of these speech acts count as performative utterances at all, how, to use the scholastic jargon, they are to count as efficacious signs. It is not just that the conventional procedures were altered in the careful revisions of the *Book of Common Prayer* (1549, 1552, 1560), but that the question of what is effected by means of such acts, and who has the authority to say and so perform them, remained fundamentally uncertain, and always open to judgment. Shakespeare's theater, I want to argue, charts from first to last, with extraordinary clarity and remorselessness, the transformed work of language in human relating that follows from this revolution in language. When authority is no longer assumed in the speech acts of a sacramental priesthood, it must be found, and refound, in the claims, calls, judgments of every person who must single themselves and others out in these calls, grant them the authority in each particular instance. So Shakespeare's theater is a search for community, a community neither given nor possessed but in constant formation and deformation. This puts him in powerful continuity, of course, with a theater he is often thought to have entirely superseded and overturned.

The result in Shakespeare's writing is an extraordinary, unprecedented expansion in the expressive range, precision, and flexibility of language as it takes up this terrible burden and gift of human relating when nothing but language secures or grounds human relations. His plays explore the finding, losing, and refinding of community through the path from performative to passionate utterance, finding and seizing words unmoored from their conventions and open to the "disorders of desire" rather than "the order of law."[9] Given the new vulnerability of certain ways of speaking, hence relating, to the improvisations of desire, the late, post-tragic plays seem particularly overcome by a consequent sense of both the depth and the fragility of human bonds.[10] Such bonds seem to rest on nothing at all but mutual intelligibility, and this seems too insecure a foundation, too liable to breakage, fracture, betrayal, and rejection. They must be forged anew and through each conversation. That is the miracle in an age where all miracles are past.

This is a picture of language which insists on the dependence of reference on expression.[11] The risks involved in the acknowledgment of this dependence may feel overwhelming, for it is a picture that makes mutual reliance in a world of unreliable others unavoidable. It is no wonder that there are concerted, serious, utterly well-meaning attempts to bypass the necessity of such voicing. If the relation of word and world could only depend on anything more reliable than our voicing, our expression of that relation, we might feel more secure in the world and we might be released from the frightening contingency and variability, the unpredictability of the actions of the others in our lives, of their fearful autonomy. But if the relation of word to world has to be established and re-established through our own voicing of it, then our responsibility in meaning might threaten to overwhelm us completely. Early moderns inherited and espoused at least two ways of evading this responsibility, both of which Shakespeare rejects. Language might operate magically outside of my particular contribution to it: this formula was precisely the object of much Reformation polemic, which attacked Catholic versions of a language that worked *ex opere operato,* the core delusion here being the "hocus pocus" of the mass itself. But Protestant polemic had its own way of bypassing human expression: this emerged in the disdain and suspicion of all forms of human mediation. Some Reformation theology, for example, insisted that it was only by eradicating all human mediations that we could be sure of the God-sidedness of grace; all human interventions stain and contaminate and infringe the sovereignty of God. The theological warrant comes along with the eradication of the human—and human acknowledgment. Forgiveness was not the province of priesthood; rather it was a speech act that had already happened. Luther's assurance was quickly undermined by the disastrous pastoral implications of the Calvinist understanding of double predestination; and Protestant "practical divinity" had to find ways of dealing with the epistemological fallout of this doctrine, one that rapidly became intellectualized as a problem of knowledge: how will we know if we are saved? The epistemological anxieties notoriously focused on this unknown but quite fundamental aspect of an unmediated relation with God. Shakespeare inherits these massive quandaries and questions and attends to them in terms of *human* speech as what makes or breaks the bonds between people. For Shakespeare, forgiveness *is* acknowledgment.

I use the term "post-tragic" here because the romances do not supersede the tragedies, but rather work through the failures of acknowledgment that form Shakespearean tragic action. Shakespeare's post-tragic plays cannot forgo what they have acknowledged: our ceaseless, relentless exposure to the consequences of our own passions and actions. But the group of post-tragic plays we have come to know as romances stage the recovery from tragedy in the renewed possibility of mutual acknowledgment. It is Stanley Cavell who has made acknowledgment central to a conception of Shakespearean tragedy. Shakespearean tragedy results from avoiding love, from failures in acknowledgment. Cavell's tragic heroes come to grief because they have substituted flattery's beguiling echoes for love's fearful mutualities and exposures (Lear) or the certainty of faithlessness for the terrifying risk of being known and loved in being known (Othello), or because of the unutterable difficulty and loneliness of taking up an identity that is yours alone to inhabit ("This is I,/Hamlet, the Dane," 5.1.256–57).[12] Acknowledgment is the ground of our relation to other minds, which skepticism intellectualizes as metaphysical lack. It is always particular; it is always of someone for something; it is not so much what we choose to do as what we cannot avoid doing. It is not a substitute for knowledge, for it includes and assumes knowledge, but it is a medium through which both response and responsibility are unendingly exacted through the commitments of human speech and action. It might include—it usually does include—self-knowledge and the ways we avoid it, recognition and the ways we avoid it, responsiveness and responsibility, and the ways we evade and avoid them. I am proposing here that the history of acknowledgment and therefore its fortunes in Shakespearean tragedy and post-tragedy can be best told in rela-tion to the sacrament of penance and its complex afterlives.[13]

A word about method. The epigraph to this introduction from Witt-genstein's *Philosophical Investigations* suggests a critical practice.[14] It is a practice that J. L. Austin called fieldwork in philosophy, or linguistic phe-nomenology.[15] To explore the grammar of forgiveness will entail thinking about the family of words connected with it: trespass, sin, offense, contri-tion, confession, absolution, reconciliation, restitution, acknowledgment—all of which are linked in their original home of the sacrament of penance. This critical practice takes as its assumption that the differences among these words will tell us about the differences we have sought to make about our cares and commitments. "Our common stock of words," says Austin, "embodies all the distinctions men have found worth drawing, and the connections they have found worth making."[16] When we exam-ine these distinctions and differences we are looking at the world as well as the words, for they are inseparable. We will begin to see that forgiveness is distinct from absolution, but also from pardon, exculpation, remittance; that it is linked to apology and acknowledgment as one of its possible pre-conditions; to forms of penalty and punishment; to a theology of grace; and to self-examination, restitution, reparation, restoration, and so to practices fully social, not just individual; to the world of harm done; finally to forms of responsibility and response. Against skeptical pictures of a gap between mind and world, Wittgenstein's remark in the *Philosophical Investigations* assumes a radical, fundamental harmony of word and world. When we pursue a grammatical investigation of forgiveness we will be reminding ourselves about how we learned to forgive and of the related practices as-sociated with it. We will be reminding ourselves how we learned such a word and how we actually use it, and in the process—because word and world are inseparable—we will learn about the histories of our cares and commitments and the differences we have tried to make in our language and in our world.[17] The notion of grammar at work in ordinary language philosophy is not the grammar of the rule-book. On the contrary, it takes it as axiomatic that meaning and use are inseparable. What words say depends on what words do, and they will lose all intelligibility if we fail to see the point of utterance on any particular occasion.[18]

For this very reason, I see a natural affinity between the practices of theater and the practices of ordinary language philosophy because each practice is committed to examining particular words used by particular speakers in particular situations.[19] Each practice understands language as situation, which is different from "context" because sometimes we understand the context only when we understand what it is that is being said.[20] Ordinary language philosophy makes the very radical claim that we will fail to understand what something means until we understand what it does, until we understand the force of the words used on any particular occasion as, say, entreaty, command, order, suggestion, permission, request, prayer. It affords us a nuanced and precise account, therefore, of the relation between the inherited ritual languages of the Middle Ages and their transformation in post-Reformation England, an account we sorely need if we want to break with the conventional accounts of periodization, whether those are subsumed under the description of "the Renaissance" or of "early modernity." Furthermore, each practice, of theater and of ordinary language philosophy, understands language as act, as event in the world, and so asks us to extend our conception of the work of language beyond the work of representation, the chief focus of historicism old and new.

In her philosophical contemplation of the nature of human action that I previously cited, Hannah Arendt talks about the boundlessness, the irreversibility of action. We do things in the world utterly unsure of their effects; they are taken up by others in ways we can neither determine nor predict. Such effects, stemming from our actions, are nevertheless uncertain and quite uncontainable. In her attempt to develop democratic and politically sustainable and just frames for action, Arendt suggested that there are two speech acts that make the boundlessness and irreversibility of action bearable: promising and forgiving. In an unpredictable world the promise is the foundation of trust, of dependability. In a world of harm the act of forgiveness allows a way of going on to new futures. It is through such acts of speech that the risk and uncertainty of action can be addressed. Both speech acts, as I will show in subsequent chapters, go through different conceptualizations in the course of the Reformation.

This book is divided into three parts. The second and third parts work as readings of particular plays in which I explore promising and forgiving as acts of making community. The first part examines the transformations in the grammar of forgiveness which follow from the abolition of penance as a sacrament.

In the first chapter, "The Mind's Retreat from the Face," I begin with a reading of one of Hamlet's most famous speeches and show Shakespeare's deep preoccupations with the split between inner and outer. "There's no art / To find the mind's construction in the face" (1.4.12–13). These words from *Macbeth* are chilling.[21] They can stand for a whole set of preoccupations in Shakespeare's theater. They suggest that there is no craft, no technique or received wisdom that might help us read from someone's face what it is they are thinking. The face and the mind are adrift in Shakespeare's image, the effort to join them daunting and uncharted. The world they communicate would be unbearable to live in, perhaps even uninhabitable. The picture of an inaccessible mind trapped in a body whose expressions cannot express that mind or soul is a picture of the human in exile from his own body and expression, and hence from all means of the knowledge of self and others. When the body stops being granted the capacity to express the mind and the soul, in Shakespeare's understanding, we don't so much protect that "inner" space (even if that's what we think we are doing): instead we lose touch with it all together. Part of the crisis and difficulty in this understanding is that we lose sense of ourselves and our communities together, in one and the same movement of self-exile from shared words and shared expressions. Once we see those words and expressions not as showing but as hiding us, we lose touch with our only means of self-knowledge and contact with others. It is this chapter that motivates the predicament that gives rise to the sense of this split. It is my belief that much contemporary criticism inhabits this very split, and so the therapeutic and diagnostic power of Shakespeare's dramaturgy is unavailable to it.

In the second chapter I flesh out my claim that the home of "acknowledgment" is the sacrament of penance, and explore some of the paths from penance to repentance.

Part 2 of the book, "Promising," looks at the language of promising by considering a play in which marriage contracts and the relation between intent and consent are particularly at issue. This play, *Measure for Measure,* has at its center a marriage contract which, with much engineering, is fulfilled, but in ways that appear to end the comic tradition in Shakespeare.

The four post-tragic plays I examine in the third and longest part of this book, "Forgiving," share certain forms, certain ways of exploring their subject matter. They survive tragic impasses by modifying the form of romance as well as the form of tragedy. I identify some of their shared patterns in the following ways:

1. In each of the plays the act of forgiving (active and passive—for the forgiver and the forgiven) must go through the circuit of self-understanding. (This is why we are in the realm of forgiveness—and forgiveness as acknowledgment—and not absolution). Self-understanding, then, is a mode of conversion, one in which past actions are seen in a transformed light, and one whose authorizing vision will necessitate and enable a change in the whole person. The change will be something whose definition and description are solely open to the one experiencing it, and its description will be a symptom of the change.

2. The forgiveness in question usually comes about by a giving over to the risks and uncertainties of relationship. This is the means and mechanism of forgiveness, and this too might distinguish it from absolution where forgiveness is granted by virtue of an office. Forgiveness in these plays is never unilateral, and so it is carefully distinguished from pardon, exoneration, and absolution. The authority of the forgiver and the forgiven must be found and granted by each to each.

3. Forgiveness must involve faith and hope in the future. In these plays forgiveness is an exchange of love, and coterminous with the growth and possibility of that love.

4. Such an exchange is usually made possible by the viewing of one's life as a gift—and so forgiveness is both an acknowledgment of separateness and a relinquishment of autonomy. The giftedness of life can be understood theologically; the idea is chiefly that we can come to receive ourselves and understand ourselves at the hands of others only by means of the conversation and friendship of others. The plays then move away from isolation or tyrannous self-enclosure (Leontes: "I have said / She's an adult'ress" (2.1.87), or Prospero's belated ability to express himself rather than assert himself in the language of imperatives, orders, and commands).

5. It is for this reason that forgiveness can only be effected linguistically. The society so arrived at is thus infinitely precious and fragile because nothing grounds or assures it beyond these exchanges.
6. Romances of forgiveness are intergenerational. The focus is never exclusively between the parental generation, but between the older generation and the younger one. The old are reborn in themselves through their recovery of the young.

Outlining the structure of the book makes clear that in parts 2 and 3 I prefer to work through the afterlives of the sacrament of penance play by play. That is because each play creates its own world and asks us to enter it. I felt that I needed to work with the logic of that created world in all its integrity, rather than picking out bits and pieces from different plays. However, my chapters on the romances should not be taken as exhaustive readings of the plays in their entirety. They tend to concentrate around the endings of the plays in particular, for two reasons. The first reason is that this is a book about the dramaturgy of forgiveness as acknowledgment and recognition, and recognitions are the last things in these plays. The second reason is related to the first: Shakespeare, I think, *meant* his endings; he took responsibility for them. They cannot therefore be subsumed under the conventions of endings, of closure, to carry their significance.

Finally, though this book explores the legacies of the Catholic sacrament of penance, I have not speculated about Shakespeare's religious identity.[22] That will always exert a fascination for all those interested in Shakespeare, but such speculation can short-circuit and even preempt the density of the embodied world of the plays and the sheer complexity of that historical, social, and linguistic inheritance. Indeed the push to the confessionalization of religious identity in the nation-state's monopoly of religion was one of the more brutal, consequential, and reductive aspects of the time in which he lived, one that extracted appalling costs and sacrifices. The legacies of the transformation from penance to repentance cannot be reduced to a question of religious identity.

I hope that this book will be read by people interested in the difficult practice of forgiveness as well as those interested in the plays of Shakespeare. It is an attempt to enact a critical practice that engages with the ethical and aesthetic as much as the historical and political dimensions that have been the preoccupation and the *doxa* of recent criticism. As such, its vision of language is one dedicated to the common and the shared as prior to any failure in sharing, any lapse in commonalty. Shakespeare, I believe, from first to last, was interested in charity as a relation between people, as a bond that was never dependent on any one individual's consent, and that worked as a relation, not a possession. This, one might say, is what he evolved his theater—the art of our shared embodiment—to restore. Such a project of recovery was never the retrieval of a static past but always a transformation of that past's deepest legacy. And it is a mode of mutual habituation, a form of participation, not a doctrine or a content—and thus fragile to, existent only in conversation, bodied forth in the gorgeous complicity of theater.

Part One

PENANCE TO REPENTANCE

It is difficult to say where conventions begin and end.

J. L. AUSTIN

1

The Mind's Retreat from the Face

I take the title of my chapter, "The Mind's Retreat from the Face," from Fergus Kerr's classic, *Theology after Wittgenstein.*[1] The phrase is a haunting, alarming way of picturing a pervasive notion of the face as a mask obscuring the mind's inaccessible internal objects. In this picture, "the mind retreats from the face, just as the immaterial soul once disappeared behind the body."[2] This picture of the relation of mind and body is most famously associated with Descartes' description in the Second Meditation.[3] It is not, however, merely a philosophical idea but a common experience of self, one intrinsic to solipsism and narcissism for sure, but prevalent too in quite common experiences of miscommunication or misunderstanding and of grief, retreat, and loneliness. Shakespeare's theater, as has often been noticed, is intensely preoccupied with what happens when the mind and soul can no longer be found in the face.[4]

The split between inner mind or soul and outer face and the fundamental denigration of expression that accompanies this split is one given point not only by the state policies of Reformation England but also by the persistent debates over ceremony that are endemic to the so-called English settlement. It is my sense that the picture still holds sway in contemporary criticism and that we will fail to understand Shakespeare's diagnosis of it as long as we remain in its grip.

I know not 'seems.'

Let's begin with some of Hamlet's most famous words:

> Seems, madam? nay, it is, I know not 'seems.'
> 'Tis not alone my inky cloak, (good) mother,
> Nor customary suits of solemn black,
> Nor windy suspiration of forc'd breath,
> No, nor the fruitful river in the eye,
> Nor the dejected haviour of the visage,
> Together with all forms, moods, (shapes) of grief,
> That can (denote) me truly. These indeed seem,
> For they are actions that a man might play,
> But I have that within which passes show,
> These but the trappings and the suits of woe.
> (1.2. 76–86)

Hamlet is describing his own sensed predicament. Though he could not have known this, it turns out that this is a *locus classicus* for a pervasive picture of the human mind, one which philosophy names as the problem of other minds. But how does it give voice to those problems and questions? What fantasies are released and expressed in them? What is the situation in which it seems necessary to voice them?

It is the second scene of the first act. Hamlet, back in the Danish court after his father's death, is in black and with the clouds still upon him is seeking for his "noble father in the dust" (1.2.71). According to Gertrude and Claudius, he has more than fulfilled the necessary mourning duties of filial obligation. Of his grief, Gertrude asks, "Why seems it so particular with thee?" (1.2.75).

In response Hamlet fastens on his mother's word, "seems."[5] What does he mean by "I know not 'seems'"? That he doesn't know how to seem? That he doesn't know what it means? That he will be who he is or no one?

That he will not participate in her world of seeming? That he insists on his authenticity and cannot comprehend or countenance a split between appearance and reality?

Hamlet is observing that his mother is reading him from his moody demeanor and mourning clothes, his "inky cloak" and "windy suspirations." There is a hint in his allusion to the "customary suits of black" that precisely because such suits are customary, conventionally assumed in the time of bereavement (though of course, rapidly relinquished by the Danish court), they can therefore not say anything "particular" about him. If everyone customarily wears them, how can they be understood to say anything about particular people or particular emotions? The common custom wipes out the expression of individuality, at least his in particular.

But perhaps we might see him as taking up his mother's use of the word "particular" here, and turning it around on her. Why are you so special? she seems to imply. For "all that lives must die, / Passing through nature to eternity" (1.2.72–73). Yes, Hamlet has said in his reply to this observation, "it is common," (1.2.73) that is, this is the case for everyone, this is common to everyone (and perhaps with the implication that this is therefore a commonplace). Her question, which prompts his famous outburst, is in response to this sardonic assent. Well, in that case, she says, why do you single yourself out in this way, *make yourself* so particular, count yourself out of the commonality? It is now that Hamlet fixes on her "seems." It doesn't "seem" particular, he might be understood as saying. It *is* particular to me because he is my father (and, implied, your husband) and so my response is indeed particular. One of the implications of his comments might be that though he is not seeming, though he does not know what it means to "seem," though his clothes actually do denote his mourning, she wishes to discard them as expressing his grief. So we might track the sheer comprehensiveness of his list, the sarcasm intensified in the hiss and precision of "suspirations," the quadruple negative that reverses the iambic rhythm of four sequential lines, the helplessness and increasingly hopeless vagueness of *"all* forms, moods, and shapes of grief," as the discovery that nothing can touch in this woman a response to his grief. Then his comments might be understood to say: if you can't know me from my expressions, my appearance, if you can't see my grief for my father, and if you, my mother, can't sympathize with it, then who can? If customary suits of solemn black, and fruitful rivers in the eye, and all the very forms, moods, and shapes of grief can't in your eyes denote me truly, then nothing will "denote me truly." I will be unknowable, theatricalized by you; you will have made an actor of me, hollowed me out. He might then be taken to be saying that if this is the case, then everything I have tried to communicate about my sadness to you, my tears, my dejection, the very habit of my mourning is useless, and *what else do I have to convince you?* What else can I show if this does not convince you? Of course a man might indeed play these actions and only your sympathy with me, your trust in me, your response to me will tell you the difference between such an actor and me, your only son. If his mother discounts his behavior and his expressions as show, all Hamlet can do is feel bereft and unknowable—and somehow, too, betrayed by the suits and trappings of woe.

Gertrude's invocation of the "commonality" of a shared finitude comes then as an utterly false comfort, one that has the effect of divorcing Hamlet from the whole of humankind, and certainly from the one who should be for him both kin and kind. Gertrude will not read, will not see, and apparently will not comfort or respond to the Hamlet before her. (In not seeing him, she will also miss something about herself.)[6] The court that Hamlet inhabits is one in which every ritual has become theatricalized. The sham rituals at Claudius's court alienate rather than give voice to the participants included in them, and in a world in which no one can see themselves in the public forms, no one can be him- or herself. In such a world of seeming, Hamlet feels himself to be unknowable, but he also has no grounds for knowing anyone else.

I've tried to motivate this famous passage in such a way as to suggest that Hamlet's insistence is not initially a statement about a metaphysically unbridgeable gap between an inaccessible mind and merely outward conventions that will never capture the utter depths of that grief, but crucially a response to a felt abandonment by the mother who has theatricalized his deepest feelings. He has lost his father, and now apparently his mother too is vanishing from him. In this plight he will leap from the possibility that his actions are potentially indistinguishable from what a man "might play" to the "necessary inexpressiveness" of "that within," its status as passing show, beyond expression.

If Hamlet's grief is constitutively beyond show—if he *cannot* give voice to it, not because the circumstances all conspire against it now, but because it is simply impossible that his outer behavior *can* reveal the "inner" workings of his mind, he will be spared both the difficulty of giving voice to that grief and the response of others to his expressions. Under some circumstances the desperate aloneness of this predicament might seem preferable to the terrible responsibility for having to account for yourself and the relentless exposure to others this entails, especially when that exposure is (mis)read as theatrical.

An alternative way of understanding the epistemological implications of the embodiment of self is provided by Stanley Cavell who has suggested that as embodied creatures, we are "condemned to expression, to meaning."[7] The picture of inner and outer is, then, also a picture of language that shields human beings from exposure to each other's responses and the endless responsibility that follows. We are "perpetually expressive." We cannot stop being expressive, and even the concealing of our expressiveness will reveal itself in the stifled yawn; in the catch in the voice when I say your name, though I don't at this stage want or need you to know that I care for you much more than I should; in the wince when, you, you bully, pinch me though I'm damned if I want to give you the satisfaction of knowing that you've hurt me; in the excessive concentration as I walk up the stairs to let you know how very sober I am; in the greater attentiveness with which I hope to distract you into not noticing that you are boring me half to death; in all the familiar, frequent ways in which we say: "I could barely contain myself." Here we cannot indeed "help ourselves." We are here, as Cavell says, "victims of expression."[8]

The hold of this picture of privacy is so pervasive that it is no wonder that Hamlet has become the icon for it. When Stanley Cavell explores the sheer grip of this picture, he suggests that the "convulsion in sensibility" of the Reformation is one factor that requires an account.[9]

The picture of inner and outer that takes hold in *Hamlet* is also one that evolves through the languages of reformed Christianity. It is this aspect that I intend to explore briefly here in order to frame my discussion of confession, absolution, and forgiveness in chapter 2. The transformations in these languages cannot be understood without a consideration of the arguments about the significance and practice of rite and sacrament in sixteenth-century England. It is not my aim to provide a comprehensive account of the complex transformation of the Reformation in England as a whole; rather I mean to shed light on how certain state policies and implementations, polemical practices, and a revolution in ritual theory and practice resulting from a changed picture of sacramental action had a massive impact on the perception of a gap between behavior and thought—or in the split vocabulary becoming more and more current, "outward" behavior" and "inward" thought.

Passing Show: Reformed Versions of Inner and Outer

Christian subjects living in the aftermath of the Reformation might have had very good reason to have recourse to a language that splits the inner from the outer. Here I isolate four interrelated factors that I regard as important. First, the use of oaths of allegiance to exact commitment and allegiance became a regular part of English state policy. For those compelled to speak words that betrayed their religious beliefs and convictions, the metaphorical language of inner and outer offered a desperately needed protection from the demand for conformity. The inner here became a place of protection, a vital retreat from coercion and constraint and a way of saving some integrity, some small sanctuary in the face of overwhelming pressure. Second, the enforcement of uniformity of religion and worship mandated in the *Book of Common Prayer* meant that once more several groups of people felt there to be an impassable obstacle between their convictions and their public expression.

Third, the polemical tradition by which the Catholic rite was derided as theatricalized ceremony re-created the language of rite as just so much empty formalism. Here inner and outer were cast in a language of doubleness and disguise, of appearance and reality; the attempt was to render Catholic ceremony incapable of saying anything at all, describing it as dumb while simultaneously rendering it dumb: both silent and stupid. Dumb, hollow, empty, vain: these were the favorite adjectives of polemical attack. Both the utterance of compulsory words at odds with religious conviction and the attempt to empty out the words of others produce an exile from words. The utterance of compulsory words that do not belong to the self-understanding of the speaker, that feel like ash in his mouth, is a terrible form of alienation not just from the enforcing state but also from the self that is forced to betray itself out of its own mouth. And the theatricalization of the words and actions of another also gives his words no carry and deprives him of so much as the ability to mean anything at all; this too is a kind of exile from words and gestures. This latter maneuver was part of a more widespread revolution in ritual theory and practice. So the fourth aspect of the increasing sense of a split between "inner" and "outer" is the language of reformed ecclesiology and the sacraments, in which the relation between the invisible and the visible church became ever more tenuous. In the subsequent sections I will show some of the historical pressures that inform this pressing sense of a gap between inner and outer.

Compulsory Words

In England's manorial courts, oaths of allegiance had been a routine and obligatory practice for centuries.[10] But the oath became a regular instrument of both Tudor and Stuart statecraft; the oath publicly elicited the loyalty of the subjects of the crown and so also identified such "loyal" subjects. Those who refused to take the oaths were subject to fines and the confiscation of property under the terms of "praemunire"; in the last resort they were subject to charges of treason. In 1534 and 1536 two new oaths explicitly linked political loyalty to confessional identity, thereby demanding a new form of allegiance.[11] The goal was for subjects to accept the king as head of church and state and so implicitly to reject the dominion and authority of the pope and his spiritual jurisdiction. "Never before had a spiritual instrument been used as a political test," says Susan Brigden.[12] The Oath of Succession was required of all men over the age of fourteen. Elizabeth extended this policy: her 1559 Act of Supremacy mandated that "every archbishop, bishop, and all and every other ecclesiastical person, and all and every temporal judge, justice, mayor, and other lay or temporal officer and minister and every other person having your Highness's fee and wages, within this realm or any of your Highness's dominions, and other ecclesiastical officer and minister of what estate, dignity, preeminence or degree whatsoever he be, shall make, take and receive a corporal oath upon the evangelist—to swear that Elizabeth is the supreme governor." The oath was later extended to members of Parliament and to all those taking a university degree.

An oath was understood to invoke God as witness and to invite divine vengeance if it should prove false. The falseness lay in the oath-taker if he thereby maligned his God; or, depending on your viewpoint, in the state commanding heretical views. If you were in dissent from English ecclesiastical polity, you were damned if you did by your own church, and damned if you did not by your nation. If a man's word is his bond, such bondage was an insufferably cruel contradiction. Such words tied their utterers to publicly witnessed promises at great cost to all sense of honor and self.

The Jacobean Oath of Allegiance (3 James 1. c. 4) was, as Michael Questier has shown, deliberately designed to divide the Catholic community, becoming in the process an even more subtle and brutal instrument of identification. This oath was intended to out Romanist dissenters after the Gunpowder Plot:

> I do from my heart abhor, detest and abjure as impious and heretical this damnable doctrine and position that princes which be excommunicated and deprived by the Pope may be deposed or murdered by their subjects or any other whatsoever.[13]

Questier argues that the oath was deliberately designed to intensify a fault-line in Catholic ecclesiology and so fragment and divide English Catholics. Those who objected to the terms of the oath tended to regard the church as "a visible commonwealth" with the temporal and spiritual powers unified in a single hierarchy. To take the oath was to accede to the right of the king to govern the church in matters temporal, and so it was equivalent to an oath of supremacy.

From the Tudor Oath of Supremacy to the Jacobean Oath of Allegiance then, to take the chronology covered by this book, English subjects had to undertake a series of vows that forced them to declare allegiance to their king, and thereby to threaten exile from their own bodies and commitments. It is under these circumstances that the split between inner and outer might emerge as a protective mechanism. "An oath taken by the outer man could not bind or compromise the loyalty of the inner man," declares Friar Forest when forced to take the Oath of Allegiance under Henry VIII.[14] The split between outer and inner here is indeed a response to crisis, to an enforcement of the conformity of the mind and the heart. It is no surprise then to see this split as the foundation of casuistical thinking whether this is expressed as local legitimations of oath-breaking such as Friar Forest's, or in the full-blown doctrine of "mental reservation." In Henry Garnett's *Treatise on Equivocation* it becomes clear that the thesis of "mental reservation" and the positive wrestling with the language of inner and outer there is designed to preserve the integrity of the utterer even when he utters words that belie his beliefs. When Garnett argues, for example, that in a mixed proposition, "part of it is expressed, part reserved in the mind," it is because he wants to save tormented souls from the accusation (including the self-accusation) that they are liars.[15] It is therefore out of deep respect for the implication of words that he evolves a theory so dangerous to the Jacobean state and to the protocols of public speech.[16]

A public life in which coercion and forms of show are the norm and in which duplicity is routinized is highly likely to lead to an understanding of the inner life as one subject to isolation and withdrawal, a life that has to be defined in opposition to the voices around it. But this means only that both public and private life are impoverished, not that we permanently and metaphysically inhabit a realm in which what we believe or think cannot be expressed. The picture of inner and outer is then only reinforced by the confessional state and its relation to the souls of its subjects.

The Elizabethan and Jacobean state had thus put itself in the following familiar position: the words it required its subjects to say were compulsory. They mandated public allegiance; yet, because the words stating that allegiance were legally enforced, they were as likely to lead to mental sleights of hand, to forms of self-splitting whereby the utterer could reconcile himself to his utterances. Under such conditions it might come to seem as if the outer man is merely a screen or a disguise for the inner man. Then the question of how to know what the other person is thinking (the problem of other minds) is indeed a practical as well as a philosophical problem.

Here is one version of the kinds of early modern fantasies that develop from this problem in the words of an anti-Catholic polemicist:

> When Jupiter had made man, being delited with such a cunning piece of workmanship, he demaunded of momus (to) find a fault, what he could spy, in so fine a feature and curious frame, out of square and worthie just reproof: Momus commended the proposition and comely disposition of the lineaments: but one thing (saith he) I like not well; that thou hast forgotten to place a window in his brest through which we might behold whether his tongue and his heart did accord. If a window were formed in the brests of these discontended catholickes, that her Majestie and the state-guiding counsell and all true friends to the kingdom might know their secret intentions . . . many

false hearts would be found lurking under painted hoods, and cakes of foul cancred malice under meale mouthed protestations.[17]

In dreaming of the perfect means of surveillance for the discovery of trea-sonous English Catholics, John Baxter produces the picture of the body as a screen to be penetrated. It is the same idea that is present in Bacon's famous phrase that Elizabeth did not like to "make window's in men's hearts, and secret thoughts."[18] John Baxter's fantasy and Elizabeth's reported demur-ral shared a common picture of inside and outside that her own state poli-cies had virtually ensured.[19]

The *Book of Common Prayer*

Elizabethan recusancy bills contained strict provisions for conformity for recusants. The Elizabethan Act of Uniformity made church attendance on Sundays and holy days compulsory on pain of a fine; repeated recusancy led to imprisonment. The 1593 bill even specified the exact words by which a recusant was supposed to recant, with special provisions for popish recu-sants.[20] The communion clause of James I's act (3 James I. C.4) furthermore required reception of communion and not merely attendance.[21] Michael Questier affirms that the requirements for conformity under the law were "hard and unforgiving."[22] Compliance with the provisions of statute law were to be effected in accordance with canonical provisions for heresy in ac-cordance with English rather than Roman canon law.[23] The 1606 act in ad-dition required the taking of the Oath of Allegiance, thus making it clear that conformity to the Prayerbook was a central part of allegiance to the Stu-art polity. The new Prayerbook compelled uniformity of religious worship in a newly national church and so created a group of newly Roman Catho-lic subjects whose modes of being in relation to their maker and preferred patterns of worship rendered them treasonous subjects, though nothing at all had changed in their modes of life. For the more evangelically minded, the new form of Common Prayer contained far too many continuities with Roman Catholicism. The long English attempt to argue for *adiaphora,* a no-tion that some modes of worship were "things indifferent," in an attempt to set a pattern of worship that might be common to all, was a failure.[24] It was clear that the words religious subjects uttered and the shapes their bodies took in worship could never be matters of indifference: they involved— and created—the most fundamental habits and dispositions. The rejection of the notion of "adiaphora" involved an insistence that words and gestures were expressive and a protest against the very notion of conventions as empty. In Peter Lake's words, Elizabeth's desire for "outward conformity," her stated refusal that she would not make windows of men's souls (a statement that is undercut by Elizabethan state casuistry), "opened up a gap between the inward and the outward, the real conviction of a person and his outward behaviour, a space, which it seemed to many contemporaries, could be exploited for all sorts of dissimulation and pretence by the faithless and the unscrupulous."[25] Here again we encounter the language of inner and outer and its logical corollary: the body screens and veils the soul, stands in its way. We must penetrate and look behind, beyond, or through it—but not at it—to grasp the workings of the mind and soul.

Dumbness and Theatricalization

The three versions of the Prayerbook were the result of extensive debate over the meaning of ceremony. In these debates polemicists developed a vituperative vocabulary whose aim was to take away the hold and the perceived efficacy of Catholic rite and the priests who performed it. This too had the effect of intensifying and polarizing the idea of a split between inner and outer, here understood as appearance and reality.

A sense of a discrepancy between the ritual words and the intentions of those uttering them was perfectly common in discussions of ritual speech. This was the focus of prolonged discussion in scholastic theory; and it was central to anti-donatism. The efficacy of the sacraments was not compromised by the ill intents of the priest because the intention of the church in the sacraments, in this understanding, could compensate for the individual failing of the priest.

In several medieval texts there is a figure called Tutivillus whose special role is to monitor accountability for words. He is a kind of demon, a collector of words spoken inattentively in the recitation of the liturgy:

> I muste eche day brynge my master a thowsande pokes full of faylynges, &
> of negligence in syllables and wordes, that ar done in your order in redynge
> and in syngynge, & else I must be sure beten.[26]

Tutivillus collects words uttered carelessly during the liturgy, but his task amplifies in different texts, and in later developments he records all idle words and talk on a long scroll that he extends with his teeth. The words he records fall under the medieval category of "sins of the tongue": gossip, slander, back-biting, words that break the bonds between people. (Medieval penitential theology here anticipates ordinary language philosophy in understanding words as making and breaking community.) In the Towneley *Last Judgment* he has a cameo role; with his fellow demons he bears scrolls recording the idle talk of the sinners whose souls are finally weighed in judgment. Tutivillus's concern might be said to be then like Nicholas Ridley's some years later. Defending the vernacularization of the *Book of Common Prayer,* Ridley says that the prayer book was englished so that "all men and women were taught, after Christ's doctrine, to pray in that tongue which they could understand, that they might pray with their heart that which they would speak with their tongue."[27]

These are fairly commonplace descriptions natural in a culture where public recitation and declaration are so central. Yet reformed polemics mounted a widespread and concerted attack on virtually the entirety of Catholic ceremonial. Tyndale vituperates in the following way:

> Judge whether it be possible that any good should come out of their dumb ceremonies and sacraments unto thy soul. Judge their penance, pilgrimages, pardons, purgatories, praying to posts, dumb blessings, dumb absolutions, their dumb pattering, and howling, their dumb strange holy gestures, with all their dumb disguisings, their satisfyings and justifyings. And because thou findest them false in so many things, trust them in nothing, but judge them in all things.[28]

This is a clarion call to open up the received authority of the priesthood to devastating judgment, and an invitation, a provocation to a world of distrust. But it is also a decisive theatricalization of the sacramental priesthood. The re-description of ceremonies as "disguisings" is a familiar and standard way of delegitimizing Catholic ritual. In describing Catholic ceremonial as dumb, Protestant polemic attempted to deprive it of voice, of the ability to say anything at all. The ritual gestures and words of the priest cannot say anything; they are dumb—silent and stupid. Tyndale suggests that Catholic ceremonial has no human voice: it is just so many meaningless bestial noises: "Where now we hear but voices without signification; and buzzings, howlings and cryings, as it were the halloo-ing of foxes, or baiting of bears; and wonder at disguisings and toys whereof we know no meaning."[29] The ascription of dumbness to Catholic ceremonial is repeated in the short introduction to the *Book of Common Prayer*, "Of Ceremonies, Why Some be Abolished and Some Retained." The ceremonies of the *Book of Common Prayer* are "neither dark nor dumb ceremonies, but are so set forth that every man may understand what they do mean and to what use they serve."[30]

If the words of Catholic priests are thereby theatricalized, so are their gestures and ritual actions; their robes are costumes, disguises that conceal the designs of priesthood. In John Bale's theater or Thomas Becon's polemics, for example, Catholic ceremony becomes theater (empty signs, vain rites, hollow performances), yet in the process theater itself has been redefined as spectacle and disguise.[31] This is, among other things, an attempt to render inefficacious the sacraments of the Catholic church since these rites *worked*—to ordain, marry, forgive, bless, cleanse, sanction, save.

The ardent desire is to move men and women to a place where they can mean what they say because they understand what it is they are saying. Reformed sacramental theology, to make complex things simple, situates the efficacy of the sacrament in the transformation of the one receiving communion, in the subjective faith—and knowledge—of the worshipper rather than the objective (*ex opere operato*) work of the priest. "You will receive so much as you believe you receive," proclaims Luther.[32] Or, as John Jewel says in his *Defence of the Apology:* "The simplest of our people understandeth the nature and meaning of the holy mystery of our Lord's Supper; and therefore they receive the same together to their great commendation."[33]

Yet as I said in my introduction, it is one of the radical claims of ordinary language philosophy that we may not understand what someone is saying unless we understand what their words are doing. Consider the different views of language enacted by Thomas Cranmer and the Cornishmen in the Western Rebellion of 1549, sometimes known as the Prayerbook Uprising. The Cornishmen who confront Cranmer think that the new prayer book is like a Christmas game.[34] Cranmer can barely understand their response. How can "the heart be moved by words that be not understood?" To Cranmer, the Cornishmen are parrots, not men: "And standeth it to reason that the priest should speak for you, and in your name, and you answer him again in your own persons: and yet you understand never a word, neither what he saith, nor what you say yourselves?"[35]

Two ideas about language seem to be operating here at hopeless cross-purposes. For Cranmer, the Catholic liturgy was meaningless and so it could not do anything; for the Cornishmen the *Book of Common Prayer* did nothing (it was not effectual) and therefore it could mean nothing. Since sacraments were signs which caused what they signified, questions of efficacy and meaning were front and center in the debates about the sacraments that informed and accompanied the Reformation.

A Revolution in Ritual Theory

In his helpful work on ritual and reformation, Edwin Muir has argued that the Reformation was a revolution in ritual theory and practice. The transformation of medieval mass to common prayer, a central part of this revolution, was driven and informed by a sense that the ritual could simply not be efficacious unless its meaning was understood; ritual became a matter for cognition. It is during this period that the word "ritual" comes into existence and it involves a "major shift in understanding of the relation of human behaviour and meaning."[36] Both functionalist theories of ritual and the long-term success of Protestant narratives in emptying out the conventions of rite indicate that this complex shift has not been given the attention it deserves. The complexity of the vast transformation in whole categories of speech acts consequent on a reformed liturgy and a transformed theology of the sacraments remains chronically underdescribed.

My earlier allusion to Cranmer and the Cornishmen should give us pause: there can be no simple opposition between words that mean and words that do something. All our words are acts of speech, and this opens us up to the sheer difficulty of sometimes determining what we mean by them and what we have done with them. In his stunning book *How to Do Things with Words,* J. L. Austin came to the conclusion that there are no grammatical criteria for performatives. One conclusion we can draw from a close attention to his work is that a major role of ritual is to make explicit what the *force* of an utterance is, how it is to be taken. The formal commendation of the Dean of Arts and Sciences is one thing and the mumbled semi-embarrassed commending of a parent who finds it hard to praise quite another. The student is commended by the Dean; but whether the student takes the parent's response as high praise indeed coming from that quarter or yet another cruel reticence is part of the history of their relations. The Dean might in fact be rather amazed that the student whom he taught himself some two years ago has made it to the Dean's list, but his views will be quite irrelevant to his commendation. The formality of ritual, by which he is invested in his office and by which he commends the student, makes it clear how the commendation is to be taken. (The student might refuse the honor, of course, say as a protest against the university's investment in companies that use child labor—conventions and rituals can always be contested and rejected—but she will still understand how it was meant to be taken.) But in the absence of the ritual assurance of explicitness the *force* of an utterance (provocation, demand, entreaty, suggestion, order, etc.) will simply have to be identified in the uncertain terrain of human conversation.

The changed role of the sacraments is a central part of what Muir has called a revolution in ritual theory and practice. Sacraments were understood to be sanctifying signs that caused what they signified. A priest whose ordination is an indelible seal is authorized to baptize; to transform bread into the body of Christ, wine into his blood; to bless, sanctify, perform the last rites; and above all, as I shall show in more depth in the next chapter, to confess and absolve. Whereas in the reformed church the proper administration of the sacraments was a mark of the true church and the minister continued to baptize, to perform radically truncated last rites, and to mediate disputes in the office of forgiveness, the reformed theology of sacraments changed the relation of his actions to the visible church. Although medieval sacramental theology had always carefully distinguished between God's act of forgiveness and the priest's role in declaring it (see chapter 2), the declaration itself on behalf of the church had the advantage in being a public, visible act. It was an act of judgment saying it was so, and because of the authority invested in the office of priest, it was thereby so. The declaration of God's forgiveness was effected. Reformed theology threatened to make the visible gestures and actions of the church accidental to justifying faith; in the priesthood of all believers the visibility of the church and the souls within it might remain fundamentally unknown and unknowable.

Sacramental Action and Ecclesiology   The desacramentalization of the Catholic church in England thus had far-reaching epistemological effects. Take, for example, reformed descriptions of baptism, the ceremony for initiation into Christian society. When the reformer Thomas Becon discusses baptism he makes a distinction between an "inward baptism of the spirit" and an "outward baptism of water" which "profiteth nothing without."[37] Tyndale makes a further distinction between "those who are baptized in the flesh and those who are baptized in the heart."[38] The epistemological quandary is immediately obvious. The primary baptism of the internal spirit and (outward) baptism by water were both deemed essential parts of sacramental action. But if the two did not necessarily coincide, how was one to know that true initiation into the church of Christ had actually taken place? Such problems were even more pronounced when justification and repentance replaced the sacrament of penance. "Repentance," says William Tyndale, "is no sacrament, as faith, hope and love and knowledging of man's sins are not to be called sacraments. *For they are spiritual and invisible.* Now must a sacrament be an outward sign that may be seen, to signify, to represent and to put a man in remembrance of some spiritual promise which cannot be seen but by faith only."[39] The state of the soul and the state of the church might both remain unknown. Thomas More saw the dangers of this picture of the internalized soul, and he worried about it in an extraordinarily prescient way. In a passage in the *Dialogue concerning Heresies* he responds to the accusation that set prayer is meaningless and that a church can be anywhere that a good man prays: "yet yf chyrches and congregacyons of crysten pepele resorting together to goddys service were ones abolished and put away, we were lyke to have few good temples of god withyn mennys soules but al would in a whyle were away clene and clerely fall to nought."[40] His perception was that the very state of "mennys soules" was dependent upon the way they "resorted together." In Fisher's critique of Luther's ecclesiology, *De abroganda missa privata,* he worried about the visibility of the church: "Who then will show you that Church, seeing that it is hidden in spirit and can only be believed in, as we say 'I believe in Holy Church'?"[41] And indeed this uncertainty remains a pressing topic of the ecclesiological discussions in the 1570s between Cartwright and Whitgift for whom the visibility of the church itself was fundamentally at issue. There were, in short, intense epistemological anxieties in how the church could be discerned and known. Luther proclaimed in triumphant defiance: "If I were the only one in the entire world to adhere to the word, I alone would be the church."[42]

Here we can see the defensive consolation familiar to Hamlet. Now the very existence of the church can be guaranteed by the lone adherence of one man to the word of God, a church founded in that heart and judged by that heart. The distinction here between a private self and a public world "guarantees the autonomy of the self no matter what happens to the external world."[43] Anyone who can confirm the mental objects in his mind through the circuit of himself alone can do without others. This is the private language fantasy. In the chapters that follow we will see many such would-be private linguists and the language lessons that ensue from forgoing the world of others.

In Luther's world, the certainty of salvation can be guaranteed only on the basis of the eradication of the untrustworthy human mediations, which will inevitably betray and traduce the work of God:

> This is the reason why our theology is certain: it snatches us away from ourselves and places us outside ourselves, so that we do not depend on our own strength, conscience, experience, person or works, but depend on that which is outside ourselves, that is, on the promise and truth of God, which cannot deceive.[44]

Compare this with Thomas Aquinas:

> The whole power of sacraments derives from the sufferings of Christ and those belong to him as man. Thus it is for men, not angels, to dispense and administer the sacraments.[45]

J. L. Austin's Inner and Outer   Medieval sacramental theology and the reformed theology of the sacraments alike defined a sacrament as the visible act of an invisible grace. When J. L. Austin explored what words do in a bravura set of counter-examples to philosophy's obsession with the statement, he clearly enjoyed disrupting and exposing the piety of the self-serious man whose profundity is, as it were, baptized by his own inner thoughts. Austin's target was, among other things, the idea that promising went on in the mind of the promiser and not in the words he uttered in promising. Speech acts are not the outward sign of an inward state that is the real key to their meaning:

> For one who says, "promising is not merely a matter of uttering words! It is an inward and spiritual act!" is apt to appear as a solid moralist standing out against a generation of superficial theorizers.... Yet he provides Hippolytus with a let-out, the bigamist with an excuse for his "I do" and the welsher

with a defence of his "I bet." Accuracy and morality are alike on the side that *our word is our bond.*[46]

Ritual action protects convention from intention because the acceptance intrinsic to ritual performance is a public act. This, as Austin so lucidly understood, is what protects us from the bigamist and the two-timer, and we could add, the mental reserver or the equivocator. If we have made a promise, our mental reservations about the matter will not affect the publicly declared commitment in our words and the fact of promising. As Roy Rappaport says: "liturgical performance does not eliminate insincerity, it renders it publicly impotent."[47]

When we hear the continuous refrain of words such as "hollow," "vain," and "empty" to describe ritual words, as if we could inject meaning into an "empty" word by a mental act of special intensity, we might remind ourselves of Fergus Kerr's words: "It is not what is going on in the radical privacy of people's minds that makes the difference between a committee meeting and a bout of glossolalia."[48] The reformers ardently desired a language in which the "outer" would conform to the "inner," where "there is ... none other use of these outward ceremonies, but as far forth as we are stirred up by them."[49] Yet their bifurcated language ended up creating an epistemological quandary that was both cripplingly vexing on a personal level and challenging pastorally. And in a cruel, unintended irony, it had the effect of intensifying a split they themselves wished to cure.

If it is inconvenient to question a convention, as Stanley Cavell has wittily suggested, then Shakespeare's culture was profoundly inconvenienced since so many of its conventions had been questioned and overturned.[50] Such questioning can, as Cavell also suggests, produce in reaction to itself the idea that such conventions are "mere" conventions, arbitrary and external, but "only a priest could have confronted his set of practices with its origins so deeply as to set the terms of the Reformation."[51] Some years ago, Bernard Beckerman remarked on the striking fact that almost every one of the Globe plays contain a public resolution.[52] Furthermore, of the fifteen Shakespeare plays produced between 1599 and 1609, only *Troilus and Cressida,* with its dour attack on stoicism and the citadel self, failed to culminate in a public and ceremonious ending.[53] This is testimony to a profound commitment to performing ceremonies in which those who have felt exiled, banished, misrepresented, or discounted by the theatricalized and forced speech anatomized on stage and in the culture at large, could find themselves spoken for and come to speak new forms of ceremony in which what they said counted.

Shakespeare diagnosed and sought to cure false pictures of the inner and the outer which render us powerless in the face of our own words. For what comes with the picture of an inaccessible inwardness is an eradication of the inherence of that inner life in the life and community with others. Shakespeare might be understood to be deeply fearful of our losing an inner life, in the paradoxical service of that inner life, thus losing our connection with others and with our own bodies and words. In the works succeeding the great tragedies he will find his way back to the possibility of restoration and forgiveness through theater, but he will do so only by virtue of understanding the necessities, evasions, and avoidance in our life with and in words. To achieve this possibility we must be able to distinguish, or be shown ways in which we do and can distinguish—not finally once and for all, but habitually and in specific contexts and situations—between sincerity and hypocrisy, between lies and truth, and between theater and theatricality.

The perceived split between "outward" behavior and "inner" thoughts is an intrinsic denigration of expressive culture and of the human voice. It is also deeply anti-theatrical because in dislocating the natural relation between words, gestures, and appearances, and "that within," the fundamental resources of theater are voided. Shakespeare lends his art to restoring the mind and the soul to the face, and in the process evolves theatrical forms in which reconciliation and forgiveness become central. Before I turn to examine the plays in which the arts of forgiveness are explored, I need to explore some of the histories of the rites of forgiveness in his culture.

2

RITES OF FORGIVENESS

Several critics have recently explored the idea that the idioms of Shakespearean theater are eucharistic. Anthony Dawson sees the actor's body shared and given, offered up to spectators, as a version of real presence; worthy reception is participation in theater and communion alike, and the actor's sharing of his flesh with spectators is a "secular enactment of eucharistic community."[1] Likewise Jeffrey Knapp suggests that Shakespeare frames *Henry V* as a sacrament whose "real power lay in the minds of its spectators" and thus represented his theater as a means not to "fight against [God's] word, but to save it from papists and preachers."[2] Thomas Bishop has also persuasively argued that "all through Shakespeare's career, questions of 'embodiment' framed in relation to the sacramental model are central to his thinking-through of the meaning of theatrical performance."[3] And Regina Schwarz in a full-blown nostalgia for the Catholic doctrine of transubstantiation has claimed that the theater became the first truly Protestant church where a community convenes and remembers sacrifice "without the *operatum* of the church."[4] Whereas there is no consensus among these critics about theologies of the sacrament, or the ways in

which such understandings inform Shakespearean theater, there is a grow-
ing body of opinion that explores the resources of a sacramental culture,
moreover a culture that has radically reformed the sacraments, for the new
idiom of Shakespearean theater. Yet, I argue, these resources are better understood when we see eucharist as intrinsically connected to penance and
its histories, for it is in the rituals surrounding communion that the community is made and remade out of acts of forgiveness. Issues of moral and
ecclesiastical discipline and issues of justice centered on the sacrament are
incomprehensible unless eucharist and penance are seen in relationship.
For the eucharist is the entire forgiven community.[5]

In the second and third parts of this book I will be examining aspects of
penance, sin, and reconciliation in a variety of individual plays, and there
I will be exploring further aspects of the speech act of confession, forgiveness, restitution as an aspect of penitential justice, and remorse. This chapter rehearses some of the attempts to redefine the nature of forgiveness in
the peculiar English settlement, when penance is abolished as a sacrament,
yet when some of the institutions and speech acts connected with it are still
an integral part of the economy of salvation.

Bud Welch's daughter died in the Oklahoma bombings of the Murrah
Federal Building in April 1995. "About a year before the execution," he
says, "I found it in my heart to forgive Tim McVeigh. It was a release for
me rather than for him."

Mary Kayitesi Blewitt lost fifty members of her family in the Rwandan
massacre of Tutsi in 1994:

> I met a woman who, after watching her husband and son being killed, was
> raped alongside one of her daughters. Her other daughters were killed at
> roadblocks. She was on the run for 100 days, meeting different people on the
> way, and was repeatedly raped. Finally she went mad and ended up in a men-
> tal hospital where she discovered she had AIDS. Now, if there was one per-
> son who had done all this and that person was found and apologized, perhaps
> you could forgive. But if there are hundreds who have hurt you, how can you
> forgive? ... You can't heal without feeling that justice has been done.

Simon Wilson was permanently disabled in a hit-and-run accident. After-
wards, he trained for the ministry:

> Some people within the church believe you can't forgive unless the other
> person repents but to me repentance isn't a condition of forgiveness because

ultimately forgiveness comes from within. Only I know whether I can forgive or not....Some people think I'm being pious telling people to forgive but actually I don't tell anyone to do anything. I simply tell people that the place I've reached is better than the place I was before.

These comments are all taken from *The Forgiveness Project,* a charity which explores forgiveness through the telling of stories. They rehearse—painfully and particularly—the moral, social, spiritual, and legal dimensions of forgiveness.[6] Who is to be the agent of forgiveness, which is an act of release as well as judgment? Each of the people I quote struggles with the extraordinary demands and possibilities of forgiveness. Each of them is confronted with questions of justice, with the terrible logic of the reciprocity of the hurt and the hurter in the same irrevocable act. Mary Blewitt would agree with Hannah Arendt: we can only forgive what we can punish. For Simon Wilson and Bud Welch, their own forgiveness cannot wait on the acknowledgment of the other no matter how desirable that act would be. They might agree with Avishai Margalit: forgiveness is not a voluntary mental act but rather a mental change.[7]

In medieval culture all these elements—the moral, social, spiritual, legal, and juridical dimensions—of forgiveness were bound together in the sacrament of penance, and medieval penitential and pastoral theology provides an extraordinarily capacious meditation on the social and psychic effects of sin and the remedies for sin. In this thinking it is impossible to separate the idea that sin is an offense against God, self, and neighbor at one and the same time. The charity whereby we love our neighbor *is* a participation in Divine charity.[8] The sacrament of penance is fundamentally concerned with justice and therefore with the machinery of punishment and correction in the cure of souls, but it is also profoundly concerned with friendship. Penance, suggests Thomas Aquinas, is concerned with justice, but it differs from vindictive justice

> because in vindictive justice the atonement is made according to the judge's decision, and not according to the discretion of the offender and the person offended; whereas, in Penance, the offense is atoned according to the will of the sinner, and the judgment of God against whom the sin was committed, because in the latter case we seek not only the restoration of the equality of justice, as in vindictive justice, but also and still more the reconciliation of friendship.[9]

The Reformation was an argument about the very nature of forgiveness. "If there is anything in the whole of religion that we should most certainly know, we ought most surely to grasp by what reason, with what law, under what condition, with what ease or difficulty, forgiveness of sins may be obtained!" declares Calvin in the *Institutes*.[10] Luther declared that no word had been as bitter to him as penitence; now, after he had formulated his understanding of man as justified by God, "nothing sounds sweeter or more agreeable to me than penitence."[11] Sins had been counted and classified in the massive encyclopedic compilations of the pastoral manuals of the thirteenth and fourteenth centuries; they were the subject of recounting in the mandatory practice of annual auricular confession before communion at Easter. In the reformed doctrine of justification, sins were no longer counted against the sinner, and it was in virtue alone of Christ's imputation of righteousness to the undeserving sinner that sin was gratuitously, graciously, divinely forgiven. The eleventh of the Thirty-Nine Articles (1563, revised 1571) proclaimed it as an article of faith that: "We are accounted righteous before God only for the merit of our Lord and saviour Jesus Christ by faith, and not for our own works or deservings. Wherefore, that we are justified *by faith only,* is a *most wholesome doctrine,* and very full of comfort."[12] These huge changes in the understanding of the state of being forgiven transformed the offices, institutions, and practices of forgiveness. I shall begin by examining the office of forgiveness and the doctrine of the keys as they work themselves out in the oddness of the English context; I then parse out some of the changing languages of confession and absolution after the sacerdotal role is radically diminished in the office of forgiveness, examine the intense epistemological anxieties accruing to penance in pre- and post-reformed practices, and the questions around human and divine agency there entailed.

The Office and Keys of Forgiveness

Can there be an *office* of forgiveness? Don't we learn the meaning of forgiveness (if not how to do it) when we learn how to speak? Surely there can be no special office into which the forgiver is formally initiated? It is a speech act that must be risked or not in individual encounters.[13] This kind of talk is unobjectionable if we forget that the forgiveness under discussion

is forgiveness for sin. Sin is an ontological category; it stains the soul, alien-
ates it from its maker. It is, as I have suggested, inseparably an offense
against God, self, and neighbor. How is that offense to each party to be
rectified, how mended? And who will or can judge such offenses? It is
precisely in virtue of the category of *sin* that there is an office of forgiveness and a rite of initiation into that office. The sacerdotal office and its
transformation in the English Reformation turns out to be an integral part
of the history of forgiveness and the landscape of penitential practice when
it is sin and not merely crime or wrong-doing that is at issue.

   The power of the keys and the sacrament of penance were concepts
whose history is intimately intertwined. The medieval understanding of
the keys circulated around a number of key texts, chiefly Matthew 16.18–19,
Matthew 18.15–18, and John 20.21–23. At Philippi, Christ had addressed
Peter:

> And I say also unto thee, that thou art Peter, and upon this rocke will I
> buylde my Church: and the gates of hell shal not overcome it. And I will
> give thee the keyes of the kingdome of heaven, and whatsoever thou shalt
> binde upon earth, shalbe bound in heaven: and whatsoever thou shalt lose
> on earth, shalbe be losed in heaven.[14]

The power to bind and loose, to forgive sin on behalf of God, was understood to be bestowed with the indelible seal of ordination.[15] By the act of
ordination, which was also a sacramental act, priests became officers and
spokesmen for the Church and dispensed forgiveness not in their own person but through the very voice of Christ, or in the preferred ecclesial formulation, "in persona Christi."[16] Christ, through the Holy Spirit, made the
sacraments holy; this was why no wicked priest could mar their efficacy
for it was objective, not dependent on the subjectivity of the priest.[17] As we
shall see below, this question of authorization and ventriloquism was extremely vexed when it came to the words of absolution. Was it possible to
say "*Ego* te absolvo?" when the agent of action was God himself? It was
the doctrine of the keys and the jurisdiction thereby claimed that made the
priest the indispensable means of sacramental absolution.

   The keys were conventionally divided between the key of order (*potestas ordinis*) and the key of jurisdiction (*potestas jurisdictionis*). The key of
order was reserved for those in orders, and it linked the sacramental action

of penance with the sacramental action, the indelible seal, of ordination. The key of jurisdiction could be delegated; thus deacons and even laymen could have this authority and could pronounce the words of absolution in the ecclesiastical courts. Indeed the ecclesiastical courts themselves constituted a further subdivision of the powers of jurisdiction; they were part of the exterior forum as opposed to the internal forum of the confessional, and these formed two parallel, overlapping jurisdictions. The internal forum was understood to be sacramental: it concerned the penitent's voluntary acts of contrition and confession; the external forum was part of the governance, and it could compel and pronounce on those in its jurisdiction. The forums were then formally distinct and performed by different authorities.[18] The pastoral reason for the division was understandable. It may have arisen from the desire to save penitents from the inevitable shame of exposure that public penance entailed, a shame that might keep them away from the practice of confession altogether. Richard Hooker suggests that the idea was to protect people "whose crimes were unknown |unless they| should blaze their own faults as it were on a stage acquainting all people with what they had done amiss."[19] The priest could administer penances and preserve the secrecy of the penitent and the seal of the confessional, and this seemed vital in trying to persuade people to come to confession in the first place. Indeed confessional manuals are full of advice to the priest about how to preserve the secrecy of the confessional in the administration of penances. Nevertheless the splitting of the two forums led to a theologically incoherent division; sin as an interior matter was "to be radically distinguished from the matters of exterior social readjustments to be dealt with in the external forum."[20] The split threatened the whole idea of sin as social, as simultaneously a sin against self, neighbor, and God in the idea of the body of Christ. Offenses against God could be taken up in the confessional, and public offenses against neighbor could be taken up in the exterior forum.[21] The doctrine of the keys and the related understanding of the sacramentality of penance gave a secure sense that God was working through the office of priesthood; after all he had through Christ given Peter the keys to the kingdom. When priests absolved sin, they did so in the name of God. Nevertheless, there was a clear sense that such absolutions were declaratory. God forgave sin; but priests declared that forgiveness on his behalf: "God alone absolves from sin and forgives sins authoritatively, yet priests do both ministerially, because the words of the priest in this sacrament (of the altar) work as instruments of the Divine power, as in the other sacraments: because it is the Divine power that works inwardly in all the sacramental signs."[22] The Holy Spirit could confer grace even through a wicked priest because it was Christ's words that were being spoken and not the priest's. The sacraments worked objectively, and so forgiveness through their agency was assured. The Council of Trent unequivocally affirmed the full *juridical* force of absolution. Absolution in the Tridentine understanding was not declaratory but a judicial act whereby a sentence is "pronounced by the priest as by a judge." In the 6th Session on Justification at the Council of Trent the dangerous notion that justification could be subjective was anathematized. "Against the vain confidence of heretics," Chapter IX declares:

> ...neither is this to be asserted, that they who are truly justified must needs without any doubting whatsoever, settle within themselves that they are justified and that no one is absolved from sins and justified, but he that believes for certain that he is absolved and justified and that absolution and justification are effected by this faith alone.... [23]

During the course of the Reformation in England, penance was no longer understood to be a sacrament. For one thing, only two sacraments were regarded as scriptural: eucharist and baptism. Penance, extreme unction, ordination, confirmation, and marriage were discounted because they were not mandated by Christ. Furthermore, the reformed understanding of sacraments as the seals and confirmation of God's promises utterly transformed the Aristotelian underpinnings of sacramental theology. In Hugh of St. Victor's definition a sacrament was a "physical or material object admitted to the perception of the external senses, representing a reality beyond itself by virtue of having been instituted as a sign of it, and containing within it some invisible and spiritual grace in virtue of having been consecrated."[24] In reformed logic, forgiveness had already happened: there was no possibility that human action itself could provide the "matter" of the sacrament as in the medieval understanding. Furthermore to bind the actions of God to the law of man was an obscenity. Medieval thinkers had in fact never understood God to be bound by sacraments, but, as Alistair McGrath has said, "the tendency to emphasize the reliability of the established order of salvation, of which the sacramental system is part, can only have served to convey the impression that the sinner who wishes to be reconciled to God must, *de facto*, seek the assistance of a priest."[25] For the reformers sacraments no longer worked objectively "*ex opere operato*" but rather were moral and spiritual instruments of reform. Thus the tripartite component parts of penance in contrition, confession, and satisfaction were transformed and dismantled.

What happens when penance is abolished as a sacrament and when the keys are fundamentally redefined in the Reformation? For Thomas Becon, chaplain to Archbishop Cranmer, in his book *The Castle of Comfort,* the very notion that men could forgive sins was obscene. Glossing over the careful distinctions made in the medieval treatises about the declaratory as opposed to judicial nature of absolution, he declares that men in so doing are taking upon themselves the office of God:

> First, I will prove with manifest scriptures that God alone forgiveth sin. Secondly, that the priest is but a minister appointeth of God, to declare free remission of sins to the truly penitent, to declare, I say, and not forgive.[26]

It is epistemological questions that come to the fore here, as I shall go on to show:

> Seeing that none can search the heart, whether it be faithful or unfaithful, but God alone; seeing also that the absolution beareth no strength but where faith is, it followeth that none can absolve me of my sins, but that Lord alone which searcheth the veins and the heart.[27]

The "shaven nation" have grossly usurped their prerogative and arrogated to themselves the very power of God. God's ministers are there to "publish" the benefit of our salvation. Absolution is the preaching of the remission of sins in the name of Christ. Becon thus, along with many of his contemporaries, redefines the keys:

> They loosen, that is to say, they preach to the faithful the remission of sins by Christ. They also bind, that is, they declare to the unfaithful damnation.[28]

The key of remission is in fact the key of knowledge, and where there is no knowledge there is no key.

John Jewel, Bishop of Salisbury, redefines the keys too. The medieval doctrine of the keys gave us many keys, he suggests: the key of knowledge; the key of order; the key of power; the key of discretion; the key of sacraments. Yet the key is the "word of the gospel and the expounding of the law and scriptures." When the word is not preached, there is no "key."[29]

Luther assimilates the key that binds to the law which reveals the nature of sin to the sinner, and the gospel which liberates and looses sin:

> Both these keys are absolutely central to Christianity, and God can be fully thanked for them. The strong, iron key which binds is for pious Christians a mighty shield, wall and stronghold against evil-doers. But it is also an effective, useful and holy medicine for evil-doers, though terrifying and frightening to the flesh.[30]

Even though the keys had been comprehensively redefined by Protestant reformers, and the office of forgiveness thereby revolutionized, the speech act of absolution remained controversial. The precise words of absolution had long been subject to controversy. Peter Lombard had argued that the words of absolution were declarative, not juridical; sacramental efficacy lay in contrition, not absolution. And the declaratory formula held sway until the thirteenth century. Should the form be "ego te absolvo" or should it be preccatory ("May God forgive you"), making it obvious that it was not sacerdotal power but the delegated authority of the church that was at issue? Such arguments never disappeared. In the *Book of Common Prayer* the words of absolution are retained in the Visitation for the Sick and in the general absolution following general confession. Here the form is deprecatory: "By his authority committed, I hereby absolve thee." In fact there is remarkable continuity between the prayer book uses of absolution and the medieval services except that there is no absolution after auricular confession and no formal restoration to the sacraments of the church. At the Hampton Court conference the form of absolution in the prayer book came up for continuing discussion. Some objected to the word in itself because it is a "forensical and judicial word importing more than a declaration," and they desired to have it corrected. The words of absolution could be even more controversial in the case of the ecclesiastical courts. There they might be pronounced by a layman much to the disgust of nonconformists and to the occasional embarrassment of the defenders of the courts.[31]

The Epistemology of Penance

When Harding argues with John Jewel in their debates of the 1560s and early '70s, he is very aware of the epistemological effects of the changing understanding of the keys. If the key was the word, how could Jewel be qualified out of his mere human resources to discern whether his preaching was effective?

> Preach ye never so much, the conscience of man being so secret a thing as it is, how can ye judge who inwardly and thoroughly repenteth and who repenteth not; and though, one repent and be sorry, and have remorse of his former life, though he look unto the light of the gospel, as ye say, and believe in Christ, what then? How can ye judge of such a person? Do you know his heart by looking in his face?[32]

If John Jewel wanted to redefine the keys as preaching rather than binding and loosing, how could one possibly be certain of forgiveness and salvation? The sacrament of penance as it was conventionally understood had been divided up into three parts: contrition of the heart (*compunctio cordis*), confession of the mouth (*confessio oris*), and satisfaction of works (*satisfactio operis*).[33] Epistemological anxieties haunted each stage of penance. If, as early scholastic theology would have it, "contritus fit contritior," how can the contrite sinner be sure of the purity of his contrition or its adequacy?[34] Yet, if not content with contrition, he confessed to a priest as was mandated annually according to Canon 21 of the Fourth Lateran Council, how could he be sure that the priest would be able to calculate the appropriate penance? It was precisely because of such plaguing uncertainties that Duns Scotus evolved his two ways of justification. Attrition, deriving less from the love of God than the fear of hell and punishment, could (*per modum meriti de congruo*), if long enough or intense enough, attain the goal of God's grace. Yet because there could be no surety here, the safer way is the way of absolution, granted in the power of the keys wherein the true efficacy of the sacrament lay. Contrition lacked a sensible sign, but Scotus located both form and matter in the priestly absolution, and this was the path to certainty. Here was room for the practices of indulgence and purgatory. These epistemological questions are then fully available in the complex, capacious medieval theologies of penance, yet it was a general medieval teaching that no one can know beyond doubt whether he is in a state of grace.[35] In the reformed discourse the epistemological questions are deeply driven, even compulsive.

This compulsion can be seen in the "Homily of the Worthy Receiving and Reverent Esteeming of the Sacrament of the Body and Blood of Christ." One of the chief reasons why Cranmer and other reformers rejected transubstantiation was that they believed it negated the act of repentance and reception. If the body of Christ was *ex opere operato* produced by a confecting priesthood, then all could receive worthily at their hands. In the official book of homilies the two-part "Homily of the Worthy Receiving and Reverent Esteeming of the Sacrament of the Body and Blood of Christ" also has as one of its central texts I Corinthians 29.11. Here Paul was addressing the divisions among the Corinthians.

When you come together, he says, it is not to eat the Lord's Supper. "For when the time comes to eat, each of you goes ahead with your own supper, and one goes hungry and another one becomes drunk." But according to Paul, it is impossible to worthily receive the body, to participate in the feast if some go hungry, if some are humiliated. This is "not discerning the body." So the homilist begins with an understanding of eucharist as memory and participation against private eating and sacrifice.[36] Yet as he goes on to address proper discernment of the body, there are emergent signs that the participation so enjoined is undercut by the very techniques encouraged to reach it. They are subtle, unwitting, yet retrospectively, in the contexts of later developments, invidious. The first is that there is a tendency to render too cognitive the mode of participation. One of the claims made in the homily is that "the ignorant cannot without fruit and profit, exercise himself in the Lord's sacraments." This seems unproblematic. But the author then claims that the Corinthian problem was ignorance: "St Paul, blaming the Corinthians for the profaning of the Lord's Supper, concludeth that ignorance, both of the thing itself, and the signification thereof, was the cause of their abuse; for they came irreverently, not discerning the Lord's body."[37] Paul actually writes, however, in reprimand of the greed and individualism that made a mockery of the body of Christ. The implication in the Reformation homily is epistemological: an epistemological problem here can have an epistemological cure. Those Corinthians did not know what the Lord's body was, just as Catholics think that the bread actually is the literal body of Christ. "For what hath been the cause of the ruin of God's religion but the ignorance therof?"[38] This constitutes a bewilderingly optimistic assessment of the situation—as if knowledge and right doctrine might dispel malice, hatred, vainglory, and contempt, as if Augustine and Calvin had never contested stoic accounts of virtue for their superficial sense of the resources of the human will. This kind of episte-mological confidence was not shared by allegorists such as Langland and Spenser or by Shakespeare, who understood that knowledge was bound up with acknowledgment and recognition and plumbed the bewildering complexity of this process, including as it did the sheer opacity of things in the world as well as in our own minds.

Secondly, in trying to insist that there will be no surrogation in wor-ship, no sacrificing of the priesthood on behalf of others ("no dumb mass-ing") the homilist comes to insist that "every one of us ought to celebrate the same, at his table, in our own persons."[39] So the notion of "in our own persons" becomes stressed to such an extent that the Pauline interdepen-dencies of the body of Christ are underdeveloped, even unwittingly under-mined, at least in the first part of the homily. The effect is to atomize the body even against the explicit desire and aim, as well as the theology of the supper: "make Christ thine own, apply his merits to thyself. Herein thou needest no other man's help, no other sacrifice or oblation, or sacrificing priest, no mass, no means established by man's invention."[40]

Finally, the homilist stresses how important it is "to prove, and try our-selves unfeignedly, without flattering ourselves, whether we be plants of that fruitful olive, living branches of the true vine."[41] Thus our feeding, our sustenance becomes dependent not so much on the participation in the supper and our enaction of the body of Christ together but on a process of introspection whereby we could check our own worthiness. It is just this eradication of a receiving community in the very act of self-knowledge and self-recognition that becomes so exceedingly problematical in this homily and where its confident tones of dispelling the darkness of ignorance only intensify and undermine its most heart-felt aims. Self-scrutiny that has lost its pastoral context in the specter of popish abuse is subject to relentlessly circular intensifications, restless anxieties of uncertainty, cravings for an impossible assurance. The religious subject begins to be gripped by an in-terminable problem of knowledge. It leads several of the subjects of John Stachniewski's fascinating book into suicides that guarantee certainty at the cost of damnation itself.[42] Despite the currents of resistance to these trajectories within the Church of England from the 1590s,[43] these powerful currents radically refigured the whole way in which human agency was conceived in relation to divine agency and significantly affected ways of conceiving self and the social.

The search for certainty, the impossibility of living with uncertainty, threatens to take over the subject completely as if knowledge can be surer than trust. Indeed what seemed to be a massive drive and determining factor in the reformed account of sin was the desperate sense of the sheer untrustworthiness of human action and human judgment. If forgiveness of sins depends on the conditions that the "Scholastic sophists" attach to it, then one will never be certain about forgiveness, and this is intolerable. "They make contrition the first step in obtaining pardon, and they require it to be a due contrition, that is just and full. But at the same time they do not determine when a man can have assurance that he has in just measure carried out his contrition," says Calvin.[44] The scholastic formulation that doing what we are capable of is enough, that God will not deny grace to the man who does what is in him (*"Facienti quod in se est Deus non denegat gratiam"*) was seen to be redundantly circular and utterly incommensurable with a picture of sin as rats ravening down their poison, as horror and depravity.[45] On this issue it is indeed hard to argue with Calvin's hard logic: "If they say that we must do what is in us, we are always brought back to the same point. For when will anyone dare assure himself that he has applied all of his powers to lament his sins?"[46] When it came to confession, how was one to know if one had confessed all one's sins? What of the ones one had forgotten? There was no consolation in the "*Facere quod.*" "Therefore that dread voice always presses and resounds in his ears: 'Confess all your sins.' And this terror cannot be allayed except by a sure consolation."[47] Furthermore there are other epistemological concerns in the whole area of binding and loosing—how do you know if you are absolved, for example?[48] Anxiety besets the sacrament of penance at every point of its medieval tripartite components: contrition, confession, and absolution. "These two things elude the knowledge of a man when he has to pass sentence upon another man. Therefore, it follows that certainty of binding and loosing does not lie within the competence of earthly judgment because the minister of the word, when he duly performs his function, can absolve only conditionally."[49] The problems are relentlessly circular: "not to know what is to be bound and loosed, yet not to be able to bind or loose unless you know"?[50] In Calvin's treatment of this question, he comes back over and over again to the question of certainty. "Why then do they say they absolve by the authority given them, when their absolution is uncertain?"[51] When it came to "satisfaction," when can he be certain of the measure of that satisfaction? "Then he will always doubt whether he has a merciful God: he will always be troubled, and always tremble."[52]

These questions of uncertainty had also famously haunted Luther. In *On the Bondage of the Will* he had asked: "What is more miserable than uncertainty?"[53] As Lee Wandell Palmer puts it: "Luther rejected all efforts to subsume the words of God to human sensibility and reason."[54] The words of man and the words of God were utterly opposed: "Human statutes cannot be observed together with the Word of God, because they bind consciences, while the Word sets them free."[55]

All uncertainties were meant to be swept away by the doctrine of justification. For under this doctrine we are justified because we are sinners, but our sins are not counted against us. In this deeply forensic model of sin, justification is the "declaration that the Christian is righteous, rather than the process by which he is made righteous, involving a change in his status before God, rather than his nature."[56]

Yet what is the agency of justification? Who declares it? The force of the priest's declarations had been rendered explicit in the ritual formulations of absolution in the confessional. Although it is plain that absolution cannot be assimilated to forgiveness, it is clear that the changed understanding of priest and sacrament has the most decisive pastoral effect on an entire cultural understanding of forgiveness.

The Eradication of the Human

The circular, painful epistemological drives for certainty in the reformed tradition are also directly linked to what I want to call "the eradication of the human" in reformed discourse. Jennifer Herdt has recently proposed that Luther demands as a starting point the utter bankruptcy of human agency.[57] In the Lutheran and Calvinistic understanding of justification, man is seen not as an ethical subject capable of growth but rather as he is seen by God, *coram Deo*. He is realized by Christ and through Christ, and the intrusion of any human agency into this picture threatens the certainty of salvation. There is to be no involvement of human virtues and habits, human laws or traditions; these could only traduce and impinge on the graceful sovereignty of God. For Luther, as he developed this perspective in his lectures on the Psalms and above all on Romans, it was a vitiating problem of scholasticism that it had viewed man from the point of view of man and not from the point of view of God. It was only if all human effort in salvation were completely obliterated as worthless that the certainty of salvation could be assured. As long as salvation depended in any degree on his own efforts, man could never be sure he had done enough, and this was an intolerable burden: "My conscience would never give me certainty. But I always doubted and said, 'You did not perform that correctly. You were not contrite enough. You left that out of your confession.'"[58] As the 4th of the Wittenberg articles puts it:

> For if, to God's judgment against sin, we were to oppose our worthiness and our merits (as a satisfaction) for sin, the promise of reconciliation would become uncertain for us, and our consciences would be driven to despair, as Paul says. (Ro. 4.15)[59]

It is not just that works were pointless and could not in any way mitigate sin or placate the righteousness of God. All forms of human action and mediation were suspect, utterly tainted. Indeed it becomes characteristic of Luther's prose that he scornfully adds the designator "human" to all kind of nouns: human traditions, human ceremonies, human inventions. He has forgotten what Thomas Aquinas said: sacraments are for humans, they speak to our embodied fleshly nature, constituting the means of grace precisely for human beings. For Luther all are worthless, and this makes any hermeneutics of human agency impossible. Berndt Hamm puts it the following way: "Luther experienced in a shattering way the deep cleft between divine and human possibilities before God—in every respect: both as an epistemological subject and as an ethical agent."[60] His sense of the chasm separating the sin of man from the goodness of God meant that he had to abandon a whole tradition of thinking about human praxis and action, one which relied on the Aristotelian notion of habitus. No human habit could ameliorate human sin, and love could no longer be the central concept in Christian life.[61] Faith alone (*sola fide*) becomes a partner in justification because if forgiveness depended on our worthiness we could never be certain of it. Justification can have consequences in human action, but it can never have causes in it.[62] This is an astonishing, impossible obliteration of the world of human action, and of the human conditions of feeling, acting, and doing. It proves paralyzing as reformed discourse binds itself in the hopeless, intensifying languages of assurance.

The Performance of Penance

In the Lutheran church confession was retained; in the reformed church the model of the consistory was put into practice, though more successfully in Scotland and Geneva than in France or the Netherlands. In this model elders of particular congregations took on the work of reconciliation in settling disputes, and were able to use the final sanction of exclusion from communion until the sinner was reconciled. Recent historians of the consistory system suggest that, at its best, the discipline could function as the medieval guilds had once done in arbitrating disputes, with the goal of charity and peace. In England, however, although reformers ardently desired to put into effect a consistory model along Scottish or Genevan lines, it was clear by the 1590s that this initiative was dead in the water. "Church discipline," while not strictly speaking a mark of the true church, was nevertheless regarded as essential to the forgiven community as the body of Christ. Diarmaid MacCulloch has recently suggested that the "lack of proper Reformed discipline was as significant as the survival of cathedrals in differentiating the English Church from the other Reformed churches of Europe."[63]

What the reformed model offered to its adherents and advocates was a system of reconciliation and justice that worked off the notion of sin as fully social, as damaging to the individual and to the community at large. Elders worked to bring the sinner to repentance and reconciliation with the whole body of the church. Where an elder could not effect a reconciliation by private admonition, the sinner was enjoined to confess to the whole church. Margo Todd's fascinating book about the discipline as practiced by the kirk in Scotland in fact discovers the greatest continuities with the medieval practices of penance.[64] She claims that the public confession of sin and the declaration of repentance expanded to become the central ritual act of Protestant worship in Scotland.

In the rites of the Scottish kirk, the penitent's performance is carefully choreographed; he or she is told exactly where to process, and the entire fabric of the church is part of the material of performance. The public confessions of penitents to the congregation were carefully coached and rehearsed because Scottish ministers had learned to their cost that it was best not to allow completely *ex tempore* performances of confession. In the reformed kirk the penitent would sit on the penitent's stool until "absolved off the stool." This was thus a "tangible, visible performance before the whole community and it made it impossible for those reconciled to violate the peace without loss of faith as well as loss of face."[65] Margo Todd claims that "the suggestion of an earlier generation that protestantism gave rise to modern individualism is given the lie by the Scottish penitential rite."

In the English context reforming ministers had to make do as best they could with the practices of the *Book of Common Prayer*. Indeed, even the *Book of Common Prayer* itself appears to lament the "open penance" of the primitive church. It suggests in the "Commination against Sinners" that the "general sentences of God's cursing against impenitent sinners gathered out of the twenty-seventh chapter of Deuteronomy, and other places of scripture" will have to suffice "until the said discipline be restored again."[66] For some reformed ministers this meant that their hands were tied in the fight against sin. They worried that their congregations were irredeemably contaminated. Stephen Denison, minister of St. Katherine Cree in London, maintained that the godly and the ungodly must take communion together, yet attempted to reassure the godly that the unworthy could not pollute the sacrament: "his being there shall not prejudice thee: he eateth and drinketh damnation only to himself."[67] Since as Peter Lake comments, "this was to introduce the mutual hostility of the godly and the ungodly into the very act of reception," this represented a manifest failure of communion as a forgiven community whose forgiveness showed them forth as part of the body of Christ.

In the half-reformed Church of England penance was also a public performance.[68] The penitent was part of the choreography of service, with his or her confession taking place usually at morning or evening service at the sinner's parish church between the first and second lessons.[69] The penitent was to perform his penance in his own parish church, and his props and costume were seen as appropriate to the drama of his sin. Henry Collin of Moze who was indicted for drunken behavior, for example, was required "to sit on his knees in the church porch with three empty pots before him till the second lesson with a white wand and then to come to the church to the minister and there to speak such words of penance after the minister as shall be delivered to him in writing."[70] Sometimes the penitential performances were in marketplace and church, as in the case of William Cock in Dedham in 1581:

> Upon Saturday next he shall in a white sheet about him, bareheaded and barefooted, about 11'o'clock in the forenoon, walk the length of the market place, holding a white rod in his hand a paper on his head describing the cause, and then stand so apparelled at the Moot Hall door (Colchester) by the space of an hour, viz, till 12 of the clock, and then confess openly his fault of fornication with Alice Chase, and shall likewise apparelled stand in the middle alley of Dedham church the Sunday following by the time of the morning prayer, and after that shall meekly kneeling on his knees confess the said fault of fornication, desiring God to forgive him.[71]

These practices seem remarkably continuous from the medieval to the reformed era. However, as I go on to explore in chapter 3, the difference lies in the fact that sins that might have hitherto been adjudicated in the interior forum of the confessional now found their way to the public, juridical setting of the ecclesiastical courts. Indeed the crucial discontinuities between medieval and reformed practices concerned the relation of the internal to the external forum of penance.

England abolished auricular confession as a compulsory annual practice, yet maintained the structure of the ecclesiastical courts. The internal, sacramental forum administered by priests disappeared; but the external forum, the juridical structure remained. The abolition of confession entailed that only public penances, not private ones (such as fasting or the recitation of prayers or psalms), were allowed. Confession was of course allowed, even encouraged in the *Book of Common Prayer*—in both the general confession in the liturgies of Morning and Evening Prayer, in the Litany, and in the general confession for the service of Holy Communion. It was also a possible implication of the injunctions to the parish priest to ensure that parishioners were in charity before communing, injunctions that might have entailed sufficient pastoral mediation including, perhaps, confession, but that also often resulted in exclusion altogether from the communion.[72]

But such confessions were no longer enjoined on all and shared by all. As Richard Hooker put it:

> The Church of England hitherto hath thought it the safer way, to referre mens hidden crimes unto God and themselves only howbeit not without specially caution, for the admonition of such as come to the Holy Sacrament and for the comfort of such as are readie to depart the world.[73]

From a practice that was mandatory at Easter, and woven into the penitential season of the liturgical year, confession was essentially relegated to the last dying speech of the criminal penitent in the context of punishment and execution.[74] Without question, the abolition of mandatory auricular confession reduced the complexity and indeed the permeability of the boundary between private and public adjudicated by the parish priest. In hardening that boundary—and in the absence of a system of discipline where admonition might work through different levels of rebuke—the abolition of auricular confession in the internal forum assured that penance would also be automatically shameful and humiliating because the resort to public exposure was unmitigated and unmediated by any prior stages of private penance. "Nothing," says Patrick Collinson, "can have made a greater negative impact than the lapse of the universal obligation to confess to a priest, as the condition both of receiving the sacrament and of remaining an acceptable part of what was still a compulsory Christian society."[75] From its original and pastoral function in the cure of souls, penance became more exclusively the means of the punishment and exposure of souls and bodies. Paradoxically, and as an unintended effect, ecclesiastical authority was further externalized. The faculty of canon law was itself ended by royal injunction by Henry VIII in 1535.[76] The reform of ecclesiastical law promised in the *Reformatio Legum Ecclesiasticarum,* a comprehensive revision of the canon law for the English polity, never took place and in the event civil lawyers took over canon law by authority of another act of Parliament in 1545, which allowed them to exercise ecclesiastical jurisdiction.[77] Thus canon law was administered often by lay officials, cut off from the living body of the law in Rome and without a university faculty trained in the continuing study of such law. The Crown in Parliament was the ultimate arbiter of ecclesiastical discipline, and loyalty to the church and to the state were indistinguishable as a result of the Erastian path taken in the English Reformation.

The abolition of auricular confession had far-reaching ramifications. Even those who thought that the precise enumeration of sins there demanded and the obligatory nature of the practice were wrong regretted its loss in the cure of souls. The early reformers such as Latimer and Ridley publicly declared the usefulness of confession, and it is clear from the Visitation records of some of the avant-garde conformist bishops that the practice was encouraged. Given that, as John Bossy has argued, it was one of the chief functions of the priesthood both before and after the Reformation to be a settler of disputes, mediating conflict and reconciling those at odds in preparation for holy communion, it was of the utmost significance that the abolition of auricular confession closed down the internal forum of the confessional. R. H. Helmholz records that canon law had in effect depended on the internal forum regulating much of men's lives. Now it was the case that conflict that had once been sorted out privately gave rise to public authority. Helmholz records that there was a great increase in numbers appearing before the ecclesiastical courts of those failing to receive communion: he thinks this is an example of the kind of issue once dealt with in the internal forum that now became the business of the ecclesiastical courts.

Confessing and Absolving

In suggesting that "men's hidden crimes" were to be referred to "God and themselves only," Hooker differentiates English liturgical practices from both the Genevan and the Roman models.[78] Quoting Tertullian, he advocates not a "theater or open court of many of your fellow servants," but rather a disclosure of the conscience before God. Every man can represent "his own particulars" in the general confession of the *Book of Common Prayer* and receive a general absolution from them.[79] It was still possible to confess to the minister privately if your conscience was troubled, but as T. W. Drury has observed: "what was habitual and what was exceptional had changed places."[80] And even that invitation is watered down in the changes from 1549 to 1552: "Let him confess and open his synne and griefe secretly" becomes "let him open his griefe." In 1549 the sinner might receive "comfort and absolution" from "us, (as of the ministers of GOD and of the churche"; in 1552 and in 1559 he might receive "the benefit of absolution, to the quieting of his conscience, and auoiding of all Scruple and doubtfulness" by the ministry of God's word.[81] Confession to a minister was thus regarded as exceptional rather than routine, and for those in special need, rather than for everyone.

The words of absolution in the Visitation of the Sick are also very carefully qualified: "by his authority committed to me, I absolve thee from all thy sins, in the name of the Father, and the Son, and of the Holy Ghost."[82] Here there was none of the confidence by which the medieval priest was understood to confess and absolve not as man, but as God. The priest in the Thomistic understanding declares man absolved of sin "not only significatorily but also effectively" because he is speaking as the church, not as an individual.[83] The priest is in effect protected from his own intentions for he speaks the intention of the church.[84] In the radical redefinition of the keys as preaching or as knowledge that follows reform, there can be no institutional surety of absolution. I will have much more to say about the general absolution and general confession of sin (in chapter 5), but it is apparent that when the office of priesthood changes so do the rites of forgiveness.

Shakespearean theater is everywhere marked by the transformation of confession and absolution. When people confess and forgive in the absence of an office of forgiveness they are newly exposed in their words. For if, as I suggested in chapter 1, the work of ritual is to make explicit what the force of an utterance is, then absent the ritual assurance that makes explicit the force of a performative, conferred in the precisely detailed conventions of the rites of confession, the act of forgiveness is both no one's and everyone's to bestow. It is no one's because the priesthood is no longer authorized to speak in God's name and a priest's intention is no longer "covered" by the intention of the church. And it is everyone's for the same reason. But precisely because priestly authority is contested there can no longer be a clear-cut distinction between what words do in the act of speaking and by the act of speaking, between the conventional and the consequential effects of the words, or in Austin's parlance, between illocutionary force and perlocutionary effect.[85]

Supposing you are a priest and you confess and absolve me. Your absolution might make me cry with relief and joy, or perhaps I resent your authority but require its effect, in which case my relief will be tinged with resentment. In either case you will have absolved me regardless of the perlocutionary effects your words have on me. But supposing you are not a priest, but you care about me. You think that I have been making some egregious and harmful decisions and you want to bring me to an awareness of them. You will, in short, be trying to confess me. But now because you have no authority to do this except for the authority I grant you in this particular instance, your attempts to confess me cannot be isolated in the same way from my response to you; there is no longer any conventional procedure whose conditions can be satisfied. We are both "singled out" in this exchange, exposed in our words to each other. Our judgment of each other is laid bare. We will be improvising, and the words we choose to address to each other will be loaded with consequence: the future of our relationship might depend on them. I might refuse the position you are assuming in speaking with me and tell you that you have no right to set yourself up as judge; you might feel that our friendship is thereby shallower and frailer that you had thought. This might be called a "rediscovery of speech," and it is the essential medium of Shakespeare's theater.[86] Cavell, drawing on the implications of J. L. Austin's work, wants to call this "passionate utterance," open to the improvisations of desire rather than the order of law. The rest of this book rehearses the implications of some of these statements, but here I will draw on a very famous Shakespearean example.

Let us turn to another conversation between Hamlet and Gertrude which I call "Hamlet's Confession" to see how questions of responsibility in meaning crowd into the scene in the absence of the office of confessor. The closet scene begins in mutual accusation as each attempts to claim moral authority and the right to name the offense:

> Queen. Hamlet, thou hast thy father much offended.
> Ham. Mother, you have my father much offended.
>
> (3.4.9–10)

These accusations involve an attempt to reposition themselves in relation to each other. Gertrude speaks as Claudius's wife, Hamlet as King Hamlet's son; both claim the name of father. When Hamlet sets up a "glass / Where you may see the (inmost) part of you" (3.4.19–20), he is laying title to the role of confessor: his task is to bring Gertrude to shame and contrition, and then to confession: "Confess yourself to heaven, / Repent what's past, avoid what is to come" (3.4.149–50). Hamlet has not been formally invested with the role of confessor; there has been no ordination. He claims the role by virtue of what he has seen, by the burden of his knowledge: that the king is a murderous usurper. So his claim is deeply revelatory of his desires for justice, his own inheritance, and moral authority, claims that can at any point be rebuffed and refused by Gertrude. Whether or not she will grant him the role of confessor on this particular occasion is precisely what is at issue, and it will involve her in the most painful revelations about herself: that she is colluding with the murderer of her husband, supping at his table and sleeping in his bed, sharing the fruits of usurpation. Hamlet as "ghostly father" (a common word for priest or friar) rests the authority for the confession of Gertrude on his own "Ghostly father," the ghost of King Hamlet whose provenance is notoriously unknown, and who now interrupts the scene. But not before the confession has been punctuated by the killing of Polonius behind the arras; the confessor is now guilty of a bloody deed "almost as bad, good mother, / As kill a king, and marry with his brother" (3.4. 27–28). Where is Hamlet's moral authority now? In this scene, the "ghostly father" is one that he alone can see; as far as Gertrude is concerned he is staring fixedly into the vacant air and he looks like a madman. As he catechizes Gertrude about her congress with Claudius, it seems as if his object is now not so much to soul-search Gertrude as to evince his own appalled disgust at her sexual depravity.

I am not so much claiming that Hamlet can confess Gertrude but not absolve her, nor that they inhabit a culture that has lost the rites of confession, as of mourning and marriage. Such accounts tend to posit too straightforward and too functionalist a relation between ritual and theater.[87] Rather I want to show that in the claims to confession as a language in which they are not formally invested as priest and confessee, they have constantly to take up their responsibility in assuming these constantly changing roles. In that endless and uncertain terrain, there is a constant struggle over where authority might lie, and who can lay claim to the "ghostly father" is constantly in play. In such play each character is newly and continually exposed to the other, and to his or her own judgment of the other.

In the complex transformations from penance to repentance, some of whose contours I have attempted to trace here, there can be no simple model of replacement, no blanket functionalism which defines and adjudicates cultural losses. Rather, as J. L. Austin says, "the total speech act in the total speech situation is the only actual phenomenon which...we are engaged in elucidating."[88] This kind of an approach requires a sensitivity to occasion; it entails that ethics pervades every act of speech.[89]

Part Two

Promising

Let my trial be mine own confession.

Angelo

3

Repairs in the Dark

Measure for Measure and the End of Comedy

In *Measure for Measure,* the marriages that conventionally end comedy are a punishment woven into the penitential investigations of the play, made necessary because sex is seen under the sign of sin. At the end of *Measure for Measure,* there are two forced marriages and an ambiguously unwelcome proposal for another. Lucio the feckless slanderer and wit is forced to marry Kate Keep-down, who has carried his child; Angelo is forced to marry Mariana, the betrothed woman he jilted and then, unknown to himself, bedded. Isabella's notorious silence at the Duke's proposal is usually read, and often played, as shock or horror. Only Claudio and Juliet, the loving couple who have been imprisoned and under the threat of death for making love before parental consent had been secured and marriage banns announced, are relieved from sentence and can bear their child into a different future. The legitimacy in marriage thereby secured is threatened by the plain fact that no desire underwrites it, and so the power of the Duke in so enforcing these marriages is brittle, utterly external to the loves and lives of those it coerces to weddings. If marriages end comedies, reconciling desire to social order, betting the world on the couples' loving consent, and showing trust in their mutual vows and promises, it is no wonder that *Measure for Measure* is seen as the last of Shakespeare's comedies, a play that comes "as the end of a development, the last word spoken in a particular kind of dramatic investigation which seems to have begun in the early 1590s and which extended itself through eleven comedies before reaching this terminus."[1] This play is based not on the energy of desire, or on the consent so carefully preserved in ecclesiastical law, but on the complexities and legalities of contracts, contracts broken or kept by ruse and subterfuge.[2] The subterfuge works to render Angelo's evil intents useless; the prevenient actions of the Duke make it impossible for him to coerce Isabella into fitting her consent to his "sharp appetite." But they also violate the principle of consent entirely because by rendering Angelo ignorant, they mitigate his responsibility for the actual act he performs. In fact, as I hope to show, the play works concertedly to violate the very principle of consent in the confessional and in marriage, two areas where the voluntary movements of the heart were historically regarded as completely central.

In the disguised ruler plays, Vincentio is unique in disguising himself as a friar, thereby introducing the interior forum back into the penitential apparatus. In this play, Shakespeare has put marriage in the context of penance. He puts on display particular pictures of sexual sin—as poison, compulsion, rapacity—and the models of law that must restrain, bridle, or otherwise discipline behavior so envisaged. The marriage contracts so carefully plotted out in *Measure for Measure* come under the jurisdiction of the ecclesiastical courts, understood in pre-Reformation England to be the exterior forum of penance. The governance of marriage is then part and parcel of the penitential apparatus of the church and state and a further reminder that penance is a juridical system.

Measure for Measure offers us a picture of sin and reformation, and in the process examines the "remedies" for sin in the post-Reformation setting when the interior forum for penance had been abandoned. Peter Lake has recently argued that the play's central question is: What would happen if power were to be trusted to the godly?—contending that the play is not only anti-Puritan but anti-Calvinist as well.[3] He argues that when sins of concupiscence are placed at the heart of the reformation of manners, and made the twin object of ministry and magistracy, sins of aversion are the inevitable product.[4] The too severe attempt to reform sexual practices can lead to disunity and a breaking of the peace that was supposed to be the object of reform in the first place. By making the disguise of the ruler a "ghostly father," a friar, a figure controversially active in the interior forum of penance, Shakespeare places these investigations in the longue durée, and the play thus becomes part of an extraordinarily penetrating exploration of the transformation of penitential practice that is an enduring and compelling facet of Shakespeare's inheritance of medieval culture.

The word "remedy" is invoked repeatedly in the play. In the *Book of Common Prayer*, marriage is itself provided as a "remedy against sin, and to avoid fornication."[5] But though Isabella pleads with Angelo using Christ as the model of one who "found out the remedy," there is, it appears "no remedy" for Angelo's severe justice in beheading Claudio. These words work like a refrain through the play. "It grieves me for the death of Claudio, / But there's no remedy" (2.1.280–81), says Escalus. And Angelo echoes these very words when he says to Isabella that there is "no remedy" to avoid his sentence on Claudio (2.2.48). Isabella's Christological response to Angelo's claim that Claudio is a forfeit of the law—"Why, all the souls that were were forfeit once, / And He that might the vantage best have took / Found out the remedy" (2.2.73–75)—is met finally by Angelo's remedy: Isabella's maidenhood for her brother's life. The word is used yet again of the clumsy manipulations of Vincentio: "to the love I have in doing good a remedy presents itself" (3.1.196). The word takes up old associations from the confessional handbooks which provide "remedies" for sin in the tradition of the virtues. What are the remedies for sin in the absence of the interior forum? It is with such far-reaching questions that *Measure for Measure* concerns itself.

Handling Sin: Pictures of Sin and Law

"I think if you handled her privately, she would sooner confess; perchance publicly she'll be ashamed, says Lucio to Escalus in the last act of *Measure for Measure* (5.1.275–76). Escalus has asked leave of Angelo to question Isabella and anticipates his questioning as an exemplary display of the workings of justice: "you shall see how I'll handle her" (5.1.273–74). Lucio's comment is a semi-apologetic gloss on his salacious aside that Escalus will handle Isabella no better than Angelo "by her own report" (5.1.273). Lucio leans on such language as he dwells on the obscene connotations of "handle" as managing and man-handling. Escalus's private handling, like Angelo's, he suggests, is erotic, but also juridical, designed to elicit evidence for a court of law. It might include other forms of handling—the racking and tousing with which he threatens Friar Lodowick a few lines later. But Lucio's comments also exploit an older usage of "handling," the penitential contexts in which sins are handled by a confessor. *Handlyng Synne* is the title of a much-read medieval confessional manual translated from the French.[6] In the confessional manuals and other medieval penitential literature sins are groped and handled, discerned and brought to light, by the priest or friar as diagnostician, healer, and absolver on behalf of the church.[7] Lucio's words refer to a practice (auricular confession) that had been abolished as a mandated, component part of the practice of penance or repentance, as I explained in chapter 2. What is sin and how is it handled if not in the confessional?

In my second chapter I described the pervasive pre- and post-Reformation understanding of sin as an offense against God, self, and neighbor. Sin is far more likely now to be understood as bad behavior proscribed by an authority conceived as wholly external to an autonomous subject in protection of his freedoms or, more metaphysically, as a merely unaccountable evil. Such a conception makes it hard to see the densely linked social and psychic explorations made possible by the medieval understanding of sin, one intimately bound up with actions, relations, and behavior. As I have argued in the first part of this book however, sin was a deeply theological category bound up not merely with social relations but also with the very structure and reflexivity of self. It was the category through which, as a human creature, one encountered and learned about oneself. It involved, as we have seen, not merely vexing epistemological questions for the priest who, as a curer of souls, was doctor and diagnostician, but also for the self and the self's relation to its past and present actions. The reformed theologies of Luther and Calvin had introduced profoundly different conceptions of sin, conceptions that underpin the changing conceptions of penance and repentance. Aquinas's great "treatise on sin" belongs to the first part of the second part of the *Summa,* known as the Prima Secundae, and Aquinas's outline of sin follows Aristotle's path in the *Nicomachean Ethics.* That is to say, Thomas considers sin in the context of the contemplation of human action in relation to its proper end (the love of God). The broadly optimistic frame of this Christian anthropology offers a picture of sin as unable to triumph over the person who seeks to live by charity.[8] Nature is fallen, but Thomas's presupposition is that of good will motivated by the charity that is the gift of God. Human action is completely central to Thomas's picture of sin: before he explores the nature of sin and virtue he first explores the nature of human acts:

> Therefore those actions are properly called human which proceed from a deliberate will. And if any other actions are found in man, they can be called actions *of a man,* but not properly *human* actions, since they are not proper to man as man.[9]

In the Prima Secundae he declares:

> Even in the lost the natural inclination to virtue remains, else they would have no remorse of conscience. That it is not reduced to act is owing to their being deprived of grace by Divine justice. Thus even in a blind man the aptitude to see remains in the very root of his nature, inasmuch as he is an animal naturally endowed with sight: yet this aptitude is not reduced to act, for the lack of a cause capable of reducing it, by forming the organ requisite for sight.[10]

The picture of sin that develops in Lutheran and Calvinist theology has a very different model of the role of human action and agency, as I suggested in chapter 2. Luther and Calvin's picture of human sin is one in which all human action is marked by total depravity. In *On the Bondage of the Will,* his extraordinary polemic against Erasmus, Luther had decried Erasmus's grotesque humanist arrogance. Free choice can lead to nothing but sinning because of the total depravity of human nature unredeemed by God's grace. All men are "consigned to perdition by ungodly desire."[11] The sinning man is a dead man; he cannot come to life alone. Justification is instant, not achieved by human action, and it involves a new creation, a total renewal of the "new man" who has put off the old in the Pauline terms of this theology. Contrast this with the view expressed in the medieval text *Speculum Christiani,* in which it is asserted that "penance gives life to the dede man."[12]

Calvin pictures the whole of humanity as totally depraved, and such corruption means that God's just condemnation is inevitable:

> We are so vitiated and perverted in every part of our nature that by this great corruption we stand justly condemned and convicted before God, to whom nothing is acceptable but righteousness, innocence, and purity.[13]

"The whole man," suggests Calvin "is overwhelmed—as if by a deluge—from head to foot, so that no part is immune from sin and all that proceeds from him is imputed to sin."[14] Concupiscence is the right word to describe the original sin in our natures on this model.[15] The way sin is pictured naturally defines the way in which "remedies" for sin are pictured. Calvin tends to prefer the imagery of the bridle, the whip, and the curb; it is just such pictures of sin and remedy that are explored in *Measure for Measure* in such a way that the remedies for sin come to be part of the fruits of sin itself.

In *Measure for Measure* the same behavior comes under a variety of descriptions. Claudio and Juliet's behavior is described by Escalus as a mere "fault alone" (2.1.40); by Pompey as "groping for trouts in a peculiar river"(1.2.90), and, in Lucio's hyperbolical euphemism, as a natural fertility that is fitting and seasonal:

> As those that feed grow full, as blossoming time
> That from the seedness the bare fallow brings
> To teeming foison, even so her plenteous womb
> Expresseth his full tilth and husbandry.
> (1.4.41–44)

The same behavior under manifold descriptions invites the audience to their own judgment of this act, their own descriptions of this behavior.

The play as a whole patterns its depiction of sin on the Calvinist model. Sin is a poisonous addiction:

> Our natures do pursue,
> Like rats that ravin down their proper bane,
> A thirsty evil, and when we drink, we die.
> (1.2.128–30)

With such a picture it is inevitable that the law required to discipline and contain such compulsive depravity will take on appropriate metaphors.

The law thus provides "needful bits and curbs to headstrong weeds" (1.3.20); it has been a scarecrow that custom has made a perch for birds (2.1.1), but now must become like whips that must cut (2.1.4–5).

Reformation theology had, as we have seen in part 1, powerfully attacked the legal basis of medieval jurisdiction; yet over the course of the sixteenth century reformed theology developed its own legal thinking, most strikingly in the notion of the two swords. Luther had rejected the notion that priests had any jurisdiction whatsoever; he rejected all canon law as a dunghill: "I shit on the law of the pope and of the emperor, and on the law of the jurists as well."[16] In his famous book-burning at Wittenberg in 1520, the Decretals and commentaries of the canonists were all thrust into the flames. Quentin Skinner claims that Luther's idea that the church was a *congregatio fidelium* entailed that it could not be understood in any jurisdictional sense at all. The rule of the spiritual kingdom for him is a rule of the soul, a "purely inward form of government" which has no connection to temporal affairs.[17] The spiritual, inward kingdom of Christ is the realm of freedom because its powers are entirely spiritual. But Luther's concept of a spiritual kingdom that is noncoercive is juxtaposed with a temporal authority which has coercive, enforcing, and punitive powers. Skinner puts the Lutheran paradox in the following illuminating way: "Luther's theological premises not only committed him to attacking the jurisdictional powers of the church, but also to filling the power-vacuum this created by mounting a corresponding defence of the secular authorities."[18] The jurisdiction of the priests is taken up by the secular authorities, and they derive their authority from God. The duty of the godly prince and magistrate, says Luther in *On Secular Authority,* is to bring about "external peace" and to govern "external things." Again it is worth stressing the splitting going on in the Lutheran conception of the subject: an inward soul is governed by Christ in the spiritual kingdom "without any laws"; the externals are governed by the godly state.[19] The law, suggests Luther in *On Secular Authority,* is not for Christians at all; it is for the unjust.[20] If the world were made up of Christians "there would be neither need nor use for princes, kings, lords, the Sword, or law" because what is right would be done freely, says Luther, quoting Paul, 1 Tim 1.9. But the unjust man needs law to compel and coerce him to do right. The hero of *On Secular Authority* is, as one of his editors suggests, not the judge but the executioner.[21] Luther would indeed have felt that Pompey's change of trade from bawd to executioner was a great use of his skills in the service of the state: "And therefore if you see that there is a lack of hangmen, court officials, judges, lords or princes, and you find that you have the necessary skills, then you should offer your services and seek office, so that authority, which is so greatly needed, will never come to be held in contempt, become powerless or perish. The world cannot get by without it."[22] Luther describes princes as "God's jailers and hangmen," whom we subjects should address as "gracious lords" just as long as "they do not overreach themselves by wanting to become pastors instead of hangmen."[23] Luther's famous doctrine of the two swords understands the spiritual sword which commands the inward kingdom of God as a place of evangelical liberty, and the temporal sword as the place of external government in which order is maintained by force, punishment, and coercion. As I want to show, this has a precise bearing on the way action is conceived in *Measure for Measure,* where human consent is, I shall argue, so flagrantly and conspicuously flouted.

Luther makes the two kingdoms theory central to his *Sermons on the Sermon on the Mount,* from which, of course, the play takes its title. Luther is glossing the following verses from Matthew: "Ye have heard that it hath bene said, An eye for an eye, & a tooth for a tooth. But I say unto you, Resist not evil: but whosoever shal smite thee on thy right cheke, turn to him the other also."[24] This is the text which is consciously juxtaposed with the Duke's invocation to retributive justice in the last scene of the play, echoing Genesis 9.6 and Leviticus 24.17–20:

> The very mercy of the law cries out
> Most audible, even from his proper tongue,
> 'An Angelo for Claudio; death for death!'
> Haste still pays haste, and leisure answers leisure;
> Like doth quit like, and *Measure* still for *Measure.*
>
> (5.1.407–11)

Luther explains that Christ's advice to turn the other cheek has given rise to many errors and questions because people have failed to distinguish properly the secular and the spiritual. Christ is here addressing himself to Christians, avers Luther, counseling them to be "uninterested" in the secular rule of government, power or punishment.[25] But he admits, "there is no getting around it, a Christian has to be a secular person of some sort." The resolution is that "a Christian may carry on all sorts of secular business with impunity—not as a Christian but as a secular person—while his heart remains pure in his Christianity, as Christ demands."[26] So when a Christian goes to war, or sits on a judge's bench, or punishes his neighbor, *"he is not doing this as a Christian, but as a soldier, a judge or a lawyer"* (my italics).[27] Christ's maxims of turning the other cheek then simply cannot be applied to the offices of the state or magistracy. Luther's two kingdoms allow him to make the astonishing claim that when a man is exercising any of these offices he is not doing so as a Christian. The splitting of the outer man and the inner man actually makes room for a thoroughly coercive and massively enhanced secular power wherein Christianity itself is consigned to the realm of the inward. That Luther takes his two kingdoms into the heart of these extraordinary texts on forgiveness is indeed an astonishing piece of exegesis, and a testimony to the hold of this thoroughly split and dualistic picture of soul and subject, Christian and citizen. When he takes the text on which *Measure for Measure* is based: "Iudge not that you be not iudged. For with what iudgment you iudge, you shal be iudged, and with what measure ye mette, it shal be measured to you againe" (Geneva Bible, Matt 7.1–2), he wants to make it very clear that Christ is here talking only to his disciples: "He is not talking about the judgment or punishment that takes place in the world."[28] It is no wonder that Quentin Skinner has traced the modern notion of the state to Luther's two kingdoms theory. We can recognize here Weber's understanding of the state as "a human community that successfully claims the monopoly of the legitimate use of force within a given territory."[29] The further highly consequential entailment of Luther's Christian anthropology is that, as Jennifer Herdt puts it, "there is no route from 'external' practices to fundamental inner transformation."[30]

The jurisdiction of sin is the question that pervades *Measure for Measure*. In England, as opposed to Geneva or Zurich, sexual sin came under the jurisdiction of the ecclesiastical courts, institutions which in the eyes of their detractors were remnants of the popish past and obstacles to the discipline which in several reformed confessions was a true mark of the church. The ecclesiastical courts historically dealt with heresy, simony, and sacrilege, with the refusal to pay church tithes, and with *defamatio*—Duke Vincentio's one place of apparent vulnerability. Indeed in the presentments of the churchwardens as a result of episcopal visitations, *publica fama* supplied the substance of ecclesiastical cases brought by the reports of neighbors, as through the practice of compurgation it could also release the defendant from the charges brought against him. After the Reformation, failures to conform to the liturgies and practices of the *Book of Common Prayer* came under the jurisdiction of the spiritual courts and provided further reasons for nonconformists to detest them.[31] They also addressed questions of usury, probate of wills, advowson and patronage, contracts where oaths had been sworn, bastardy and matrimony—these latter also the complex terrain of the play's investigation of legitimacy and consent in marriage, as I shall show later on.

Apart from the probate business of the court, church court business was divided between "instance" cases, which involved the hearing of cases brought by one party against another, and the significantly more controversial *ex officio* cases, in which sins were judged and corrected by a judge in virtue of his office. In *ex officio* cases the laity were refused the right of compurgation and were unable to confront their own accusers.

The abolition of auricular confession paradoxically had the effect of separating the internal from the external forum of confession. Canon law has, as I suggested in chapter 2, since the twelfth century distinguished between the internal forum of confession (the court of conscience) and the external forum of the ecclesiastical courts. The first was governed by the power of orders (*potestas ordinis*) and was largely the domain of the priest in the confessional imposing penances in the cure of souls. The second forum was properly speaking in the jurisdiction of the bishop and his officers, rather than the priest, and had the power to punish in the ultimate medicinal aim of curing the soul. Precisely because after the abolition of compulsory auricular confession there was no regular mandated recourse to the priestly admonitions and the penances that might result from such private confessions, penance became more punitive, public, and juridical in ways that could have been neither intended nor anticipated. The sorts of minor offenses that might once have been dealt with in the internal forum of confession to a priest were now brought before the courts, as I mentioned in chapter 1. Those who refrained from participating in communion for reasons of conscience because they were "out of charity" with their neighbor were referred in increasing numbers to the courts where those reasons might be brushed aside as they were coerced to participate in communion.[32] Helmholz suggests: "By closing the confessional, Protestantism opened wider the doors of the spiritual courts to new sorts of public regulation."[33]

In *Measure for Measure* the public and humiliating exposure of those who are escorted to prison by the officers of the law is part of the play's display of justice. "Fellow," says Claudio, "why do you show me thus to th' world?" (1.2.116) Pompey is similarly displayed to the on-stage audience when he is paraded across the stage for the second time by Elbow and escorted to prison. "Art thou led in triumph?" mocks Lucio (3.2.44), an implicit stage direction that is often used to great effect in productions. Mistress Overdone is also exposed to public view in act 3, scene 2, and put on the stage of humiliation, the fourth such parade across the boards under the escort of the officers of the law. "In infamy," says George Herbert in *A Priest to the Temple,* "all are executioners, and the law gives a malefactor to all to be defamed."[34]

Promises and Consent

Consent is conspicuously evacuated in *Measure for Measure.* We might find Angelo and Lucio disturbing and unsavory characters, but they do not appear to consent to their own marriages. Secondly, the bed-trick nullifies Angelo's attempt to rape Isabella, but it also nullifies his actual activity—having sex with Mariana—since he thought Mariana was Isabella. Thirdly, the Duke as friar earns the trust of those he employs in his plot, but his disguise once again changes the nature of the actions they have undertaken and violates their consent.

Ecclesiastical law historically placed an absolutely central emphasis on the notion of consent in the making of marriage. Gratian had established the exchange of words of present consent as the initiation of marriage, and sexual intercourse as the completion of it and had been emphatic that "no woman should be married except by her free will."[35] Using the scholastic terminology of the sacraments, Peter Lombard stated that "the efficient cause of marriage" is consent, "not any consent, but expressed in words: not concerning the future, but in the present tense."[36] It was the words of husband and wife, in the absence of any witnesses or priest or church ceremony, that made the marriage.[37] It was not even necessary to specify particular words to make the marriage licit. John Mirk in his *Instructions for Parish Priests* makes some proposals: "Here I take þe to my weddyd wife" is his suggestion.[38] As Lianna Farber has recently written, the exact words are never specified because the exact words were important only insofar as they were the external sign of an inward consent: "If there were an agreed upon formula, it would be equivalent to declaring not that consent created a marriage but that particular words created it—the words would be akin to knowing the password that opened a door."[39] This meant that if mutual trust broke down one person might understand one thing by the words uttered and another something else entirely, if there were no witnesses or publicly verifiable evidence to draw on. Since the words spoken were only evidence of inward consent, it was not even "he said, she said" that was important, but rather what "he thought, she thought." No less an authority than Thomas Aquinas had declared, "if mental consent is lacking in one of the parties, on neither side is there marriage."[40] This was tantamount to opening up the potential of mental reservation: I spoke the words of present consent but in my heart I did not consent.

It was just such an understanding of the promise that Austin had complained against in his assessment of the pseudo-profundity of the man who declares that marriage cannot be a matter of mere words but must rather be one of deep inner convictions (see chapter 1). Such a philosophy of ritual words gave perfect harbor to the welsher and the bigamist, for they could say that their hearts had not inwardly consented to their own marriages. The Carmelite friar Thomas Netter had made mincemeat of Wyclif's similar views that marriage should not be a matter of mere sensible signs. In the *Trialogus,* Wyclif had argued that *verbum mentis* (words of the mind) are more important than words of the mouth, *verbum oris.*[41] As for the vaunted distinction between the words of present and future consent, Frederick W. Maitland's famously witty comment says it best: "of all people in the world lovers are least likely to distinguish precisely between the present and future tenses."[42] The legal problems with such law are easy to predict.

The canonistic doctrine of consent in marriage produced some astoundingly perplexing questions. For in establishing that a binding sacramental marriage was instituted by the single exchange of consent between two parties, without any other formalities, canonists had developed a form of marriage that was incapable of proof. For if two witnesses required to establish the fact of the marriage themselves disagreed about whether a secret marriage had taken place, such proof was impossible to establish. One historian charmingly described the situation: "many couples all over the Christian world may have been uncertain whether they were actually married or not."[43] "A marriage made alone by the words of present consent without witnesses was unprovable in a court of law. As Shannon McSheffrey has said: "The distinction between the contract made privately between the two parties and a properly witnessed one was well recognized by late medieval Londoners. The former, enforceable only in the internal forum of the conscience, was called 'marriage before God,' emphasizing both its sacramental and its unprovable nature."[44] McSheffrey suggests that the ecclesiastical courts routinely recognized that they had no jurisdiction over what God himself alone could know and parties were to "be released to their consciences."[45] These unprovable marriages were to be distinguished from clandestine marriages, which were defined as contracts "not subsequently solemnized or improperly solemnized."[46] The problems around such marriages also focused on the division between an interior forum of confession and conscience and the external forum of the church courts, which could only use the visible and verifiable as its aegis.

Medieval marriage theology was obviously subject to considerable modification in Reformation theology and legal practice. Reformation theologians wanted to insist that the consent of the parents was essential, that without it marriage was void, and that the promises must be made publicly and repeated in church. They wanted, in short, to insist that marriage was a public institution. Luther for one could not understand that although marriage had been regarded as sacramental there seemed to be so little supervision of it. Above all, reformers sought to eradicate the idea, current from Gratian onward, that sexual intercourse might complete a marriage made by future consent, and also that a marriage might retrospectively ratify the prior sexual relations of the parties involved. In dealing with the massive increase in poverty and bastardy, the reformed church wished for a concerted attack on the immorality it saw in contemporary practice. John Witte has recently suggested that the idea of the magistracy pioneered in Luther's political theology "helped to trigger a massive shift in power and property from the Church to the state."[47] The intense preoccupation with sexual sin in Genevan discipline sprang from Calvin's concern to prevent the pollution of the Lord's Supper. But the preoccupation with sexual sin in England precedes English Calvinism, as Marjorie McIntosh has demonstrated, and is part of a reformation of manners that intensifies in the fifteenth century.[48] The vast majority of matrimonial causes that came before the ecclesiastical courts concerned the validity of marriages. Lay people

began to be prosecuted for attending the contracting of a clandestine marriage, and every attempt was made to bring marriage into the publicly
ordered apparatus of the church and state. Marriage was to be a public
institution and premarital unchastity, once regarded as retrospectively nor-
malized by matrimony, became a punishable offense.[49]

Comedy conventionally bets the future on the bonds of trust made between dizzy and variable people and their trust in each other. In *Measure
for Measure* desire is not so much accommodated to law as subsumed by
its legal niceties. Worse, it becomes a question of contracts which must be
maintained by trickery and coercion. The forced comic ending depends
upon the coercive external jurisdiction to be brought about in the first place.
Julia Reinhard Lupton in an illuminating recent treatment of *Measure for
Measure* has argued that Claudio and Juliet's "secret consensual union" performed outside the sanction of the church and state is "an exercise or an
experiment in civil society, taken as those forms of public association that
elude the direct supervision of the state and its church, but also occurred
beyond the household or oikos."[50] In her reading, Isabella is the citizen
saint who refuses or threatens to refuse the terms of the Duke's sovereignty
seen in his offer of marriage, which in royalist understandings is a picture
of the subordination of subject to state, as of wife to husband. She rightly
comments that the marriages at the end of the play are "commanded" by
the Duke: "go take her hence and marry her instantly" (5.1.377). She points
out that here "the outward order of the church-state alliance appears in de-
nuded form, as a pure operation of the public office."[51] Performed by fiat on
the unwilling subjects under its purview, it exposes the extrinsicist fate of
sovereignty. Reinhard Lupton argues that Angelo's consent has been performed by the bed-trick. But how can Angelo have consented to sleep with
Mariana when he thought he was sleeping with Isabella? Consent cannot
be retroactively granted without violating all norms of action. Consent is
part and parcel of what makes an act a voluntary act. Human actions must
proceed from a deliberate will, Aquinas had said, as I suggested earlier.

The bed-trick indeed turns out to be a trope of long duration, and it
is used to think through a range of questions about the nature of human
agency and desire.[52] It is fascinating that Aquinas actually mentions what
has come to be known as the bed-trick as part of his dialectical and capacious investigation of intention in the *Summa*. Could a man be held responsible for adultery if he slept with another woman thinking her to be

his wife? The footnote of the Blackfriars editor finds the example naïve, but its presence there is an indication of the longevity of its role in the history of narrative, a role precisely guaranteed by the question of what constitutes a human act.[53] This version of the conundrum is of course reversed in the case of Angelo: can a man be held responsible for rape when he has not so much violated his chosen object but rather slept with the woman to whom he is betrothed, who, moreover, wants to marry him? This play ends in marriages then, but the very principle of consent that makes a marriage valid has been violated. One of the very agents of that violation is the Duke-friar who turns out to embody a two-bodies in one conflation of the agency of the church and state.

The Duke as Friar

Disguised rulers appear in a number of plays produced in the opening years of James I's reign. Middleton's *The Phoenix* and John Marston's *The Fawn* and *The Malcontent* all feature disguised rulers, or sons of rulers.[54] But in no other play is the ruler disguised as a friar. Why did Shakespeare choose this disguise and what are the implications of his choice?

In *Measure for Measure,* the Duke's disguise as a friar gives him metaphorical jurisdiction over the internal forum as well as the external forum. And it gives him access to the character and virtue of those he purports to confess, and grants him a virtually impenetrable plausibility: "I have confess'd her and I know her virtue" (5.1.527). As friar, the Duke can procure the secrets of the soul so that they become fully available to the sovereign state. The Duke and the state (which claimed it did not want to make windows into the souls of its subjects) now have access to the interior forum and are privy to the secrets of the confessional.

The "confessions" in the play traduce the speech act of confession altogether. During the course of the play, the Duke-friar will solicit the confessions of Juliet, Claudio, Barnadine, and Mariana. His tactic systematically converts the discourse of self-knowledge and transformation into the acquiring of information.

It is as confessor that he garners the trust of Isabella—and this is absolutely central to her shock at his reappearance at the end of the play. Scholars have viewed her silence at his proposal but perhaps not sufficiently registered the force of his betrayal of her trust. It is as a father confessor that she is anxious to trust him and to accommodate herself to his desires even at the cost of publicly proclaiming herself as the one who had slept with Angelo. When he asks her to marry him, he is violating all understandings of himself as a friar and the fraternal and spiritual friendship offered in that relationship. Whereas it might indeed seem strange to her that he comes up with the bed-trick scheme, it is in the service of protecting her chastity. Now it might seem as if he had other, hidden motives and other interests in her chastity. In McBurney's Theater of Complicity staging, one of the most moving scenes in the play is when the Duke has told us that he will not tell Isabella that her brother has after all been saved by the "accident" provided by Ragozine's head:

> But I will keep her ignorant of her good,
> To make her heavenly comforts of despair,
> When it is least expected.
>
> (4.3.109–11)

Isabella's response is devastating in McBurney's gripping staging. In her grief she moves forward to gain comfort from the consoling friar whose gratuitous cruelty is the very cause of her grief. Forgoing her customary control and restraint, she rushes forward and, almost prostrate, clutches hold of the friar, beating her fists on his back. They are thus framed in a sort of pietà where the friar is definitively imaged as mother church. But he does not embrace her. In fact, aware of her physical proximity, he keeps his arms and body separate from her, stretching them out into thin air. After a long moment he deliberately encloses her in an embrace that unites calculation with withholding in a deeply disturbing combination. There is not one ounce of natural warmth in this movement and no grain of compassion; the sheer viciousness of his retention of this piece of information is drawn out to expose its inherent sadism. It richly informs Isabella's sense of shock and betrayal at the end of this production of the play, and her sense of despair and entrapment. Indeed it seems clear that Isabella's trust is in the friar as friar; it is unlikely that she would have gone along with the scheme had a layman proposed it.

Utterly hidden himself and so incapable of being known by others, he can, or so he thinks, discover them in the truth of the confessional. The confessional is then for him a form of effective espionage, a useful means of surveillance. It is of course very easy to fool those whose trust you already have, and it is this sort of trust that the Duke as friar abuses. As confessor, he has no compunction in casually breaking the seal of the confessional, a secrecy enjoined again in the canons of 1604, even in the utterly reduced and confined new circumstances of post-Reformation confession. He lies to Claudio and Isabella later on that he has confessed Angelo and "knows" that he is only testing Isabella (3.1.165–66). To him the confessional is the mechanism by which "all difficulties" are "but easy when they are known" (4.2.204–5).

So the role of the friar and the Duke, once kept separate in two different jurisdictions, are collapsed into one. The king turns out not to have two bodies but one as he subsumes the friar's tasks as confessor into his own. If, as Julia Reinhard Lupton has said, Isabella is a citizen saint and *Measure for Measure* experiments with horizontal relations against the Duke's remodeling of his own sovereignty, then it is also apparent what the human costs are in the terrible exposure and humiliation of his subjects. Here the secrets of the confessional are not so much protected as used as part of the state apparatus. And it is confession itself that has collapsed entirely into the coercive external apparatus of the state.

The consent that is historically as central to marriage as it is to the essential idiom of comedy, and the consent, the willing contrition of the penitent in the internal forum of the confessional, have both been rudely violated. Indeed the violation of consent in the confessional is the very means to enforce the marriages at the end of the play.[55]

In the long genealogy of anti-fraternalism, which is turned to new uses in Protestant theater, friars are conventionally associated with pretense, disguise, and deceit. The most notable examples can be found in the work of John Bale, particularly his longest and most sustained piece of agitprop drama, *King John*. But the conceit is by no means confined to Protestant theatrical texts alone; it is the central accusation against Catholicism itself.[56] For the later middle ages, friars cathected many of the problems associated with voluntary poverty and spoke to the contradictions and convictions of a religion that had at its heart a notion of sanctified poverty.[57] Yet friars were also traditionally confessors, often to kings, and worked outside the parishional system, directly under papal authority. In John Bale's theater, the friar is the quintessential conspirator and suborner of England by

Rome, and the figure, par excellence, of disguise. Indeed in Bale's theater, fraternal identity is only possible precisely as disguise because it is essentially duplicitous, essentially histrionic.

Shakespeare's own friars, prior to *Measure for Measure,* are emphatically not in this tradition. On the contrary, the friar is the figure who benignly circumvents the problems paternal authority brings to the legitimate desires of the young. The friars in Shakespeare generally help the young to marry, or engage in providential fictions; above all, they are not busy manipulators but the trusters of time. Their fictions have the effect of halting the rash, destructive, and violent impetuosity of false judgments—such as Claudio's viciously public denunciation of Hero in *Much Ado About Nothing,* or the revengeful animosity of the parents in *Romeo and Juliet.* In these plays, friars are represented not as a royal priesthood, but as a church unsubordinated to the state and capable of acting quite independently of the state's jurisdiction. In transforming his prior treatment of the figure of the friar to the Duke as friar in *Measure for Measure,* Shakespeare reverses the import of Protestant theater's deployment of this figure. Against this background it becomes clear that the figure of the Duke-friar is now directed not at the "theatricality of the church" but at the theatricality of the crown/dukedom/monarchy; it is precisely an inversion of anti-Catholic theater using its own techniques. The wolf in sheep's clothing is not friar but Duke. For here confession (transitive) has become utterly theatricalized and fake. The contrition and confession of subjects are deployed in an epiphany of ducal/monarchical power enacting a fantasy of itself as "grace divine," and pardon becomes a one-way donation which substitutes for forgiveness and reconciliation. One has only to compare this scene with the last scene of *Cymbeline* to observe the utterly different effect of the king's "Pardon's the word to all." For in that scene every reconciliation comes about because of the heartfelt utterances of the protagonists, and their mutual revelation of themselves restores them to themselves and each other.

The Duke as friar is part of a discourse on dominion which anciently pairs the notion of sexual and political consent, and which therefore sees sexual ethics as an intrinsic part of the exploration of tyranny where tyranny is understood as the ruler who acts for his own personal pleasure above the common good.[58] It is also a thorough-going critique of the inseparability of church and state invested in the person of the monarch as supreme governor of the church, a critique incidentally shared by Catholics and nonconformists alike, though for different reasons. Finally it is an economical and hilarious theatrical joke on the king's two bodies.

The Duke's Dénouement

The hole-and-corner secrecy of the Duke-friar's confessions are provocatively juxtaposed with the emphatically public staging of the last act. The Duke declares that he is "bound to enter publicly" (4.3.95), and he sends a message to Angelo that soberly puns on procession as both trial of justice and public entry:

> Him I'll desire
> To meet me at the consecrated fount,
> A league below the city; and from thence,
> By cold gradation and weal-balanc'd form,
> We shall proceed with Angelo.
> (4.3.97–101)

The pun is preceded and underlined by another one on the notion of gradation as both step and status.

The whole of the long last act of *Measure for Measure* takes place at the gates of the city and thus draws on some of the conventions of the royal entry.[59] In medieval cities with their parcelized sovereignty and mixed jurisdictions, the protocols of entry to the formal frontiers of the city were elaborate and minute in their observations of deference and preference. Sometimes, for example, the mace, or other symbols of authority vested in the most senior office of the city, would be relinquished to the visiting sovereign, kissed, and returned. In this economically eloquent gesture, authority is ceded and then granted again. It is a renewal of trust, authority, and delegation; it marks out borders and territories in a ritual that lays bare the structures of governance, displayed and reaffirmed mutually by the giver and the recipient. These forms of ceremony were invented in the Middle Ages alongside the processional drama of Corpus Christi. Royal entries borrowed from the advent liturgy as they stage the coming of the king as the coming of Christ. In such kingly appropriations of Christology, a fully developed sacramental understanding of kingship is modeled.

Vincentio is staging an entry then, an entry that stops at the gates of the city to reveal the structures of governance there. We think we are about to witness the ceremonial and public transfer of authority; what we see is a scripted performance that stages the epiphanic presence of the Duke—like "grace divine."

The last scene depends on Angelo revealing himself as corrupt because his saintly reputation is the best cover for his depravity. No witness will have credibility against such a visibly upright man. Justice in these circumstances will be seen to be done only once that depravity is revealed, and this is the point of Vincentio's metadrama. It is an exquisite setup. Vincentio greets Angelo and Escalus and informs them that only a properly public thanks could afford them due "requital" for their administration of justice. The requirement that Isabella say that she has slept with Angelo is designed for Angelo: it is a lie that he thinks is the truth. In becoming the judge of his own cause (5.1.166–67) he will reveal his deep corruption, as he uses his own unblemished reputation to scar Isabella as mad or unstable. The plot becomes even more exquisite as Angelo imagines that he will find the "mightier member" who set these women on, and his probing leads eventually to the revelation of the mighty member as Vincentio himself. It is the splitting of the Duke into the two figures of friar and duke that allows him to "reveal" the corruption he has witnessed.

Yet the double genealogies of Christ and king evoked in the royal entry, the Christological motifs of advent, are remodeled through the inventive theatricalization of the king's two bodies. The theatrical joke in *Measure for Measure*'s last act is precisely that an actor can only play in one body at a time. That body can stand in for the friar's body. It can stand in for the Duke's body. It cannot stand for both at once when both need to be present. Vincentio has spent most of the play in his disguise as a friar; his theatrical problem at the end of the play is that these putative two bodies (Vincentio and the fake friar) must both be produced at once. The Duke has to disappear for the friar to reappear ("I for a while will leave you," 5.1.257). Even in the dizzying substitutions of *Measure for Measure* where, beginning with Angelo's deputizing for Vincentio, one body is so often standing in for another—Mariana's for Isabella's, Barnadine's for Claudio's, Ragozine's for Barnadine's, a maidenhead for a brother's head—the friar's stand-in for the Duke can operate only for as long as they never have to appear together.

The legal fiction of the king's two bodies gives the king one body that dies and one that is immortal and incorruptible, thus allowing for the permanent legal existence of kingship in the absence of a mortal incumbent, or during the passing from one mortal incumbent to another.[60] Here the king's two bodies are not so much a glorious fiction of inviolable monarchy as an instance of, and an insistence upon, the real limits of embodiment—that even as actors we can be only one body at a time. The appropriation by the Duke of the friar and the model of power thereby implied reaches its limit here too.

In his speech to parliament in 1603, James VI and I brings into conjunction precisely the connections of the king's two bodies so richly explored in *Measure for Measure*. Using the language of the marriage service, anticipating at once the union of Scotland with England and the union of crown and people, James says:

> What god hath conjoined then, let no man separate. I am the Husband, and all the whole Isle is my lawful wife; I am the Head, and it is my Body; I am the shepherd, and it is my flocke.[61]

The pastoral image of the shepherd, the conjugal image of husband and wife, and the image of the body politic are benignly united, but it is the underside of this appropriation of church by king that is explored in the play.

In *The Castle of Comfort*, Thomas Becon had made an interesting analogy:

> If sins be forgiven of God, and the ministers commanded to declare the same to the people, then doth it follow that they forgive not the sin, but only are ministers appointed of God to publish the benefit of our salvation. If a prince pardoneth his subject for treason committeth against his person, and sendeth his letters of favour to the traitor by one of his faithful servants, commanding him to declare his pitiful mercy to the guilty; who forgiveth the fault, the messenger or the king?[62]

Becon's rhetorical question produces the comparison that God stands in relation to the priest in the same relation that a king stands in relation to his messenger. The priest and the messenger merely deliver the authoritative words of God or king. The analogy not only asks its listeners or readers to liken the king to God but in the process altogether obscures the question of agency. It is this question that is central in *Measure for Measure,* and one of the questions it asks is: how does authority take on a body? How is this body subject to the viewpoint of others? It turns out there is no such thing as a simple deputization or substitution of one body for another such that one body is a mere cipher for the other.

The Duke's theater has its costs. "Let my trial be mine own confession" (5.1.372), declares Angelo, and thereby pronounces the play's deepest logic. There can be no true confession where confession is an instrument of a state which has made "thoughts" its subjects. In *Measure for Measure,* Shakespeare imagined a society which had lost the institutions, understandings, and capacities for confession. In converting confession into accusation and surveillance, it is precisely vulnerability to others that the Duke denies. For it is the thrust of the Duke's own confession to the friar who aids and abets his disguise that he wishes to be invulnerable to the perception of others. In surrogating Angelo he wishes to escape from his own past actions and their consequences. This is the import of the "confession" he makes to the friar in a conversation that, even here, he attempts to script and control: "Now, pious sir, / You will demand of me why I do this?" (1.3.16–17). What the play explores, then, is the sort of state and the sort of theater that occur when interiority is hollowed out, when the consent of the heart is vitiated both in contrition in the confessional, and in marriage. In short, this is a theater of exposure and humiliation which stakes itself on shame.

The Duke's theatrical "remedy" which has theatricalized confession and evolved a form of theater to replace it has a cost. The cost is, of course, the bypassing of the volition of those involved in his theater whether by making them instruments of a wider plan of which they are in ignorance, or by neglecting their consent in the matter of their own marriage. It is recognition and acknowledgment that are forgone in this externalized "remedy," a remedy that has bypassed the self-transformation of those requiring reform. And it is of course the slanderer and the saint, Lucio and Angelo, both traders in reputation, who are shown in this play to be incapable of transformation and to require both the coercive justice of the Duke and the love of the women who might make honest men of them, "moulded out of faults" (5.1.439).

So *Measure for Measure* gives us marriages in which the very principle of consent is violated. The bed-trick relieves Angelo of the consequences of his own actions and in consummating a marriage it weds him to Mariana, but only by abrogating all responsibility in action. The legitimacy of marriage turns on a legality; there is no harmony here between desire and the law. What hope there is in this play lies in the forgiveness of women and the possibility that best men might be molded out of faults. In this it looks forward to the later plays in which marriage, or rather remarriage, is a question not so much of future promise as of the forgiveness of past actions. Shakespeare's preoccupation in the theme of marriage is now not with promising but with forgiving and with the theatrical forms in which forgiveness can be modeled and embodied.

Part Three

FORGIVING

Who among philosophers has a theory of forgiveness and whether it is giveable? It would be a theory of comedy.

STANLEY CAVELL

4

THE RECOVERY OF VOICE IN
SHAKESPEARE'S *PERICLES*

And words can be wrung from us,—like a cry. Words can be *hard* to
say: such, for example, as are used to effect a renunciation, or to confess
a weakness. (Words are also deeds).

LUDWIG WITTGENSTEIN, *Philosophical Investigations*

In this chapter I will not be so intimately concerned with the resources of
penance and its transformations. Instead, I will be examining Shakespeare's
exploration of the wording of the world in *Pericles*. This chapter then explores the "post-tragic," a term I have already used, but so far not defined.
It also shows how Shakespeare develops in *Pericles* a new form of romance
in which a community is re-created through the recovery of voice.

To understand *Pericles,* we must begin with *King Lear.*

Romance, "The Fair Unknown," King Leir, and King Lear

Gloucester's eyes are out. There is nowhere to be led except to the place
from which he will not need leading. This is Dover cliff whose "head /
Looks fearfully in the confined deep" (4.1.73–74), the place from which he
wishes to fall to a death that releases him from a life quite beyond endurance. Here is where Edgar stages his morality play. Gloucester is Despair.

But what is Edgar? The good priest who counsels him against despair and turns him back to life? The figure of mercy who redeems him to a life it would be merciful to leave? And what are the remedies against despair or the resources of theater in this endeavor?

From the point of view of the penitential tradition despair is the most corrosive aspect of accedia or spiritual sloth because it renders impossible its own cure. Despair is unbecoming; it is the privation of the only resource by which the hopeless person might be released from its deadly, annihilating force. In Spenser's stunning treatment in *The Faerie Queene* the clinching argument that persuades the Red Crosse knight to want to kill himself is the knowledge of his own blemished life, the litany of his betrayals and failures and the bald fact that they deserve condemnation.[1] What despair obliterates, of course, is the sensed availability of grace. The Red Crosse knight will have to be tutored in the House of Holiness by the theological virtues, Faith, Hope, and Love, to feel that light again, and to be relieved of the bitter, excoriating logic of his own merits and deserts.

In the face of Gloucester's despair, Edgar attempts to restore him to his own life. Gloucester's blindness makes him easily deceivable. The word picture of the cliff's edge that Edgar paints for him as they stand on flat ground shows Gloucester's dreadful dependency on the kindness of strangers. Only the stranger is his estranged son. Gloucester jumps down the vertiginous cliff onto the flat stage and Edgar persuades him that he had been tempted to despair by a fiend now exorcised.[2] Edgar through his morality play has staged a miracle play too: "Thy life's a miracle" (4.6.55). It is a miracle performed dramaturgically, not supernaturally, and thus it is an ordinary miracle. Yet Edgar has thereby tricked him into living; in staging this sideshow, trifling with his despair to cure it, he has withheld himself and thereby theatricalized his relations to Gloucester.[3] This prompts the question: to what sense of his life might Gloucester have been restored had his son shown himself and acknowledged his father as his?

In the final act of this morality and miracle play, Edgar is the vehicle of a third medieval genre. Entering as the "fair unknown," he stages himself as the hero of romance. The fair unknown is the characteristic figure of medieval romance who assures us that virtue and force can be reconciled; the threat of violence in an honorific culture is thereby both challenged to embrace virtue and seen to uphold it. In the process the unnamed redeemer turns out to be noble, military valor retains its privilege, and gentility is preserved for gentles as a class as well as a moral attribute. In the last act of *King Lear,* Edgar seeks to "prove" that Edmund is a traitor. This is the archaic justice of the ordeal in which God's agency can be enacted through the victor in combat.[4] Edgar's anonymity takes up the resounding theme of the last two acts—acknowledgment:

> Dost thou know me?
> > (Gloucester to Lear, 4.6.135)
>
> I know thee well enough.
> > (Lear to Gloucester, 4.6.177)
>
> Sir, do you know me?
> > (Cordelia to Lear, 4.7.48)
>
> "To be acknowledg'd, Madam, is o'erpaid.
> > (4.7.4)

So what does it mean in a tragedy about what Stanley Cavell has termed the avoidance of love, whose theme is the remorseless enaction of the capacities of each of the characters for acknowledgment, that Edgar enacts this romance part? When he claims his name from Edmund and reveals himself he tells his audience that it was a fault not to have revealed himself to his father sooner. He does so when he is armed and ready for battle, and the news is enough to kill Gloucester dying between "two extremes of passion, joy and grief" (5.3.199). There is thus no reconciliation of might and right. Edgar vanquishes Edmund but too late to preserve Cordelia. Romance recognition is given retrospectively in Edgar's belated revelation of himself to his father. Nothing is born again from this revelation because it is the cause of his death by joy and grief. The form of romance that this play inherits and explores simply cannot contain the extremes of emotion engendered. That Edgar continues unknown to his father is a cause for deep regret rather than wonder, the cause of a death rather than a rebirth; it is an acknowledgment that in the world of King Lear every failure of acknowledgement will be remorselessly tracked down and exposed.[5]

In the romance trope of the "fair unknown," the unknown (un-named, unidentified) presents a threat to the honorific code and its cult of gentility, but there is trust that the insignia of identity will once again make the protagonists knowable, recognizable. In Shakespeare's version of the Lear story, taken from the *Old Arcadia,* Edgar's desire to be unknown is first of all a conscious disguise that is necessary to protect him from the murderous ambition of his brother and the befuddled yet dangerous gullibility of his father. But he is now completely safe from this utterly broken man on the cliffs of Dover. His decision to maintain his disguise, to remain unknown to his father, is now not a disguise for the sake of safety: it is a conscious theatricalization of himself which deprives his father of the possibility of response. Edgar chooses to remain hidden so that he can reveal himself to his father not as a fellow broken man but as the hero of a romance, just as he has cast himself in a miracle and morality play. But the fortunes of Edgar and Gloucester, as of Lear and Cordelia, indicate that such forms will no longer answer to the paths of unknownness in King Lear. No revelation of the insignia of knighthood will answer to the forms of recognition that this play sounds and requires, paths which stem from the repudiation of language as a public form, an attempt to suborn it into the expression of naked flattery to a sovereign will. The revelation of a social identity cannot cure, resolve, or relieve the forms of unknownness the play has sounded. The revelation must undertake the risks and particularities of acknowledgment. Edgar must reveal himself not as a fair, chivalric knight but as Gloucester's son, tricked and deceived by his murderous brother, disowned and hounded by his father, and hiding in the most displaced and outcast figure as the only place of safety. Edgar's romance plot, like his morality and miracle play plots, is an avoidance, its narrative modes unanswerable to a world in which humanity preys upon itself like monsters of the deep. *King Lear* shows us a graceless world, a world which God or the gods seem to have abandoned, a world in which virtue is initially indiscernible to those in power.

In rehearsing these well-trodden themes I mean to show how the recovery of grace and the resources of romance are again at issue in *Pericles.* So too is the recovery of speech. *Pericles* is a rewriting of *King Lear.* Lear gives away his kingdom; Pericles is exiled from his. King Lear loses a beloved daughter and discovers that his other daughters are monstrous; Pericles imagines that his daughter has died and so loses her. Both plays inherit and test out the capacities of the romance form. Both plays feature recognition scenes which beg to be seen in the light of each other; the one with a king who is moving in and out of sanity; the other in which both father and daughter regain their voices together. *Pericles* is Shakespeare's first post-tragic play: not only is it written after *King Lear* but it works

through the tragic impasses of *King Lear.* If *King Lear* is a tragedy of acknowledgment, *Pericles* is a romance of acknowledgment. Both plays have
a complexly evolving relation to the form of romance. I will argue that
the romance forms in *King Lear* are motivated by a relation to speech and
that this highlights the work of recovery in *Pericles,* a play which one critic
has noted seems to have been written for its recognition scene alone.[6] The
more normal route taken in romance recognition scenes is the revelation of
identity through tokens and signs. This is sometimes a mark on the body:
Odysseus' scar, the mole upon the cheek of Viola and Sebastian's father. Or,
in the form of the fair unknown, it is sometimes an unveiling where the
incognito knight reveals who he is beneath his mail, hauberk, and armor.[7]
The recognition in *Pericles,* I want to argue, does not merely supply the
identity of the protagonists and so restore them to each other and to themselves. The recognition in the exquisite scene in which Pericles and Marina
are begotten again happens not through the displaying of tokens and signs
of identity, but through the sharing of a story that belongs to them both.
It is a recovery that emerges from painful silence. The telling of the story
comes as a revealed truth that incarnates the accidents of their histories.
Their stories could so easily have not been told, and it is the telling that
makes the play a profound exploration of what it means to tell a story and
to find yourself in one. The recognitions involved here are about the basic,
usually unspoken bonds of trust in speech.

In working the recognitions through the fundamental act of speaking
rather than through the tokens or signs that ratify social identity, Shakespeare is making the form of romance into something new. In this play,
with its extraordinary focus on the fact of utterance itself, Shakespeare finds
the recovery of self and community all at once, and this becomes central to
the grammar of forgiveness as it is explored in the subsequent three plays
on which this book focuses: *Cymbeline, The Winter's Tale,* and *The Tempest.*

But if *Pericles,* as I am arguing, is a play that stages the recovery of voice,
how is a voice lost? The abdication scene of *King Lear* might provide one
response to that question. At the beginning of *King Lear* a daughter finds
that she has nothing to say. Words of truth and of love are alike impossible
at Lear's court. The play will show relentlessly, remorselessly, what a culture comes to look like when the paths to truthful expression are lost. In the
famous first scene of *King Lear,* Lear has devised a "love-test." This is dis-
tinctively different from the test contrived in the old *King Leir* play where

the point is to trick Cordella, his favorite child, into allowing her father to choose her husband. In *King Leir,* Cordella wishes to choose her own husband, but the King anticipates that her response to the love-test—that she loves him best—will force the emotional logic that he then must choose for her. Shakespeare's version of this scene is entirely different. Most important, it is staged as a public ceremony. In Stanley Cavell's influential reading of the abdication scene, Lear sets the public test not because he wants to choose her love for her, but precisely because he cannot bear the utterance of love; he is avoiding acknowledgment. To be loved, he must be known, and so to speak love is to reveal that knowledge, to acknowledge it. Flattery does not need to know its object; its aim is mutual aggrandizement, and so it obscures both truth and the particularities of an actual relationship. His public ritual of competitive flattery makes any true declaration of love impossible, unspeakable under those conditions. Cordelia cannot declare her love precisely because she does really love him. Goneril and Regan can declare their pseudo-love precisely because they don't. They are willing to participate in the charade of flattery because that is their currency. Goneril, as Stanley Cavell has said, shows her contempt for "human speech as such" and not alone for her father.[8] Lear has staged a public ritual in which it is impossible to speak words of love and he loses—has already lost—the capacity to distinguish between flattery and love. Lear reads her "nothing" as a rejection, but "nothing" true can be spoken here. Lear has enforced a kind of silence on Cordelia: "Love and be silent" (1.1.62). The love she bears him can have no voice here. And in theatricalizing love, stifling its expression, Lear loses his ability to learn differences. He cannot discern love from its imitation, and this, Shakespeare shows us, is tragic.

The abdication scene in *King Lear* is thus a primal scene of silencing, a scene that expropriates public ceremony to private fantasy and thus disables ritual from its work of participation. The interruption, suspension, or appropriation of ritual work is characteristic of Shakespeare's explorations of the form of tragedy. At the court of King Claudius Prince Hamlet's expressions of grief and love are also unspeakable. "That within" cannot find expression in the "maim'd rites" of the play. What people learn of each other is through surveillance, eavesdropping, subterfuge, or through Hamlet's attempts at dramaturgy. As I shall suggest in a subsequent chapter, the truthful speech known as confession is also stifled and travestied in Othello's devastating "confession" of Desdemona in the death-bed scene. When the paths to the natural expression of emotions are foregone, there are no ways of knowing oneself or others.[9] The results are catastrophic, the stuff of tragedy. Cordelia cannot heave her heart into her mouth; Hamlet's natural expressions of grief and love pass showing; the plays in which their natural voices are silenced are plays in which it is impossible to know anyone or be known because trust in words as the home of such knowledge has all but disappeared. Once public rituals are made to echo the private and mad fantasies of a man powerful enough to mold ceremonies around those fantasies, no one can be knowable within their forms. Shakespearean tragedy takes up the cues of the history plays in examining the subsumption of ritual languages under the fantastical imaginings of vain or tyrannical men. When public ceremonials are suborned to private fantasy we get the logic of Leontes: "I have said / She's an adult'ress, I have said with whom" (2.1.87–88). What Shakespeare shows us in act 1, scene 1 of *King Lear* is the kind of stifling of speech consequent upon these suborned ceremonies which try to speak one and not many voices.

Critics have certainly noticed the preoccupations of the tragic plays with "maim'd rites."[10] But one of the remarkable things about such readings, illuminating as they have sometimes been, is the way in which a kind of functionalist talk (never far away when ritual is at issue) comes to define Shakespeare's relation to received traditions. Rites always assumed to be stable are said to be lost, and the lostness and the stability work in perfect counterpoint. The stability of ritual can even be understood as a back-projection of that lost-ness. The problem with this kind of generalizing language is that it loses the specificity of speakers and the occasions on which they speak, and even more the specificity of Shakespeare's own occasion. To miss that specificity is to fail to ask why speakers say just these things in these situations and thus to miss what they say.

When Shakespeare rewrote *The Chronicle History of King Leir,* a play deriving from the late 1580s or early '90s and newly printed again in 1605, he was rewriting a romance. Indeed *Pericles* was written during a revival of romance. *Mucedorus* had recently been restaged as had the old *King Leir* (in 1605).[11] *The Knight of the Burning Pestle,* itself first produced in 1607, though not printed until 1613, had been apparently too scathingly sophisticated about the popular revivals of chivalric romance to be well received, but it is a testimony to the popularity of the form and the sophistication with which it is revisited.[12] Versions of *King Lear* appear to be written on either side of *Pericles* (a dating which makes *King Lear* a late play too). *The History of King Lear* (Q) and *The Tragedy of King Lear* (F) appear to have been written in 1605–6 and 1610 respectively, with *Pericles,* as well as *Macbeth* and *Antony and Cleopatra* coming between.[13] It is clear, then, that Shakespeare was profoundly interested in the form of romance as a post-tragic drama. Romance is present in *King Lear* not only in the Gloucester/Edgar subplot, added from the *Old Arcadia* and absent in *King Leir,* but in the fact that it is so pointedly and remorselessly a deliberate inversion of the romance form. *King Leir* is of course a romance: Cordella is reunited with her father, the kingdom is regained, and right triumphs. In fact the play is a morality play about the evils of flattery and unkindness. Above all in this play, the heavens answer the trust of those who call on them.

When Regan's messenger is sent to murder Perillus (the Kent character in King Lear) and King Leir, he asks the messenger to prove that he is doing this on Goneril and Regan's orders and there ensues a discussion about whether he should swear by heaven, earth, or hell. He should not swear by heaven because Perillus proclaims the guiltlessness of heaven in "such haynous acts"; he should not swear by earth because King Leir declares that "the mother of us all…abhors to bear such bastards," and he should not swear by hell. There ensues a long scene in which Perillus and King Leir submit to the will of God and pray for forgiveness. Each attempts to save the other by standing in his stead. At this point thunder and lightning come in as the *deus ex machina,* and the messenger's knife poised to kill them falls. At each point where the gods are called upon in this play they respond to the call of humans; the agency of heaven in restoring justice to the world is vindicated through the work of romance. In Shakespeare's *Lear,* this romance is systematically inverted to indicate that the gods have left the stage. Romance is the form that systematically converts chance into providence, but there is no such conversion in King Lear. In the play, the gods never answer the prayers of those who call upon them.

In *Pericles,* Shakespeare explores the notion that with the return and renovation of romance can come a restored faith in the possibilities of grace. Yet the miracles are ordinary. Although it is clear that the overarching agency of heaven is supervising human action, it is the agency of the human voice that is the medium of redemption. In this way, both the form of romance and the form of tragedy are profoundly revised through the sounding of human acknowledgment as miracle.

Pericles is a ragbag of romance effects and techniques, and as such it explores the mutuality of narrative and community.[14] If King Lear begins with a ceremony where truthful speech cannot be uttered—can say only "nothing"—then Pericles makes a different kind of silence central to its workings. Its romance resolution operates not through the traditional body marks and tokens but through the slow dawning of speech in which one person is encouraged to tell her story to another who longs to hear it.

In *Pericles* we are presented with a man who refuses to speak. The death of his daughter, following on the death of his wife has made him an exile not just from Tyre and the murderous fantasies of the incestuous Antiochus, but from all of human society. *Pericles* is a post-tragic play both because it sublimely stages the recovery of voice—Pericles', Marina's, and Gower's too—and because it bets the possibility of any goodness in the social order on such recovery. *Pericles* is a profound exploration of the resources of acknowledgment, of recognition, and of the power of stories, shown and told.

In what follows I propose to examine anew the relation of *Pericles* to one of its source texts, John Gower's *Confessio Amantis,* an examination that will reveal how central the question of voice is to the play.[15]

Pericles and Gower's *Confessio Amantis*

Two of the recent editors of *Pericles* ponder the notion that in George Wilkin's draft of the play, Shakespeare found the paths to the late great plays, *Cymbeline, The Winter's Tale,* and *The Tempest.* Says Philip Edwards: "It would be curious indeed if Shakespeare had discovered, in a poor play that he started tinkering with, the kind of plot, the kind of art, the kind of themes, which he was to spend all the endeavour of his last years of his writing life trying to develop. It would be curious indeed, but it has to be admitted it would not be impossible."[16] Roger Warren, the editor of the Oxford World Classics edition of *Pericles,* puts the point more positively: "Wilkins's outline of his draft may have provided Shakespeare with a stimulus for all his late work."[17] Shakespeare, however, enters the world of the late plays through Gower rather than through Wilkins. I will be arguing that Shakespeare found three related things in a renewed encounter with Gower's *Confessio Amantis* and in particular with Gower's version of the Appollonius of Tyre story in Book VIII of the *Confessio.* First, against the Calvinist consensus that we inhabit an utterly depraved nature that can only be redeemed by God's grace, Shakespeare found in Gower's rendering of the Appollonius story grace at work in and through nature as Appollonius finds the world restored to him in the lineaments of his lost daughter's face. Second, he found an engrossing and thoughtful contemplation of the nature of stories and their authority in Gower's frame narrative, a narrative that makes time and the possibilities of an internally motivated, not externally imposed recognition central to both the power and vulnerability of stories. Third, and above all, he found a shared fascination with the question of voice, and what it means to come to speech and to lose it. The third aspect is my focus here.

Shakespeare had used Gower's Appollonius of Tyre story before as a source for *The Comedy of Errors,* where his placing of Egeon's lost wife as abbess in the temple of Diana indicates Gower as his source.[18] The play is an astonishing exploration of the poetics (and theatrics) of incarnation and, as in *Pericles,* the sea is the very solvent of human identity:

> I to the world am like a drop of water,
> That in the ocean seeks another drop,
> Who, falling there to find his fellow forth,
> (Unseen, inquisitive) confounds himself.
> (1.2.35–38)

That Shakespeare returns to Gower's Appollonius story again several years later and with such pointed and rare fidelity indicates that Gower is a pervasive and generative resource for him. Helen Cooper claims that this return is characterized by a "faithfulness to his source so unusual in his work as to turn the play into an act of homage to the traditions of romance transmitted through English."[19]

Blown by chance winds, Gower's Appollonius harbors at Mytilene in an extremity of desolation. Reduced to a virtual catatonia by the loss of his wife and daughter, he refuses to talk with anyone and keeps inside the hold of his ship weeping all alone, wishing neither to see or to be seen:

> For he lith in so derk a place,
> That ther may no wiht sen his face.
> (*CA* 8.1642–43)

He wants, it seems to be a hole in nature, to lose his sentience. It is at this point that Thaise is called upon to "glade with this sory man" (*CA* 8.1663), but although she sings like an angel and though she tells him many tales and strange riddles, he refuses to speak. At last there is some response: half-mad with wrath and grief, he asks her to leave:

> But yit sche wolde noght do so,
> And in the derke forth sche goth,
> Til sche him toucheth, and he wroth,
> And after hire with his hond
> He smot.
>
> (*CA* 8.1690–94)

Thaise is struck into a forceful reproach. Almost despite herself she begins to reveal her identity:

> Avoi, mi lord, I am a maide:
> And if ye wiste what I am,
> And out of what lignage I cam,
> Ye wolde noght be so salvage.
>
> (*CA* 8.1696–99)

And thus it happens that the stories that had isolated each of them in their worlds turn out to be one and the same story. They are doubly shared— because it is told at all and because it is the *same* story. What Genius (the priest of Venus, Amans's confessor, and the tutelary genius of procreation from Gower's major intertext, the *Roman de la Rose*), wants Amans to see in this story is:

> What is to be so sibb of blod.
> Non wiste of other hou it stod,
> And yit the fader ate laste
> His herte upon this maide caste,
> That he hire loveth kindely,
> And yit he wiste nevere why.
>
> (*CA* 8.1703–9)

In a poem that has explored the range and reach of loving according to one's kind, where loving kindly had threatened to be overwhelmed by incestuous longings, compulsively static fantasies, and an inability to see beyond the mirror of self-reflection, this mode of kindly loving is given redemptive force and wonder and allowed its full extended play. I think the word "kindely" carries its Middle English sense of "thoroughly, completely, effectively, well."[20] Above all, it animates the meaning of the word not simply as appetite and feeling but of course as "family" and "offspring" as well as with benevolence and revealed created nature.[21] Thaise now freely offers what "sche hath longe in herte holde" (*CA* 8.1726) and what ensures is a "newe grace" (*CA* 8.1739) so that Appollonius can emerge from the "derke place" (*CA* 8.1740) that is both literal and metaphorical. The shadows of Antioch are dispersed and whereas the contagion of that riddle solved but not spoken had been to breed flight, exile, and a contaminating "privete," this encounter will be towards openness, community, and in this story, sound government too: "And out he cam al openly" (*CA* 8.1748).

Gower's rendering is pellucid and simple. Its power to move and its complexity derive from its setting as the last of a whole sequence of stories told by Genius to Amans. Amans is hardly an ideal interlocutor for these stories. Although he is scrupulously honest to the mandates of the confessional in giving his response to these stories, minutely examining himself for sloth, envy, and greed, for example, and though he is occasionally prompted into some curiosity that momentarily takes him out of the obsessive and sterile circularity of his thoughts toward his lady, he mostly, and sometimes hilariously, misses the point. (Amans's obtuseness and relentless referring of all stories toward himself, his inability to recognize the otherness in them and in himself is not just a local problem but structured into the models of exemplarity at work in the confessional.) Terence Cave has read Shakespeare's Pericles as the exemplary listener to Marina's role as story-teller: he encourages—hangs on—her every word, trusts her beyond probability, beyond what is strictly reasonable, trusts her relation of the story before he has any intimation of their actual relation and, weeping with joy, he sees that her story is his.[22] Shakespeare's version of this scene reveals what is implicit in Gower's scene of story-telling too. As William Robbins has recently said: "Thaise's story moves Appollonius not out of intelligence or pity or persuasion, but out of kinship: not because it offers an *analogy* to his own predicament, but *because it is part of his story*" (my italics).[23] Amans's response to Genius's culminating tale is bathetic:

> Mi fader, hou so that it stonde,
> Youre tale is herd and understonde,

As thing which worthi is to hiere,
Of gret ensaumple and gret matiere,
Wherof, my fader, God you quyte.
Bot if this point myself acquite
I mai riht wel, that nevere yit
I was assoted in my wit,
Bot only in that worthi place
Wher alle lust and alle grace
Is set, if that Danger ne were.
                              (*CA* 8.2029–39)

How a story will touch you is a function of its place in your history and a function of the extent to which this can be recognized. This is as much a question of acknowledgment as that growth from ignorance to knowledge celebrated in Aristotelian *anagnorisis*. And in Gower's recognition scene, the kindly knowledge that Appollonius has of Thaise, the fact that he loves her kindly without knowing why, crucially precedes the revelation, the unfolding of her actual identity: "Bot al was knowe er that thei wente" (*CA* 8.1709). It is then the full resources of kind that Genius can finally draw on when he counsels Amans "what is to love in good manere, / And what to love in other wise" (*CA* 8.2010–11) and when he can invoke "loves kinde" (*CA* 8.2228). It is important in the last of a series of exemplary tales that we're given a primal scene of recognition that might be understood as itself exemplary of the conditions of self-recognition in a story. It is a scene which transposes such self and other recognitions as vulnerable to the chance of an offshore wind, and to the terrifying risks of self-exposure—in this case prompted by a violent rejection, which is nevertheless the stuff of gift and wonder.

The Voicing of Recognition

Shakespeare takes these cures and the short lines of the recognition scene (less than a hundred) in Gower, and expands Gower's spare, limpidly economical lines into a drama of two and a half times as many lines in which the recognition is drawn out to suggest the difficulty and centrality of what it means to come to speech. Each of the protagonists of this scene has been silent in different ways. Marina is supremely articulate; indeed she seems to be a goddess of the expressive arts. She can sing like one immortal and dance and compose artful canvases with her needle. She can confound deep clerks like the articulate female saints of the hagiographic tradition. In the brothel it is her ability to speak that has preserved her. Indeed it is important that when we first meet Marina she tells us in the most natural way of her parentage and her loss made new because of the loss of her nurse Lychorida:

> Ay me! poor maid,
> Born in a tempest when my mother died,
> This world to me is as a lasting storm,
> Whirring me from my friends.
> (4.1.16–20)

Her very first words bespeak a loss just passed and one about to happen: like Proserpina, she will rob Tellus of her weeds to strew Lychorida's grave with flowers.[24] She goes on to rehearse the story her nurse has told her of her birth at sea, and she mimes out the storm, lending her voice to her father, to the storm, and to the sailors who man the boat. It is a mini-story of his endurance and her survival. But in Mytilene there is no one to trust with her words. There are no declarations at all that might reveal who she is.

This contrasts with one of the sources of the play, Lawrence Twine's *The Patterne of Painful Adventures,* in which Tharsia (Marina) declares her heritage to Athanagoras (Lysimachus) and tells him the story of her abduction.[25] If she cannot tell her story in Mytilene, a place which does not encourage stories, where words are for advertisement and sale and in which all flesh is commodified, she is the lightning rod which converts others. ("Thou hast the harvest out of thine own report" (4.2.141). Again, Shakespeare takes a motif from hagiography—the saint in the brothel, St. Agnes—and turns it into a property of speech. Her indefatigable yet unlabored honesty helps others to name and thereby come to see what they are doing. Her exchange with Lysimachus is a case in point. She is told Lysimachus is an honorable man; and she holds him to the standards of that honor. Honor is thus an ethical category, not a class code, as in the old hag's speech of *The Wife of Bath's Tale.* She takes the words of others and holds them to their meaning so that all equivocation, hypocrisy, all the euphemisms that cover over sin are shown to be pitiful evasions of the fundamental evils they purport to describe. Hence Lysimachus imagines he is making idle conversation in which she is paid to indulge him when he asks her how long she has been at "this trade." He will cause offense if he names it, but she encourages him to do so and in this way he will start to see himself in the act of naming his actions. (4.1.75–125). Now she forces him to live out the honorable title he claims: "If you were born to honor, show it now" (4.6.92). In this and other ways Marina survives the brothel, but in so doing she brings others to name the deeds they do and so to understand and take responsibility for their own actions. Though she cannot help but be a touchstone of honesty, she has never revealed herself in her words in Mytilene. She is, one might say, powerless to make herself known.

The reasons for Pericles' silence are different. Pericles refuses to speak at all. He cannot see the point in speaking. This means, I suppose, that he has nothing to say, nothing he has found worth saying, no one to whom he wants to speak, and no position from which to speak, because he believes that there are no listeners who might understand. His grief at the terrible loss of his wife and daughter has made him feel so alone that he cannot believe that anyone else might have experienced anything similar. (It is this that Marina gently contests when she suggests there might be one whose grief "might equal yours, if both were justly weigh'd" [5.1.88].) The point here is not the magnitude of the suffering but the unassuageable isolation to which it gives rise. The first production I ever saw of *Pericles* was put on in a huge old warehouse in Old Street, London, by the RSC and Cardboard Citizens, a homeless people's theater troupe. The play had been developed in workshops with asylum seekers throughout England during the previous year and began with a set of stories about exile and wandering. One story concerned a man who had lost his wife and daughter in an accident who left home and simply walked and walked in a silent world without speaking.[26] The production brought out in remarkable ways both the loneliness of grief and the terrible commonalty of the experience among the dispossessed.

So both Marina and Pericles fear to give voice; there is no one to hear and therefore nothing to say. It is worth slowing down at this point to stay with these silences. They are silences that negate or deny the grounds of human sociability and hence of the capacity for self-knowledge that is intrinsic to language use and to the ability of any community to go on. If talking is the wording of the world, if what can comprehensively be said is what is found to be worth saying, then no world is worded, no word worlded for Pericles.[27] This is what makes their eventual mutual act of speaking so world-giving and so regenerative. Pericles' isolation is identifiable in the traditions of despair, exile, and the wild man. He dons sackcloth and ashes and vows never to cut his hair. But Shakespeare's version makes his speechlessness the most important thing about his exile, and mounts his integration back into forms of human sociability as the recovery of his voice simultaneous with the recovery of Marina's. The mutuality is key; to tell someone something one must have something to tell, something the other must be in a position to be struck by.[28] Shakespeare parses out the very conditions of telling and shows two people finding themselves and each other in that act. The relief is of a mutual intelligibility that restores a sense that their lives are common, shared, and no longer uniquely isolating. Let us now return to the scene of recognition.

It is structured like an interrupted story. The governor of Mytilene entreats Pericles' chief adviser to recount the "cause / of your king's sorrow" (5.1.63), but he is interrupted by the arrival of Marina herself, summoned by Lysimachus, the governor, to revive Pericles' spirits. As in Gower's version, Pericles' downright violence in pushing Marina away elicits her spirited response. Though she has come to revive him, she is also prompted into a rare disclosure and a rare desire to be seen, a response that has been utterly submerged in the conditions under which she has hitherto been "gazed at." Tentatively and with dignity she begins to outline the lineaments of her story, one that she has kept hidden in the world of Mytilene. Initially she can only tell her story in the third person. Perhaps the challenge of those words to Pericles' sense of his own suffering as literally unmatched by any other's can only be approached without the claims of the first person:

> She speaks
> My lord, that may be hath endured a grief
> Might equal yours, if both were justly weigh'd.
> (5.1.86–88)

She has seen something in his own grief to match hers and now tells him that hers might equal his. She then begins in the first person to tell him about her derivation and her fortunes. His voice now begins to echo her: "My fortunes—parentage—good parentage…" (5.1.97). And he asks her to speak again. When she does so, he asks her to turn her eyes upon him (the choreography of glances and sightlines is intricate, painful, and central to the scene). And he starts to see the likeness of Thaisa: "you're like something that..." (5.1.102). He now begins to interrogate her breathlessly, prompted by this likeness. From his terrible withdrawal he now yearns for her language like a starving man who has found nourishment. Her words now become something to feed on, and by the end of his next speech it is no longer clear whether he is talking about his wife or his daughter:

> My dearest wife was like this maid, and such a one
> My daughter might have been: My queen's square brows,
> Her stature to an inch, as wand-like straight,
> As silver voice'd, her eyes as jewel-like
> And (cas'd) as richly, in pace another Juno;
> Who starves the ears she feeds, and makes them hungry
> The more she gives them speech.
>
> (5.1.106–13)

In both Gower's and Shakespeare's versions of this story then, the preternaturally perceived fact of likeness is underwritten by a further act of telling. Before he recognizes her as his daughter he recognizes her as truthful and outlines the conditions of what Terence Cave calls the perfect audience for a story:

> Falseness cannot come from thee, for thou lookest
> Modest as Justice, and thou seemest a (palace)
> For the crown'd Truth to dwell in. I will believe thee,
> And make (my) senses credit thy relation
> To points that seem impossible; for thou lookest
> Like one I lov'd indeed.
>
> (5.1.120–25)

The move here is from what looks like something ("thou lookest"), the mode of simile and analogy, to an extension of his mind to an utter trust in her language. And now he moves on to concrete, specific questions as he approaches not what she is like, but who she is. When she utters the simplest of words, to which his questions have finally brought her, her plain and literal declaration: "My name is Marina" (5.1.142) can have a long-delayed impact.[29] And now echoing back her language to her, he prompts more from her: "Tell thy story" (5.1.134).

The celestial music that Pericles now hears as he drifts into sleep is the answering echo, the divine attunement to the harmonies established through the human voice. There is no competition here between divine and human agency. For if, as I earlier proposed, romance is the form in which chance is converted into providence, this has happened here through the touching of human voices. In violently rejecting Marina in his act of pushing her away, he prompted her to cry out, to declare who she was. The sound of her voice, the look of her; this is how grace breaks his refusal of the world and opens him up to another. It is a grace that works through nature in a felt wonder, a pattern of slow recognition that is utterly marvelous, yet utterly natural. The fact of Thaise's/Marina's life can now be felt as the miracle it is, and grace found and felt in the mysteries of generation. Such a wondrous yet ordinary miracle comes about by a soliciting attentiveness, a palpable hunger, and a felt desire for disclosure.

Amans's response to what I have called a primal scene of recognition in the *Confessio* is, under the circumstances, hopelessly bathetic. In response to this lovely story, by far the longest in the structure of 88 odd narratives that make up the *Confessio,* he seems to say: "Lovely, well done, father, you've told a lovely story. But you don't have to worry about me in this regard. Incest is not one of my problems. No, I'm far too in love with the one and only to bother with that kind of thing. Look, you're supposed to be a clerk of love, can't *you help* me?"[30] His own scene of recognition comes later when Venus gets him to look at himself in the mirror in a reverse Narcissus scene. She has tried to tell him kindly, though some things are hard to hear and some knowledges hard to remember:

> So sitte it wel that thou beknowe
> Thi fieble astat, er thou beginne
> . . . .
> This toucheth thee; forget it noght:
> The thing is torned into was.
> (*CA* 8.2428–35)

With the mirror comes a memory of his passed and past days, and he is released from the timeless allure of his fantasies into a sense of his position in the cycle of nature and labor as he imagines himself in the seasonal calendar. As a lover Amans has been all too immune to the stories told him, but when he recognizes himself, he is revealed as the very teller of the stories we are hearing: the poet John Gower who is an old man.[31]

And it is as an old man, incarnate again, "assuming man's infirmities" (1.1.3) that he returns to Shakespeare's stage, the guardian and keeper of stories for the tribe for whom he wastes his life like a taper light (1.1.16). To tell a story Gower must be mortal, he must assume a human body with all its vulnerabilities and pleasures.[32] Stories are "restoratives" (1.1.8), but they may be refused by the wit ripe enough to be on the brink of rottenness, as Gower says in his choric prologue. They can restore us to ourselves, but only if *found,* not if imposed from without.

To make the recovery of voice so central to the rehabilitation of Marina and Pericles, Shakespeare posits a new community founded on mutual attunement. Its fragility and depth both rest on the possibility of just this immensely delicate rendering. It is this kind of community that is at stake in each of the so-called romances that follow. Shakespearean romance offers the slow discovery of the ordinary chancy and occasional miracles of human communication. Their joy is fragile, open-ended. In finding this ordinary miracle of human story-telling and sharing, of human speech, he is not only decisively repudiating the eradication of the human in the reformed discourse of forgiveness which obliterates all human agency in that act; he is also decisively breaking with a model of language as private property enclosing a sovereign will. He is parsing out a grammar of recognition and acknowledgment, one which will allow him to perform acknowledgment itself as forgiveness in the late great plays to come.[33]

5

ACKNOWLEDGMENT AND CONFESSION
IN *CYMBELINE*

Vladimir: Suppose we repented.
Estragon: Repented what?
Vladimir: Oh.... (He reflects.) We wouldn't have to go into the details.

SAMUEL BECKETT, *Waiting for Godot*

Confession is a speech act that seeks its completion
in the acknowledgment of another.

JAMES WETZEL

What is it I can confess? I can confess that I envy that man's art and this man's scope, the anger I failed to suppress at the last faculty meeting, that I have been wasting my time. To whom am I confessing this? If I have been unfaithful I can confess this to my husband; if I am Bill Clinton, I must apparently confess this to the nation. Who will then forgive me or him? Can I confess that my very existence here and now takes up far more than my fair share of the world's resources, and so I harm others, specific others, every day just by living the life I live? I can confess all the things—but only the things—for which I am accountable. I can hardly confess your sins, though it might, at times, in certain moods, be tempting to accuse you of them.

And what is it I can forgive? Can I forgive, say, my uncle's alcoholism, my rapist, my husband's betrayal? Will my uncle, my rapist, my husband be forgiven because of my forgiveness? Who is to say? Who can say?

Confessing is a speech act and so it is more closely akin to declaring, revealing, admitting, avowing, allowing, telling, than it is to lamenting, sorrowing, regretting.[1] The latter was encompassed in an older theological language of attrition and contrition, but the difference between contrition and feeling sorrow for something lies in the fact that contrition keeps the reality of the harm I have done before me, whereas I can be sorry for a million and one different things that do not involve my own responsibility in hurting. We have all been at the other end of: "I am sorry you feel that way." Perhaps we have even said it. Contrition keeps the reality of someone else's pain, a pain connected to my actions, before me, and it is this sense of the harm of the other that keeps me from the many possible corruptions (and consolations) of remorse as a private language, including a fascination with the cleanliness of my conscience, or the complexity of my own mind. Confession in short must be *performed;* it is not something that takes place inside the mind.[2] And the kinship, the family resemblance of confessing to admitting, avowing, revealing, acknowledging, shows why it is hard to do.[3] In confessing I have not only revealed something about myself, but committed myself to a different future.

In the last chapter I concentrated predominantly on the last "recognition" scene in *Pericles;* in chapter 6 I shall do the same for *The Winter's Tale.* As with *Pericles,* the recognition scene in *Cymbeline* is predicated on the fact or act of speaking and the new community that comes into being as a result of these acts of speech. As with *The Winter's Tale,* a self-involving remorse is overcome publicly: however spectacular and histrionic the divine intervention is, remorse is addressed through the overwhelming response to human others. The last extraordinary scene of *Cymbeline* links the languages of confession, acknowledgment, and recognition to create the unprecedented peace that is the "mark of wonder" in this play, the play that harmonizes Britain with ancient and contemporary Rome. Is it a pax romana or a pax Britannia? Pardon, in any case, is the word to all.[4] In this pointed Christianization of Aristotle's "anagnorisis," in the multiple recognitions that come so thick and so fast in this bravura scene (twenty-four in all), in the crescendo of self-disclosures and the infection of truth-telling that overcomes the protagonists, in the narrow path between the ludicrous and the wondrous, and between delight and dangerous risk, Shakespeare once again parses out an astonishing exploration of the grammar of remorse, acknowledgment, and the recreation of a new community through forgiveness. Once again we might see this as a eucharistic community because it embodies forgiveness, and because it imagines the restoration of each person to him or herself as inseparable from, intimate with, the restoration of that community. In the multiple confessions that end the play, the expression of each person's remorse engenders further truths, and these truths are seen to be part of a shared story that makes sense only when told together, a story whose each individual part turns out to be part of the same whole, a whole not visible until each individual part of those stories is told. It is, in short, a re-membrance.

Posthumus's Keys: The Penitent Lock

Posthumus speaks the inherited languages of sin and repentance and begins to show us the contours of remorse, a remorse that is vital to the acknowledgments of the last scene. The linking of remorse and acknowledgment here is key. Just as in my chapter on *The Winter's Tale,* I am depending on a particular understanding of remorse as an awakening to the reality of an other.[5] That is why confession is not about the revelation of a past belonging to me, but a recognition of the reality and effects of my speech and action in the lives of others. As James Wetzel has said in a passage I use for the epigraph to this chapter, confession is a speech act that seeks its completion in the acknowledgment of another.[6] It is not an inward language at all, though of course it must be voiced in the language of acknowledgment.[7]

It is Posthumus who asks: "Is't enough I am sorry?" (5.4.11), and his question might be said to sum up a few centuries of penitential discourse in one highly economical query. For the question of sufficiency, as I suggested in the first part of this book, haunts penitential discourse. Early medieval contritionist understandings, such as that of Peter Lombard in the *Sententiae in IV libris distinctae,* on which every scholastic commentator cut his teeth, held that contrition was sufficient for God's forgiveness; for others it was priestly absolution that constituted the "matter" of the sacrament of penance, a penance that could be administered only through the church's officers.[8] For Luther nothing could ever be enough, there could therefore be no language of sufficiency or accounting, no earning or calculating, meriting or measuring to limit or usurp God's one-sided, utterly gratuitous, preemptive and prevenient gift of grace. Posthumus's own language in the prison scene in act 5, scene 3 here is shot through with the language of accounting and with a vocabulary straight from the medieval confessional. I quote at length:

> My conscience, thou art fetter'd
> More than my shanks and wrists. You good gods, give me

The penitent instrument to pick that bolt,
Then free for ever! Is't enough I am sorry?
So children temporal fathers do appease;
Gods are more full of mercy. Must I repent,
I cannot do it better than in gyves
Desir'd more than constrained. To satisfy,
If of my freedom 'tis the main part, take
No stricter render of me than my all.
I know you are more clement than vild men
Who of their broken debtors take a third,
A sixt, a tenth, letting them thrive again
On their abatement. That's not my desire.
For Imogen's dear life take mine, and though
'Tis not so dear, yet 'tis a life; you coin'd it.
'Tween man and man they weigh not every stamp;
Though light, take pieces for the figure's sake;
You rather, mine being yours; and so, great pow'rs,
If you will take this audit, take this life
And cancel these cold bonds.

                                        (5.4.8–28)

I count: bonds, coins, audit, render, debtors, worth, repent, clement, satisfy, and a jumble of possessive pronouns trying to work out what belongs to whom. This is the logic of penance as counting and accounting, and it has an old and scandalous history, the history that prompted Luther's liberation from the impossibly exacting cost of sinning and its ruthless, insatiable demands. Here this penitential logic is rendered aporetic through the image of a life that is "coin'd." The very most Posthumus can render for Imogen's life is his own. But Posthumus ends up caught in a dilemma which is also a discovery: how can he pay in a coin (his life) which it is not in his power to give, even though that is the utmost he could ever tender or render:

For Imogen's dear life take mine, and though
'Tis not so dear, yet 'tis a life; you coin'd it.
                                        (5.4.22–23)

The image of the sovereign's coin hovers between an understanding of himself as a creature, made in the image of God, therefore gifted, gift and recipient at once, and one of despair.[9] He can't pay, because nothing will be enough and the coin he might wish to pay in is not his to give. So he can only say: "great powers / If you will make this audit, take this life / And cancel these cold bonds." The language of contrition is like the words with which children appease their temporal fathers; it can't possibly be enough to be sorry, he thinks, and the language of payment is hopelessly inadequate. How could even his life pay for his taking of Imogen's? Neither Imogen nor Posthumus own their own lives. So the prayer to the "great powers" ends by turning to Imogen. His remorse leads him again and again to his sense of the utter particularity of the woman he imagined he has murdered and his soliloquy ends with an address to her: "O Imogen / I'll speak to thee in silence" (5.4.28–29). Here he is like Leontes: "Whilst I remember / Her and her virtues I cannot forget / My blemishes in them, and so still think of / The wrong I did myself..." (5.1.7–10). Here is the perspective in which the meanings of what one has done, what one has become through doing it, and what victims have suffered are inseparable.[10]

The "cold bonds," as both Martin Butler and Roger Warren note, stand for prisoner's fetters, the bond of life itself, and the bonds of old legal agreements.[11] In the penitential context of this speech they also stand for the chains of sin. What, then, is the penitent instrument? The language of the keys, of binding and loosing and its theological and doctrinal fortunes tends to be traced around a series of scriptural passages: Luke 24.47–48, Mark 16.15–16, Matthew 28.18–20, John 20.21–23, and especially Matthew 16.18–19: "and I say unto thee, that thou art Peter, and upon this rocke I will build my congregation: and the gates of hel shal not prevaile against it. And I will give unto thee the keyes of the kingdome of heaven: and whatsoever thou shalt binde in earth, shal be loosed in heaven."[12] These keys are defined by medieval theologians as the apostolic authority granted to the church to confess and absolve. But the authority "of binding and loosing," as I suggested in the first part of this book, is redefined by reformers (for whom sinners are always already forgiven) in a range of ways: for Tyndale, the gospel is the key; for Becon, the key is preaching; for John Jewel the keys are not of confession but of "instruction" and "correction" and so on.[13] The point here is not to locate what particular doctrine of the keys is held by Shakespeare, a reductive and pointless, probably impossible endeavor. It is rather to show how the language of imprisonment and release is displaced from the physical fetters to the pinching, excoriating dilemma of a conscience in chains; to see, moreover, how such language is inextricably bound up with questions of the relationship between human effort and divine will, of despair, and of the felt anguish of acknowledgment without grace; and finally to see how deeply engaged such a predicament might be to the most central and agonizing questions around guilt, responsibility, and salvation in his culture.[14] The scene poses itself as a felt and existential question for a haunted soul confronting the results of his own murderous rage, for whom there appears to be no recourse but death.

The medieval theology of the keys would have stressed the tripartite nature of the sacrament of penance in contrition, confession, and satisfaction. The penitent lock would have consisted in the contrite sinner confessing to a priest, and the sacrament of penance encompassed both his speech act and the speech act of the priest in absolving him. Sins, says, Aquinas, are like bonds which must be loosened or dissolved; the priest's words "I absolve you," "derive from Christ's own words to Peter: *Whatsoever you shall loose on earth... and is the form used in sacramental absolution.*"[15] Calvin too consistently imaged sin itself as bondage.[16] The longevity and purchase of this figure is apparent in the fact that sin as bondage is used by Lancelot Andrewes in "A Sermon Preached at Whitehall upon the Sunday after Easter, being the Thirteenth of March, AD MDC." Linking the texts from Luke 4.18 and Isaiah 61.1, Andrewes comments on the word "captive":

> The mind of the Holy Ghost then, as in other places by divers other resemblances, so in this here, is to compare the sinner's case to the estate of the person imprisoned....The very term of "the keys"—wherein it was promised, and wherein it is most usually delivered—the terms of opening and shutting, seem to have relation as it were to the prison gate. The terms of binding and loosing, as it were, to fetters or bands. And these here letting forth or detaining, all and every of them to have an evident relation to the prisoner's estate, as if sin were a prison and the case of sinners like theirs that are shut up.[17]

Andrewes's sermon defends the work of the ministry in the act of absolution. In a long gloss on the grammar of John 20.23 the sermon says that "remiseratis" stands first, and "remittuntur" second. Thus "it begins on earth and heaven follows hereafter." It is important, states Andrewes, that the Scriptures set this down in two words. The Apostle's part is delivered in the active and his own part in the passive, and thus "it is so delivered by

Christ as if he were content it should be counted as the Apostles agency" in the act of the remission of sins. This is Andrewes's avant-garde conformity and defense of the central office of priesthood in the act of reconciliation.[18] But Posthumus has no priest to confess to, no friend, no human other. So he calls first to the gods, and then to his dead lady: "Imogen, I'll speak to thee in silence."

The Incorporate Past: Confession in the *Book of Common Prayer*

In the massive reevaluation of the ritual language of Catholicism, the *Book of Common Prayer* may be understood both to extend the penitential reach of the liturgy and to contract it. How is it possible to make both these claims at once? Annual auricular confession had been inaugurated as a legal requirement for all Christians at the Fourth Lateran Council of 1215.[19] This practice was associated with the rites of Easter. To imagine it as some hole-in-the-corner affair, some "ear-shrift," as Tyndale put it, would be to accept the polemical description of its most ardent enemies.[20] Confession as practiced by the vast majority of parishioners was a preparation for the Easter eucharist, and as such a part of the mass and, with the eucharist, one of the only other repeated sacraments incorporated into the liturgical year. It was never, for such parishioners, a particularly private event since it was done mostly on Maundy Thursday, Good Friday, or Easter Sunday when parishioners queued up in a crowded line to kneel before the parish priest. This kind of mandatory annual auricular confession associated with the Rites of Easter is abolished in English reformed practice, as I explored in part 1 of this book, but in the revised rites of the *Book of Common Prayer,* parishioners are repeatedly beseeched to consult their minister if, after examining their consciences, they felt themselves to be out of charity with their neighbor and so not ready to receive the sacrament worthily. There is still a form of private and auricular confession and absolution in the Order for the Visitation of the Sick, but as far as able-bodied people were concerned, it was only those who found that they could "not quiet their consciences," the ones who "requireth further comfort of counsel," who were encouraged to "come to me or some other discrete and learned minister of Gods woorde and open his griefe, that he may receive ghostly counsaile, advice, and comfort, as his conscience may be relieved."[21] The rite was thus exceptional rather than routine. The difference here is that the onus falls on the sinner alone and consultation of the minister is at the sinner's discretion. As Patrick Collinson has memorably said: It was "as if the great unwashed public had said to the clergy, 'don't call us, we'll call you.'"[22]

Nevertheless the *Book of Common Prayer* allowed considerable scope for the minister to decide whether his parishioners were in a position to participate in the eucharist, and it is clear that the extra-liturgical practices of the ministry of reconciliation continue almost unbroken from the Middle Ages.[23] The Morning and Evening Prayer, adapted from the medieval Breviary, begins with a collection of scriptural quotations all of which concern amendment of life, any of which the minister is to read during the service. These readings (from Ezekiel 18, Psalm 51, Joel 2, Daniel 9, Jerome 10, Matthew 3, Luke 15, Psalm 143, and 1 John 1) form a patchwork of petitions for mercy, acknowledgments of sin, desires for amendment, and they weave together both the penitential psalms and the central parables of forgiveness in the New Testament. Even more important, they are immediately succeeded by a general exhortation of the minister: "And although we ought at all times, humbly to acknowledge our sins before God: yet ought we most chiefly so to do, when we assemble and meet together...."[24] John Booty, the editor of the Elizabethan BCP, has said that the penitential introductions to Morning and Evening Prayer (which resembled the Order of Communion of 1548) "changed their spirit, if not their nature."[25] What follows is a general confession, a speech act made together in which the whole congregation kneels and is generally confessed and generally absolved.[26] That is, the congregation are confessed and absolved all together and of all that they have done and left undone: "We have left undone those things which we ought to have done, and we have done those things which we ought not to have done."[27] "Forgive us," says the general confession in the "Order for the Administration of the Lord's Supper, or Holy Communion," "all that is past."[28]

The ostensible intent of the reforms was, of course, to realize the communal aspects of eucharist as a prayer of thanksgiving, rather than to see it confected by a sacrificial clergy; the reforms worked against both the notion of a secret ear-shrift to a priest and the idea that a priest could, for example, celebrate a mass on his own.[29] But there has been a quiet revolution in the nature of the speech acts of both confession and absolution.

In the rubrics which specify the preparations for holy communion, each parishioner is called upon to examine his own conscience (rather than with an interlocutor), to think where he/she might have offended, and to "confess yourselves to Almighty God." What is the consequence of making confession a private utterance to the deity rather than a speech act to an individual? Does it not have the effect of putting a rift between the notion that an offense against neighbor *is* an offense against God and vice versa, and so the guiding concept of the simultaneity of sin against God, self, and neighbor. Might the effect not be to render sin more abstract, as it were, a private thought?[30]

"I confess to God, not to Tutu," declares General Tienie Groenewald as he chafes against the protocols of the Truth and Reconciliation Commission in South Africa. But here is Tutu's reply:

> Jong, if you've had a fight with your wife, it is no use you only ask forgiveness of God. You will have to say to your wife you are sorry. The past has not only contaminated our relationship with God, but the relationship between people as well. And you will have to ask forgiveness of the representatives of those communities that you've hurt.[31]

There is no separation for Tutu between the actions committed by Groenewald in his criminally ugly defense of the apartheid regime and the actions committed against God; their separation is a corruption of Christian justice.

In the abolition of auricular confession, the vast, subtle and capacious literature of classification of the sins and their remedies in the manuals for confessors, and penitential literature, a literature that was at once theological and psychological, was simply dispensed with. The new theology regarded the enumeration of sins in auricular confession as both intolerable and superfluous.[32]

I am reminded of George Eliot's brilliant depiction of Bulstrode's downfall in *Middlemarch*. Bulstrode had committed a great sin in his youth, when he had hidden the existence of a daughter who was likely to inherit the wealth of the widow he had married. Now the man who found the daughter, and then concealed her identity, and who has been blackmailing him on the strength of it ever since, is in his medical care, a care he neglects in such a way as indirectly to lead to his convenient death. Eliot makes it clear how comforting to his sense of holiness, how sweet to his nonconformist heart, is the confession of general sinfulness and unholiness that he makes regularly in the quiet of his own conscience and in the face of his maker. How different this is from the kinds of hard particularity he must face when his misdeed becomes public. Here, Eliot stresses, "his struggle had been securely private, and…had ended with a sense that his secret misdeeds were pardoned and his services accepted."[33] Here, Eliot continues:

> Sin seemed to be a question of doctrine and inward penitence, humiliation an exercise of the closet, the bearing of his deeds a matter of private vision adjusted solely by spiritual relations and conceptions of the divine purposes. And now, as if by some hideous magic, this loud red figure had risen before him in unmanageable solidity—an incorporate past which had not entered into his imagination of chastisements.[34]

This is a brilliant description of the difference between the ruminations of a private conscience no matter how demanding it might appear in its own best lights, and the nature of that "incorporate past" when it is confronted by the effects of that past in the actual lives of others. This is indeed the difference between a confession which is a speech act, one which says something to someone about something, and one which speaks of a general and ubiquitous sinfulness and therefore confesses either nothing in particular—or everything all at once: "forgive us all that is past."

Debates over confession remained central to doctrinal, liturgical, and disciplinary concerns in the first three decades of Elizabeth's reign because of the concerted, but in the end failed, attempt to reform the structure of the ecclesiastical courts into a classis structure. Something of this understanding of a mutual proclamation and mutual absolution is understood in some of the proposals for "church discipline" put forward in the "Admonition to Parliament" (1572) and constantly sought after by Thomas Cartwright and others in his arguments with Whitgift.[35] Excommunication was a sanction that Cartwright saw as grossly abused by the ecclesiastical courts, and taken therefore so lightly as to be useless. Excommunication should be left to elders in the classis structure of a proper consistory, enacting a discipline which was one of the marks of a true church.[36] Confession should therefore be "to the church" and penitential discipline from first to last a public performance, not a private contract between priest and penitent. Shakespeare had of course brilliantly examined what it might mean to make this a state policy in *Measure for Measure,* a searing indictment of the enactment of the presbytery.

But, as I suggested in my introduction, in the later plays the search for forgiveness *is* a search for community, and the language of forgiveness, of confession and absolution, is made available for passionate utterance.

Passionate Utterance

It is time to explain what I mean by passionate utterance. The language and the crucial vision here belong to Stanley Cavell's recent work on the legacy of J. L. Austin and Wittgenstein. In a richly suggestive essay Cavell has revisited some of the key distinctions by which Austin had anatomized performative utterances. Austin had (famously) attempted to isolate some features of language in which something is done in the saying of words, and he had further divided performative utterances into the illocutionary, in which something is done *in* virtue of saying something, and the perlocutionary, in which something is done *by* virtue of saying something. Cavell notes that whereas Austin had lovingly and lavishly and minutely parsed out the forms of illocutionary verbs, he was both vague and parsimonious when it came to discussing perlocutionary verbs: "Clearly, any, or almost any, perlocutionary act is liable to be brought off, in sufficiently special circumstances, by the issuing, with or without calculation, of any utterance whatsoever."[37] *"Any, Almost? Liable?"* responds Cavell. "Why is that roughly the end of a story rather than the (new) beginning of one?"[38] He starts over again with Austin's distinctions and begins to map out a realm of speech about which Austin was skittish: the expression of desire.[39] He calls this "passionate utterance," and notes that it may include illocutionary and perlocutionary verbs in equal measure. It is striking that Austin did not name perlocutionary effects. Moreover, it is characteristic of perlocutionary verbs that their effects are not named in the saying as for illocutionary utterances.[40] The perlocutionary act is "not...built into the perlocutionary verb."[41] And this is because the second person essentially comes into the picture. I do not, suggests Cavell, generally wonder how I might make a promise or, if I am a judge, render a verdict, or, if I am a minister, declare this man and woman man and wife, whereas I might well give considerable ingenuity and attention to how I might persuade you, or console you, or seduce you, and as I do so the possible parameters of your response are constantly before me.[42] If I am a priest I do not generally wonder how I absolve you, but I may well wonder how I confess to you if you are not a priest. And how, then, will you hear my confession if you cannot absolve me? Absolution is an office, as I explored in chapter 2, but confession—even if it is made to an absolving priest—is not. Perlocutionary acts "make room for, and reward, imagination and virtuosity"—and "passionate expression makes demands upon the singular body in a way illocutionary force (if all goes well) forgoes."[43] Austin had described six necessary conditions for the felicity of performative utterance, and Cavell shows how these may be extended or overturned in the case of passionate utterance. If in performative utterance, there is a conventional procedure, in passionate utterance there is none. If I confess my sins to my parish priest in the Middle Ages, I will enumerate my sins according a particular schema, the "forma confitendi."[44] I will be asked how I have sinned against the ten commandments, the seven sins, how I have not performed the seven corporal works of mercy and so on.[45] Of the circumstances and contexts of my sins, I will be asked: "quis: quid: ubi: quibus: cur: quomodo: quando" and sometimes "per quos" and "quotiens."[46] But if I am confessing something to you, there will be no set form to follow. I am at the mercy of my own conviction, my own eloquence and honesty, and of your ability to bear and hear my words, and so I am also at the mercy of your response. If, in performative utterance, the particular persons and circumstances must be appropriate for the invocation of the procedure, now who has the authority, or the standing, is precisely what is at issue. Auricular confession, of course, *must* be to a priest.[47] But I might have to dare to confess something to you, and you may well think I have completely overstepped the mark and transgressed an unspoken rule of our relations, and so refuse my right to speak to you in this way. My confession will involve a claim to a particular standing with you, and it will risk refusal and rebuff. So, "establishing standing" and "singling out" are now the second conditions of passionate utterance. If, in performative utterance the procedure must be executed correctly and concretely,[48] such requirements are utterly moot in the case of passionate utterance for there is no agreed procedure. For example, a condition of auricular confession is that it must be complete, a particularly troubling, demanding, even impossible requirement for the scrupulous such as Luther.

In the medieval practice of the sacrament of penance, confession had been intrinsically linked with absolution. The sacrament of penance is begun when the penitent is moved to confess, and completed when the words of absolution have been said over the penitent. But if there is no such procedure, we will have to improvise, make it up as we go along. You may forgive me, but you will not absolve me. Austin's fifth condition—where the procedure requires certain thoughts and conditions, the parties must have those thoughts and feelings—is also applicable to passionate utterance: the one declaring passion must be moved to declare it. The sixth condition—a requirement of subsequent conduct—is, in passionate utterance, a requirement for response in kind and now. "Unlike the performative case, it is open to the one addressed to resist the demand" such that "what is at stake is the question whether a 'we' is or is not in effect now."[49]

Now, the "we" in the *Book of Common Prayer* is meant to instantiate rather than describe a pre-existent "we." But I am suggesting that the paths from the "I" to the "we" are constantly in the process of interruption and derangement. The ejection, isolation, and estrangement, not to say madness, withdrawal, resentment, and frustration, of the Renaissance protagonists who strut and fret their way across the stage point to the immense dissatisfactions, to the premature coercions of a preemptive "we." *Cymbeline* tries a different pathway from the "I" to the "we," one enacting a fantasy of communal truth-telling which is itself an exploration about the conditions under which truth-telling might be possible.

Absolution still exists, of course, in the practices of the reformed English church. It exists not merely in the general absolution, but also in the service for the Visitation of the Sick. But in general it tends now to be associated with the discredited (at least to some) church courts, therefore sometimes administered by lay people, and notoriously subject to financial commutation. In the Sarum Use, the word "absolvo" is used of God and the minister: "Deus...absolvat: ego te absolvo." But in the *Book of Common Prayer,* God *forgives* but the minister *absolves.*

We might say that in the grammar of forgiveness a king pardons, a priest absolves, but only humans and God forgive. And the Christian God (along with the ministers who must administer the *Book of Common Prayer*) has been banished from the stage. The Shakespearean grammar of forgiveness is up to humans. But perhaps the theater, or at least Shakespearean theater, can teach the church a thing or two about forgiveness.

Scenes of Confession

Before I return to the last act of *Cymbeline* and its multiple confessions, I want to examine some scenes of confession both in medieval drama and in Shakespearean tragedy. In medieval drama Confession is a personification who offers shrift and absolution. Two onstage confessions are worth mentioning here, one in *The Castle of Perseverance* and one in the late medieval morality play *Mankind.* It is worth exploring these to show the consequences of a drama that no longer has such figures. In medieval drama, confession is more likely to happen offstage, and the work of the drama is often to bring its audience to an appreciation of the rite of penance.[50] Yet in *The Castle of Perseverance* we get an onstage confession from Humanum Genus to Confession. Confession seeks out Humanum Genus after he has sinned and begs him to confess:

> If he wyl be a-knowe hys wronge
> And nothynge hele, but telle it me,
> And don penaunce sone amonge
> I schal hym stere to gamyn and gle
> In joye þat euere schal last.
> (ll. 1328–32)[51]

The logic of the play is that mercy is available for the man who asks for it: "Whanne Mankynde cryeth," says Confession, "I am redy" (l. 1430). In *The Castle,* Humanum Genus confesses according to the schema of the ten commandments, the five wits, etc., and he is absolved by Confession:

> If thou wylt be a-knowe here
> Only al thi trespass
> I schal the schelde from helle fere
> And putte the fro peyne, unto precyouse place.
> (ll. 1455–58).

The Castle stages the repeated necessity of confession in the context of mankind's indefatigable perseverance in sin.[52]

In the morality play *Mankind,* the speech act of confession itself is given a more specific focus in a play that thematizes accountability for speech. Indeed Mankind is reciprocally understood when the nature of Mercy is understood. Mankind is a creature in need of mercy; he will know himself only when he calls upon mercy. Both these plays then centrally stage acts of confession. The personifications are not priests (though they may of course be dressed in the costume of priests), but part of the point of these penitential plays is to explore the efficacy of penitential ritual. Both plays may be understood in the context of the polemical status of penance as a sacrament and the office of forgiveness in the judgment of confession. Wycliffite attacks on the necessity of confession and the sacrament of penance had contested the authority of the priest in the act of confession and absolution because Wyclif had argued that true penance exists in the mind alone. Such a view, as I mentioned earlier, had been ridiculed by his opponent, Thomas Netter, who had profoundly grasped the theological and epistemological as well as ecclesiological and political implications of such a statement, but Wyclif's view was widespread among Lollard communities.

When Mercy explains to Mankind that for "every ydyll worde we must ȝelde a reson" (l. 173), he is invoking Matthew 12.36–37: "But I say unto you that every idle word that men shall speak, they shall give account thereof in the Day of Judgement. For by thy words thou shalt be justified, and by thy words thou shalt be condemned." The play explores the horrors, challenges, and difficulties of this terrifying judgment, in languages which move from the scatological to the sublime. In exploring the extent to which we are creatures who express or evade our cares and commitments in words, the play exposes us to the difficulty of saying certain words, and of the necessity of our implications in what we say and do.

It is worth paying close attention to the play's acts of naming since this is where the chief work of the play is located—in the move from naming to calling. The dramatis personae, Mercy and Mankind, announce who they are; they name themselves to the audience offstage and on (ll. 17; 113–15; 194–95; 219; 221–25), but the work of the play is to get the audience to see that they can be understood only reciprocally, through their mutual relationship and recognition. As Mankind is suborned by the vice characters, Titivillus, Mischief, New Guise, Nowadays, and Nought, he comes to ask their mercy for the beating he has originally given them (ll. 650, 658). Seeking mercy from a place where it cannot be granted, where it is negated, he is brought to despair. Such despair, as I mentioned in chapter 4, was always considered one of the most troubling and vitiating sins because it disappears the mercy of God and so imperils the salvation of the immortal soul. "Certes, aboven alle synnes thanne is this synne most displesant to Crist, and moost adversarie," as Chaucer's Parson's Tale has it.[53] In despair mercy is unavailable; it can no longer be a felt presence and so it cannot be called upon. Such is the vicious and intensifying hold of despair that it renders impossible the very thing it is most in need of. It thus obviates its own cure, and this is not quite true of any of the other sins. When Mankind seeks mercy from this confederacy of thieves and murderers—"I crye yow mercy of all þat I dyde amysse" (l. 658)—he is "noughted" and a few lines later tempted to kill himself at Mischief's suggestion.

Mercy re-enters and in the formal language of confession asks him to "aske mercy":

> Dyspose yowrsylff mekly to aske mercy, and I wyll assent.
> ȝelde me neythr golde nor tresure, but yowr humbyll obeisance,
> The voluntary subjeccyon of yowr hert, and I am content.
>
> (ll. 816–19)

Mankind cannot bring himself to utter the words: it is a "wyle petycyun," a "puerilite" (l. 820) to ask for mercy again and again. But Mercy wants him to articulate words that seem such a long way from his sanguine and perfunctory, superficial invocation of mercy at their first encounter. Now the words will be sheerly difficult to say, but it is part of the discourse of confession that they must be spoken. Mercy exhorts Mankind time and time again to articulate the words that must come from his mouth to mean anything at all: "ȝet, for my lofe, ope thy lyppes and, sey, 'Miserere mei, Deus!'" (l. 830). And finally Mankind, who has been unkind, is brought back to his own kind, to his own nature, and utters these words:

> Than Mercy, good Mercy! What ys a man wythowte mercy?
> Lytyll ys oure parte of paradyse, where mercy ne were.
>
> (ll. 835–36)

With these words he acknowledges his specific relation to the character Mercy (that he is direly in need of him), to himself (that *he* is in need), and to God (this is what it means to be one of his creatures, mankind) at one and the same time. Mercy and Mankind are coincidently understood because mankind is a creature in need of mercy.

This is a crucial moment in the play to which the careful patterning of Mankind and Mercy's address has been leading all along. Mankind only recognizes Mercy at the same time as he knows himself; but he can only bear knowing himself under Mercy's loving gaze. It is not simply an identification of mercy, but one which is only utterable and conceivable as a self-recognition—a self-recognition, moreover, that comes not through introspection but through mercy received at the hands of another. The play dramatizes a dawning process of recognition and self-recognition, a self-recognition dependent not on introspection, but on relations with others. The play thus brilliantly charts what Wittgenstein calls "the dawning of aspects," in which something is read as an instance of something else. To know yourself as a member of the species mankind in the Christian anthropology of this play is to know yourself as a creature in need of Mercy. It is in this way that the recognition of Mercy depends on the self-awareness of Mankind. The recognition of Mercy is not so much a naming *of* him as a call *to* him. This means that there is a history of theatrical recognition, of acknowledgment in the morality play tradition, and that it almost invariably involves the sacrament of penance.[54] This history has been submerged because critics have substituted naming for calling and in so doing underestimate both the difficulties of learning and the seriousness of speaking. But in successfully banishing the particularity of voice they fail to see that the point of uttering words and the circumstances in which they get uttered are an intrinsic, indispensable part of the significance of those words.[55] When we are tempted to speak outside of language games in this way, we lose not what the words mean in our saying them, but what we mean in saying them.

I have been suggesting that the work of the play is to bring Mankind to contrition so that he might confess his need for mercy. So confession and the recognition of mercy are coterminous. I have also been insisting that our analysis of *Mankind* must work at the level of the utterance, which is irreducibly social and circumstantial, and not at the grammatical abstraction of the sentence, suggesting that this is the burden of the ordinary language philosophy of Wittgenstein and Austin as well as the insight and idiom of the play itself.[56]

Now *Mankind* and *The Castle* can confidently allude to a penitential ritual that is still available, though it might be under heretical and reformist attack. Confession is still a component part of the sacrament of penance;

there are authorized agents who can hear confession and make absolution for individual sins. That is what these plays stake themselves on as they explore the efficacy of that sacramental act. They seek, in short, to bring their spectators to confession, and to see the need for its utterance.

In my chapter on *Measure for Measure* I have already had reason to look at the disappearance of the friar from Shakespeare's stage. After *Measure for Measure,* which annexes the confessional either to ducal/monarchical surveillance or to a purely juridical function, there are no more priests or friars to hear confessions. "Let my trial be mine own confession," says Angelo, thereby substituting a judgment descending on him from on high for the humbling, contrite acknowledgment of need and humility that are central to any confessional act of speech. He thereby obviates the central requirement of a confession that it needs acknowledgment in the response of another, an understanding central to the play *Mankind.* It is beyond my scope here to give a full theatrical history of confession, but it is worth revisiting another crucial scene, one from Shakespeare's own work, because the tragedies seem intent on exploring a world where confession is unavailable, and that absence informs the ethical world of these plays.

In chapter 2, I explored the famous closet scene in which Hamlet catechizes Gertrude, as a confession scene. But Hamlet, I stressed, has never been initiated into the office of confession. He takes up this position in relation to his mother who is invited to acknowledge her behavior under the name of sin. It is precisely because Hamlet is not a priest that he reveals himself in this action. (The friars who have performed confession have all disappeared from Shakespearean tragedy.) His judgment of his mother is in this instance inevitably a revelation of himself to her. In the tragedies, marked as they are by stifled speech, as I explored in my previous chapter, Shakespeare seems to give us instances of failed confession in which the confessor is precisely seen to be taking on a position where his authority in so speaking is constantly in question, and as Stanley Cavell has suggested, what is constantly at stake is whether a "we" is or is not in effect now, and the terrifying ways we are exposed to each other in our acts of speech.

Shakespeare gives us a further instance of "tragic" confession in Othello's deathbed confession of Desdemona in the play's last act. Acting as a demonic agency of justice, Othello believes that it is Desdemona's acknowledgment of guilt in confession that will make his killing an act of sacrifice and not murder. Confession is what links truth to reconciliation, and yet here we are given a scene in which it is impossible for Othello to hear any truth because he has convicted Desdemona in his mind. Only her admittance of guilt will count as a confession for him, and so Desdemona is rendered dumb. There is nothing she can say that might count as a confession except that which would be a lie. So the scene appears as a hideous quasi-blasphemous travesty of confession, in which Othello is a usurper of the role of priest. If you confess someone, you must grant them authority in their own speech act—that is the whole point of confession, and it is why confession is seen to be so necessary in the travesties of justice we call show trials and also why we feel the terrible injustice in such attempts. Othello will accept as confession only what we already know is blatantly untrue. There is simply nothing Desdemona can say—her words are rendered utterly impotent because she has been granted no authority in their saying. And before she is stifled, her speech is. Desdemona might here say with Hermione: "My life stands in the level of your dreams" (3.2.81) as Othello might say with Leontes: "I have said / She's an adult'ress, I have said with whom" (2.1.87–88). Both have turned language itself into a private possession.[57] Embedded within this confession scene is another one: Desdemona imagines that Cassio's confession will reveal the truth and show her innocence, but Othello stifles this avenue of escape too:

> Othello: He hath confess'd.
> Desdemona: What, my lord?
> Othello: That he hath us'd thee.
> (5.1.68–71)

Desdemona's dying confession is the most merciful, saving of lies. To Emilia's question, "O, who hath done this deed?" she responds: "Nobody, I myself. Farewell" (5.1.123–24).

Infectious Confessions: The Gift of Speech

So let me now turn finally to the last scene of *Cymbeline*. The people collected together in that scene are unknown to each other in a variety of ways. Some are in a literal disguise: Posthumus as a Briton peasant, Imogen as Fidele, Belarius as Morgan. Some do not know their own identity and in this sense are unknown to themselves. This is true for Guiderius and Arviragus, but it is also true for Posthumus, who thinks he is a murderer, though he is not one. All, in any case, have mistaken or confused views of each other. It is a situation ripe for exposure and discovery. And it reworks some of the most romancey forms of recognition where the "fair unknowns" of medieval romance turn out to be gentle after all, where the creation by kingly knighting is confirmation, not creation, of prior identities that reconcile virtue with honorific status. All these delights inform part of the sense of playful recognition on the part of the audience, as Shakespeare revives his "mouldy old tales." Yet what informs the sense of fragility and wonder in this last scene, and its extraordinary investigation of response and responsibility, is that this particular community is restored through the speech act of confession. The scene is structured by means of five confessions, the deathbed confession of the queen, the long, cluttered, self-interrupting confession of Giacomo, the confession of Pisanio completed by the outburst of Guiderius, and the confession of Belarius.

The reported confession of the queen is central to begin to un-poison the speech of the community, and the fact that it is a deathbed confession means that there can be no question at all of its veracity. "She alone knew this," says Cymbeline, "And but she spoke it dying, I would not / Believe her lips in opening it"(5.5.40–2). This confession, whose truthfulness is guaranteed only by virtue of the fact that there is nothing at all to be gained for the queen by virtue of it, begins the un-poisoning of the court through further truthful speech.

It is the ring that motivates the second confession, the one by Giacomo. The ring, metonomy of Imogen, is just one of the complex signs in the play, and it is embedded in the central narrative turn of the plot because it is the ring that is transformed from a token of fidelity to the sordid, competitive marketplace of Giacomo and Posthumus's degrading fantasies. The ring is not only the pledge of Imogen's fidelity but the sign and pledge of their clandestine marriage, a marriage that is the only instance of truth and value in the entire corrupt court where all have to mimic the displeasure of the king in her choice of husband. But it is also "the jewel," made the subject of a hideous barter with Giacomo in act 1, scene 4. The suddenness of this overturning is precisely an indication of the extreme fragility of even the deepest human bonds, bonds that rest alone on mutual intelligibility and trust, both of which can turn with remarkable rapidity to pervasive misunderstanding and deep suspicion.[58] The ring, like the bloody cloth, changes its meaning. The bloody cloth, like a relic, is first of all the (spurious) sign of Pisanio's murder of Imogen at Posthumus's bequest. It is therefore also the sign of Pisanio's fidelity. It is certainly not what it seems to Posthumus, for whom it becomes first of all the sign of his desired revenge, then the very sign of his repentance. It is not until the end of the play with the revelations by truthful speech that its real meaning can be established. The signs need to be placed in a community of trust for the new, true significations to become clear. For Imogen has been understood by Posthumus up to this point as the gift of the gods. When Imogen gave him the ring she had said:

> Take it heart,
> But keep it till you woo another wife,
> When Imogen is dead.
> (1.1.112–15)

And his response to this was: "How, how? Another? / You gentle gods, give me but this I have / And cere up my embracements from a next / With bonds of death!" (1.1.114–17). This same language of gift is repeated when he at first perceives that Giacomo has made his wife and his jewel equivalent: "The one may be sold or given, or if there were wealth enough for the [purchase] or merit for the gift; the other is not a thing for sale, and only the gift of the gods" (1.4.82–85). Giacomo's scornful response—"Which the gods have given you?" (1.4.86)—points to his shrewd perception of Posthumus's sense of his lack of desert. Gifts may be hard to receive. Giacomo has no difficulty with the next devilish plant: Imogen may be only his in title. It is in the doubt about his desert, not the doubt about Imogen's merits, that Giacomo finds rich soil for his new covenant. Imogen is reduced from gift to title in that fissure, and then even that title is shown to be unstable, perhaps ill-founded. As soon as Posthumus's anxieties get to work in this direction he—and Imogen—are lost. I mean by this the following: if one sees life as a gift, that is not because one first sees life as a gift and then speaks in accents of gratitude. Rather "a sense of life as a gift comes from speech and action which are in the key of a certain kind of gratitude."[59] The value of gift and gratitude are seen only in the way they deepen the lives of the people who live in this idiom, in this accent. Indeed as Lewis Hyde has said: "true gifts only constrain us as long as we do not pass them along—only, I mean, if we fail to respond to them with an act or an expression of gratitude."[60] The suddenness of Posthumus's reversal is a terrifying instance of how easily and subtly that spirit may be debased, how seemingly casual, yet utterly destructive, that degradation is. The new covenant, the new wager is a hideous parody. The reversal of the first exchange of tokens, and the sacred bond between Posthumus and Imogen, posited on the giving of their words to each other, has "turned" swiftly to this. Each will find cause bitterly to renounce not only the other, but the whole of femininity, or the whole of masculinity for which they have stood in. When the bonds, the troths of their exchanged vows have been traduced, betrayed in this way, it is as if language itself is lost. The dense pun on bonds in Posthumus's penitent declamation in prison now opens out to another use of the term "bond." Our word is our bond: to speak at all is to commit ourselves in our words. That is why linguistic competence is essentially an ethical matter.[61] To redeem language itself: this is the burden of confession in the last scene.

Giacomo's confession is in every sense what a confession should be in the medieval confessional manuals: bitter, self-accusing, complete, particular.[62] Though Cymbeline compels his confession and thus enacts one of the incoherences of coerced confession—confess freely or else—he is "glad to be constrained to utter that / Torments me to conceal" (5.5.141–42). He leaves out nothing. He gives the occasion, the circumstances, the motivation of his actions. He is so self-accusing that it is hard to understand the grammar of his speech at times. The consequent revelation of Imogen's innocence to Posthumus prompts Posthumus's own bitter outburst and self-accusation, which in turn outs Fidele as Imogen. Then, in the absence of the fear released by the Queen's confession, Pisanio can now speak truthfully about the whereabouts of Cloten. "Let me end the story" (5.5.287,) says Guiderius, and confesses his killing of Cloten. This is itself a confession that in putting him under threat of execution prompts the confession of Belarius's true identity, and thus the restoration of the kingdom's heirs and the reuniting of the family. But Guiderius's words, "Let me end the story," are testimony to the fact that their individual confessions are part of a shared story, a story which can only be told together. No individual confession in itself makes sense, but all in all, and all prompting all, they tell a story in which each understands his or her individual role. Guiderius's mole comes like Odysseus' scar, as the "donation of nature," but the stock mark of romance recognition is gently and delightfully superfluous. The "donation" has been the speech of each to each.

And speech as donation was exactly how Augustine had defined confession. Confession, for Augustine, is the exact opposite of a lie. A liar seeks to own language as a possession, but confession is speech that in abjuring and disowning itself returns itself to the giver who is God. So confession instantiates language as gift, according to Augustine, because it is only in saying what confession says that one is rightly related to God.[63] Or one might say, as Cymbeline does: "See, / Posthumus anchors on Imogen; / And she (like harmless lightning) throws her eye / On him, her brothers, me, her master, hitting / Each object with a joy; the counterchange / Is severally in all" (5.5.393–97). It is this shared joy that frees "all those in bonds," as all the prisoners are released and "pardon" becomes the word to all (5.5.424). This counterchange, this reciprocation, is the new economy; it is gift, not wager. For Posthumus once saw Imogen as "the gift of the gods," but was deeply susceptible to Giacomo's piercingly scornful question: "Which the gods have given you?" So language returns as gift through the offerings of truthful speech, speech animated by the realizations, the making real of each to each in remorse.[64] This is Shakespeare's real presence, his remembrance which finds its own complex fidelity, and its own peace, with a discarded and vilified past, a past whose rejection has seemed structural to the thought of so many of his contemporaries.

6

SHAKESPEARE'S RESURRECTIONS

The Winter's Tale

Grace is forgiveness.

KARL BARTH

Grace, inasmuch as it is given gratuitously, excludes the notion of debt.

THOMAS AQUINAS

You pay a great deal too dear for what's given freely.

THE WINTER'S TALE 1.1.17–18

The Grace of Christ, or the holie Ghost by him geven dothe take
awaie the stonie harte, and geveth an harte of fleshe.

ARTICLE X OF 42 ARTICLES

Let's forget about the ghosts that have troubled Shakespearean theater in recent years. Let's for the moment lay to rest Clarence, the ghost of
Hamlet's father, and other haunted and haunting spirits.[1] Such ghosts are
conjured in *The Winter's Tale,* the subject of the present chapter, but though
they lend the play their title, they are not finally its subject or its medium
(no pun intended!). Hermione's ghost is twice conjured in the play. When
she appears to Antigonus to name her child Perdita, she is strictly provi-
sional, for Antigonus has "heard (but not believ'd) the spirits o'th' dead/
May walk again" (3.3.16–17) "If such thing be," Hermione's appeared in
a dream more like waking than sleep; in Antigonus's report she melts
shrieking into the air after delivering her message (3.3.17–18). She is stage-
conjured once again by Leontes as he imagines the response of Hermione's

ghost to the prospect of his remarriage: her sainted spirit would "again possess her corpse, and on this stage / (Where we offenders now), appear soul-vex'd / And begin, 'Why to me?'" (5.1.57–60). Why have you done this to me? And Paulina joins the conceit: were she the ghost, she would shriek "Remember mine." (5.1.67). But the play, even—perhaps especially— in such conscious echoings of *Hamlet,* refuses such hauntings, or rather they function as pure memorials, tokens to chastise the guilty soul, and not as realized spirits.[1] The ghost story whispered to Hermione by Mamillius is private, interrupted, and finally superseded by Leontes' Lenten penitence and the public rite of participation in the "awakening" of Hermione, which is also the awakening to faith in all gathered around her, a ceremony that brooks no recusance. *The Winter's Tale,* I want to argue, consciously replaces the memory theater of the ghost world with the memory theater of a new theatrico-religious paradigm of resurrection. If Shakespearean ghosts have been concerned with forgettings, the new paradigm articulated in *The Winter's Tale* is concerned with recollection, re-imagined through the paradigm of repentance and resurrection.[2]

Shakespeare's resurrection theater is intimately linked to an exploration of both penitence and repentance as modes of recollection and redemption, mediated through a profound and resonant engagement with the puzzling, concertedly bewildering resurrection narratives of forgiveness in the Gospels, the Easter liturgy, and the Mystery Cycles. The resurrection narratives are, after all, paradigmatic texts for the exploration of recognition.[3] In this memory theater it is recognition and acknowledgment that become central. And it is key that in this new paradigm in which response, responsiveness, and responsibility are all important, the returning figures are *actual*—flesh and blood. What the play offers us instead of ghost stories is the most spectacular in a series of instances in which those supposed dead appear precisely to those who have harmed them. Such characters are not in fact dead at all, but they are specifically dead, indeed metaphorically killed, by those to whom they appear.

Return and Recollection

Consider the following *dramatis personae,* all presumed dead during the course of the plays in which they feature:

Claudio in *Measure for Measure*
Helena in *All's Well that Ends Well*

Marina in *Pericles*
Hero in *Much Ado about Nothing*
Imogen in *Cymbeline*
Prospero (to Gonzales, Alonso, and Sebastian) in *The Tempest*.

The drama of their return is always a theater of memory and recognition. The "resurrected" characters burst into the present as reminders of an ineradicable past that must be confronted in the lives and thoughts—in the self-recognition—of those to whom they so hauntingly return. The intensity of their return is particularly felt by, and, I would argue, particularly directed toward, those figures most profoundly implicated in their disappearance.

When Claudio reappears after his reprieve from execution, his sister must greet him as the woman whose last words wished that execution swifter.[4] When Helena enters the court, the question of the spectre is raised once again by the king: "Is't real that I see?" (5.3.306). Bertram's response, uttered, we presume, to Helena, is at once a claiming of her as shadow and substance, as name and thing of wife, and almost in the same instance an "O, pardon!" (5.3.308). Her unanticipated reappearance jolts him back to a past in which he has dispossessed her, a past he imagined was his alone to recount. Hero, after a falsely reported "death" and full funeral rites, returns to the man who has brutally and publicly defamed her on her wedding day as his once and future bride;[5] and Imogen returns to the man who has, so he thinks, arranged for her murder (5.5.228–29). Marina's return to Pericles is differently understood: the power of the great recognition scene in *Pericles* lies in the discovery that she and Pericles share the same story, as they share the same flesh and blood.[6] But this discovery might never have been made were they not to come to speech, an act full of massive risk and painful recollection for both of them, as I explained in chapter 4. Posthumus's encounter with Imogen in the last scene of *Cymbeline* demonstrates how little recognition has to do with sight. He fails utterly to recognize her even though she stands right in front of him protesting her name. Prospero stands outside the charmed circle in which Alonso and Sebastian are immobilized; this encounter with the man they must have thought was long drowned fails to bring the unrepentant Sebastian to penitent recognition (5.1). But it brings Prospero to take on his humanity in one of the most metatheatrical renderings of theater as a memory palace, a place of redeemed memory and the possibilities, difficulties, and promises of reconciliation.

The returns in such resurrections, unlike the ghostly returns of earlier plays, offer the opportunity for transformation, but a transformation that will take up and redeem the past.[7] They offer too, the opportunity for a new accounting in which the *responsibility* of the one who has caused harm is utterly bound up with the *response* to the person harmed. It is because such reappearances involve the most complex encounters with the past of those to whom they reappear that I call these reappearances resurrections. They utterly and completely violate the fantasies in the harmers' minds that the past is subject to their will, their possession. The resurrected subject once thought dead is the vehicle for the resurrection of the one whose actions had appeared to lead to an irrevocable harm.[8] And of course it is just this *mutuality* that differentiates these encounters from the ghostly returns of the unavenged in earlier plays. Their putative deaths are nearly always mechanistically contrived, involving complicitous friars, or potent drugs capable of inducing a sleep that mimics death, or, most outrageously, of statues that appear to come to life. To pursue the whys and wherefores of these means is to dissolve the kinds of trust that are being rebuilt in the new communities and identities forged through such returns. Leontes' puzzled inquiry at the end of the play: "Thou hast found mine, / But how, is to be question'd; for I saw her / (As I thought) dead and have (in vain) said many / A prayer upon her grave" is parenthetical and belated (5.3.138–42). It is not how Hermione has survived that is important but *that* she has. Her recovery depends on the renunciation of epistemology as our mode of access to others. For the insistence on knowing others as the very basis of our access to them, as Stanley Cavell and Shakespeare know, will make the others in our lives disappear, petrify them, or turn them into nothings. It will cloud the basis of our relations to each other in response and acknowledgment, even as it compensates for the sometimes intolerable responsibilities for the maintenance of our relations with each other when they rest on nothing more secure than such responses.[9]

It is the resurrection narratives from the Gospels, mediated liturgically in eucharistic worship, and in medieval Corpus Christi theater, that provide the paradigm for these encounters as narratives of forgiveness, of redeemed memory and the possibilities of mutual presencing. In incorporating the deep structure of these narratives, Shakespeare creates a grammar of theater capable of countering both the Protestant suspicion of fiction and the kind of papists who would "grossly palpabrize or feel God with their bodily fingers," in Nashe's striking phrase.[10] Resurrection narratives take us deeply into an understanding and enactment of memory that denies individual possession and ownership. Such a view is not doctrinal; it does not articulate a set of beliefs about the Resurrection. That would be far too literalistic a reading. Its truths will exist as story because the condition of faith is, in any case, a narrative condition.[11] This new grammar of theater will seek not so much to communicate new ideas as to construct shared possibilities to which the understanding of grace as forgiveness will be central.

Penitence/Repentance

In a characteristically witty turn of phrase, David Steinmetz has written that the Reformation began almost accidentally as a debate about the word for "penitence."[12] The Reformation preference for the term "repentance" over "penance" sought to replace the Vulgate reading "penitentiam agite" with its uncomfortable, even blasphemous works theology. Yet the early reformers were far removed from the antinomian willfulness perceived in them by their opponents who could not conceive of the excess and gratuity, the utter one-sidedness, of Reformation grace. The early reformers would have thought that it was precisely those who have progressed in the love of God who could see sin in the first place, and understand their own behavior under its sign. As Steinmetz puts the matter: "It requires some growth in grace in order to repent properly."[13] Yet, when the remorse, call it contrition, of the sinner becomes detached from the power of the keys, as it threatened to do in medieval contritionist theology, Wycliffite heresy, and the structures and institutions of the post-Reformation settlement, there was no *formal* declaration of forgiveness, no office of forgiveness, no agency authorized to speak God's forgiveness through the church, as I have been arguing. In *Of the Lawes of Ecclesiastical Polity,* Hooker makes the distinction between God's forgiveness and ministerial absolution:

> Wherefore having hitherto spoaken of the vertue of repentance required, of the discipline of repentance which Christ did establish, and of the Sacrament of Repentance invented sithence, against the pretended force of humane absolution, in sacramental penitencie, lett it suffise thus farre to have

> shewed, how God alone doth truly give, the vertue of repentance alone pro-
> cure, and private ministeriall absolution butt declare remission of sinnes.[14]

The priest as confessor had exercised the power of the keys in offering
absolution as both verdictive and exercitive—in J. L. Austin's terms, as
both verdict and sentence.[15] In the absence of that verdictive and exercitive role, the problem of assurance—a medieval as well as a Reformation
pre-occupation—became increasingly pressing. So having asserted the
merely declarative nature of absolution, Hooker continues: "Now the last
and sometymes hardest to bee satisfied by repentance are our mindes."[16]

In *Measure for Measure* Shakespeare had explored the project of a political and social reformation of sin, yet the conclusion that, as Lucio says,
"grace is grace, despite of all controversy" (1.2.24–25) is hardly made read-
ily available in that play; indeed that play might be understood to exhaust
hope in any such social and political "solution." *Measure for Measure* might
be understood to thematize the exhaustion of extrinsicist conceptions of
grace as it does the resources of comedy for Shakespeare. Even if one ac-
cepts, as I do not, the Duke's dispensation of pardon as "pow'r divine"
(5.1.269), the play has so concertedly sundered will from intention in
the plot that it becomes clear that change is imagined less as a complete
transformation than as an external imposition.[17] It is in the late plays, *The
Winter's Tale* and *Cymbeline,* that Shakespeare evolves new ways of making manifest the presence and possibility of grace and forgiveness. In this
chapter I want to explore the presence of these topoi in these late plays, and
then seek to outline why it is the resurrection narratives that provide the
paradigm, the deep structure of this theater and, finally, show how those
narratives inform Shakespeare's sacramental theater.

Is't enough I am sorry?

"Is't enough I am sorry?" As if to confirm Richard Hooker's insight, this
is Posthumus's anguished question in *Cymbeline* (5.4.11). "Sir, you have
done enough," is Cleomenes' response to Leontes in *The Winter's Tale*
(5.1.1). The question of sufficiency haunts penitential discourse as it haunts
Shakespeare's last plays. What is enough and for whom? What are the
agencies of forgiveness? God? The person wronged? The priest on behalf

of the church? To Cleomenes' assertion that he has redeemed his faults, "paid down / More penitence than done trespass," that he should now "as the heavens have done, forget your evil / With them, forgive yourself," Leontes replies: "Whilst I remember / Her and her virtues, I cannot forget / My blemishes in them, and so still think of / The wrong I did myself; which was so much / That heirless it hath made my kingdom, and / Destroy'd the sweet'st companion that e'er man bred his hopes out of" (5.1. 3–4, 7–12). Cleomenes' confident language of sufficiency is cast in the language of a measurable debt, a debt which once paid permits the forgetting of evil and the forgiving of self. Cleomenes is also complacent that heaven's actions in the agency of forgiveness are transparent, fully readable to him, if not to Leontes. But Leontes understands enough about the grammar of forgiveness to know that he cannot forgive himself, that the grammar of forgiving yourself is in fact nonsensical. To forgive himself would entail absolving himself, and this would imply that he could, by an act of his will, reclaim his acts and their effects on others back from the lives of those others and order them by dint of that will.[18]

Forgiving, then, like promising, requires the presence of others; and in the acknowledgment of that mutuality lies the truth that others have reality in a past that is no one's individual possession.[19] In remembering Hermione, Leontes will remember what his relation to her has been—it is part of the particularity and the hard faithfulness of his memory that he must acknowledge his relation to her. This is what fidelity now is. To know his deed, to paraphrase Macbeth, is to know himself. That is why, as Raimond Gaita has suggested, the natural expression of remorse is: "My God what have I done! How could I have done it?"[20] For Leontes, his remorse is the path to finding the independent reality of Hermione. It is the way he refinds her.

Raimond Gaita has described remorse as a "recognition of the reality of another person through the shock of wronging her, just as grief is the recognition of another through the shock of losing her."[21] Leontes' remorse shows the lucidity of his suffering. It shows that the only true remembrance of her will, mortifyingly, involve a remembrance, blasting and perpetual, of his own folly in harming her. The causes of the death of Hermione and Mamillius will be marked on their graves, and in visiting them he will constantly be faced with the mark of his own actions. The two memories are coterminous; this is why remorse is a form of proper memory. It is also why it is so radically isolating and lonely in its fearful lucidity, expressed in the compact grammar of "Come, and lead me / To these sorrows" (3.2.242–43). Lifted out of the mad fantasy that has turned Hermione to stone, for Leontes to know Hermione is to acknowledge *his* relation with her.

The plays in which these questions are asked and prematurely answered stage their own tentative responses. In *Cymbeline,* as I explored in chapter 5, the response comes in a bravura recognition/reconciliation scene whose revelations begin their unfolding by virtue of the truths revealed in a deathbed confession, a scene that holds the moving and the ludicrous in exquisite tension, in which virtually every single character on stage is restored to him- or herself, as they also encounter each other. And in *The Winter's Tale* it appears in an astonishing scene in which a statue seems to come to life, a scene in which the agencies of both religion and art are deployed to embody the ravages of time and the possibilities of a reconciled community.

Posthumus's anguished question, expressed in the form of a prayer, exposes his new sense of creatureliness discovered in the very act of repentance; only the gods' forgiveness can give him the "penitent lock" that will pick the bolt of his conscience. Posthumus's sense of indebtedness is complete; it pertains to his very life, a life that, even if rendered, would not restore or repay hers. In these late plays the understanding of grace and forgiveness is intimately associated with what it means to be human creatures. The costs of the denial of creatureliness in fantasies of autonomy, in denials of dependence, in the creation of others in conformity to our own will, in the negation, therefore, of the condition of createdness, are what the plays must recover from. The discovery of others, of self, and of God is in these plays often part of one and the same movement.

It is central to my understanding of this endeavor that the languages and discourses for thinking about such peace are primarily liturgical. They entail an understanding of the body of Christ as liturgically enacted and not institutionally guaranteed. That is why in medieval practice and penitential theology, the sacrament of the eucharist and the sacrament of penance are incomprehensible except by means of each other. Indeed the abolition of penance as sacrament and the incorporation of confession into general confession at Morning and Evening Prayer and Holy Communion in the Book of Common Prayer services might have placed even more emphasis on the eucharist as the place of reconciliation. For the body of

Christ in this understanding, as it is elaborated in some of the most central medieval cultural forms, is precisely not the wafer held between the hands of the priest, whether understood as the transubstantiated elements of bread and wine, or as a memorial enactment of Christ's redemption. It is the reconciled community. The church as reconciled community might be occluded or betrayed, it might cease to become visible just insofar as a peaceable kingdom is lost, and its lineaments will be restored where such a peace is glimpsed or embodied in its practices. This understanding, which sees the church itself as a performance of the body of Christ rather than a possession of it, has certain consequences. To understand some of the depths of the transformation of Renaissance theater we need to see it in the light of the revolution in ritual and performative culture entailed in church and theater together.[22] For the church to perform the body of Christ means that the church itself will become visible or invisible as these bonds of community are made and broken. That is why the discourses and languages of penance and repentance are an intrinsic part of Shakespearean reconciliation, and need to be understood in all their complex longue durée. It is why, I think, in the creation of a theater that is post-tragic, Shakespeare turns with a renewed intensity to the structures and practices of penitence. If Shakespearean tragedy has been about the consequences of the denial of acknowledgment, then the late romances will find in an exploration of the languages of penitence and repentance an exploration too of the possibilities of acknowledgment. We might recall what Hannah Arendt has said: "Without being forgiven, released from the consequences of what we have done, our capacity to act would, as it were, be confined to one single deed from which we would never recover."[23] Forgiving, as I earlier suggested, following Hannah Arendt, is a redemption from the predicament of irreversibility.

Resurrection Narratives: I

To understand, in Karl Barth's terms, grace as forgiveness is to understand the deepest implication of the resurrection narratives in an exploration of memory. In order to see Christ as risen the disciples must recognize themselves as the ones who abandoned him. Recognition of Christ is for them bound up with a self-recognition that must involve a painful confrontation of the past and its diminutions. In a moving exploration of the resurrection narratives, Rowan Williams examines the way in which God's memory can hold open the past for the apostolic community. To be able to see Christ, for example, Peter must accept his role as denier. He has denied Christ three times as he warms himself before the charcoal fire (John 18:18); in John 21 when the risen Christ is on the shores of Galilee, Peter jumps into the sea to go to him and "Assoone then as they were come to land, they saw hote coales, and fish layd thereon, and bread."[24] Peter is called to recognize the risen Christ in front of the very object by which he had denied him, and he is asked three times if he loves Christ. The reprise of Peter's actions is essential to the granting of his new apostolic identity: there is no new identity without the redemption of that memory of betrayal, but it is the presence of Christ that allows such a memory to be borne in the first place. The resurrection stories create forgiven persons.[25]

Peter's remorse is made a focus of the treatments in some of the resurrection narratives of the mystery cycles.[26] In *The Towneley Plays,* for example, Peter dismisses Mary Magdalen's witness as foolish carping, and Paul joins in with his misogyny here by assimilating 1 Cor. 15.9–11 to John 20.18–19: "And it is wretyn in oure law / 'Ther is no trust in womans saw."[27] When Peter begins to believe Mary, he is filled with remorse, and his thoughts immediately turn to that moment before the burning coals when he denied Christ: "I saide I knew not that good / Creature, my master" (Thomas of India, ll. 87–88). He rehearses the moment of his betrayal. But when Christ comes with his wounds freshly bleeding, Christ's forgiveness of his disciples becomes central to his establishment of their apostolic mission. As he breathes the Holy Ghost into them, he grants them the power to bind and loose sin:

> I gif you here pauste:
> Whom in erth ye lowse of syn,
> In heuen lowsyd shall be;
> And whom in erthe ye bynd therin,
> In heuen bonden be he.
>   (Thomas of India, ll. 236–240)

Their mission to forgive others is indissolubly based on their own forgiveness, so that their past may be faced and not prove annihilating.

In *The Chester Mystery Cycle,* the race to the tomb between Peter and "the other disciple" from Luke 24.12 and John 20.2–10 also prompts Peter's remorse, now tinged with wonder at the emptiness of the tomb and the discarded shroud which he takes as a sure sign of resurrection. Once again he recalls his betrayal of Christ by the coals and his felt lack of worth and is comforted by John.[28] In the meditational play from E museo 160, *Christ's Resurrection,* the fully penitential dimensions are enlarged even further as Peter enters weeping bitterly and confesses his denial "with teres of contrition."[29] Here the ecclesiological dimensions are drawn out as Peter, first apostle and future pope, reflects on the name given him by Christ:

> *Petra* is a ston, fulle of stabilitee,
> Always stedfaste! Alase! Wherfore was I
> Not stabile accordinge to my nam, stedfastlye?
> (*Christ's Resurrection*, ll. 297–300)

The church is founded not in triumphant glory but on the basis of the taking up of just this sinful past. Here, as Leontes remembers Hermione, so Peter remembers Jesus and so also his own cowardice, fear, and lack of fidelity: "When it commys to remembrance / In my minde it is euer!" (*Christ's Resurrection*, ll.327–28).

In *The Towneley Plays,* the intertwining of the eucharistic and penitential is further elucidated by the use of the central text of John 6: "I am the bread of life." In Towneley's *Resurrection* play, as the soldiers sleep, Christ emerges from the tomb as angels sing "Christus resurgens" and, displaying his bleeding wounds, he links the Johannine words to the offering of his body in the mass, a scene usually treated in the Last Supper plays in the other cycles:

> I grauntt theym here a measse
> In brede, myn awne body.
> That ilk veray brede of lyfe
> Becommys my fleshe in wordys fyfe:
> Whoso resaues in syn or stryfe
> Bese dede foreuer,
> And whoso it takys in rightwys lyfe
> Dy shall ne neuer.[30]

Yet if resurrection both requires and releases remorseful remembrance, what is being substantiated in Christ's apparitions is an open question in the plays. Is he a ghost? Both Peter and Thomas ask the question.[31] Thomas's hand deep into the wound of Christ and his sharing of fish and honeycomb materialize his resurrected body for the apostles, but the question of his "ghostliness" plays on the signification of the word as spirit, third person of the Trinity, and the "soul of a deceased person," appearing in visible form.[32]

What is being founded is a new community and a new kind of self in which memory can be redeemed, not through the counting and recounting of sin, but through a new form of intersubjectivity. In Shakespeare's version of resurrection, it is the agencies of both art and religion, of religion working through the agencies of theatrical art, that have become essential to the workings of these narratives.

Resurrection Narratives: II

The trope of resurrection is far from being unique to Shakespeare. Indeed it is very widely used. It appears in *Antonio and Mellida, A Chaste Maid in Cheapside, The Lady's Tragedy, The Dutch Courtesan, The Knight of the Burning Pestle, A Trick to Catch the Old One, The Jew of Malta, The London Prodigall,* and *The Widow's Tears,* for example, and this list is very far from comprehensive.[33] Peter Womack helpfully describes the motif and its immense popularity thus:

> To die is to deploy, as it were, a power which exceeds that of the ruler; death is the outside of the network of relationships that constitute the society of the play. Those who return from death, then, are impossibly able to exercise this uncanny, asocial authority *within* ordinary society. It is a fantasy of justice.[34]

This is a perceptive comment, and it is borne out, I think, by Thomas Middleton's extraordinary play *The Lady's Tragedy,* a play performed by the King's Men shortly after *The Winter's Tale* in 1611, and which presents a sustained interaction with *The Winter's Tale.*[35] Each play features a tyrant; each play flirts with funerary and statuary art, and with the language of superstition, idolatry, and iconoclasm; each has a lady in a sequestered "tomb." In Middleton's play, "the tyrant" usurps Govianus's throne and seeks to satisfy his lust on the lady betrothed to Govianus. The Lady prefers to die than to submit to his depredations and in a grotesquely staged scene kills herself just before the tyrant's men enter to abduct her. But if Womack suggests that the motif of resurrection stages a "fantasy of justice" by exercising an uncanny authority within *ordinary* society, the justice remains "wild" in Middleton's version. The tyrant, seeking to deny the very limits of death, breaks into the cathedral, kisses her effigy, and breaks open the tomb in which she is kept. Govianus disguises himself as a painter ordered by the tyrant to make the lady look as if she is still alive. Painting her lips with poison (in a bizarre reprise of *The Revenger's Tragedy*), he ensures that the lady, so "disguised" as a painted idol, will be the instrument of his death when next the tyrant kisses her. The play works in counterpoint to the medieval tropes of Easter; the tyrant is Herod, and his soldiers are sent not to guard the empty tomb to prevent a resurrection, but to violate and rob the sacred space of the church. The lady "all in white, stuck with jewels, and a great crucifix on her breast" resembles nothing so much as the images of Christ reserved with the sacrament in the Easter sepulcher until Easter Sunday in the medieval rites.[36] But she is also a conscious reprise and reversal of Hermione. In the one play a living woman poses as a statue: in the other a dead woman is treated as if she were living, and herself delivers death through the necrophiliac desires of the tyrant. Though she is cold in one play, the amazed response to her warmth constitutes the wonder of the other. In one play the hand of art is used to conceal, and the tyrant's perverse pleasures are secret; in the other art is revelatory and the event of its disclosure is a *public* event in which the participation of all present is constitutive of the art of theater.

In Middleton's reversal of the usual energies and directions of the trope, we are very far from any return to the "ordinary" in Womack's phrase. Indeed the camp, expressivist horror of the play is an insistence on the difficulty, not to say impossibility of that task. In short, there is no "resurrection" in *The Lady's Tragedy*. Justice is revenge, and the lady is the *instrumental object* (her agency as passive as a dead person can be) of Govianus's device. "I am not here," says her ghost, a "voice within" the tomb, when Govianus visits her now empty sepulcher (4.4.40). This is the "non est hic" of the angels on the empty tomb announced to the visiting Maries in the Gospels. The absence of Christ there is the sign of his resurrected presence which must be disseminated in the witness of his apostles. The absence of the lady here can only seem like a stage joke; she is now the material ghost who must be there to give voice to itself, the actor doubling the dead and living bodies—the grammar of "he is not here" and "I am not here" so ludicrously different. Middleton's brilliantly iconoclastic play allows us to see anew the commitment to the miracle of the ordinary in Shakespeare's play.

Peter Womack goes on to say that these tropes are authorized by Christ and borrow the "gestic vocabulary of the theatre...which came to an end only twenty years or so before Juliet died and rose again."[37] But the authority of those tropes is unavailable in Middleton's play. Let us now, finally, turn to Shakespeare's great resurrection scene to test out the authority of inheritance there.

Leontes' Shame

However protracted Leontes' penitence, however drawn out his sadness, however deeply he repents, his actions and his words cannot secure him forgiveness. Though they are necessary indications of the depth of his repentance (for us as audience, for his audience, most especially for Hermione) they cannot in themselves secure any release from the responsibility for the damage he has caused. The discourse on forgiveness in *The Winter's Tale* makes it clear that it must come, like grace, through the very medium of religious theater. The stillness of Hermione's life (her still life, the still life of her) and Leontes' past actions as set in stone are coterminous. That is why no understanding of the scene is complete without an appreciation of the centrality of Leontes' tears as the sign of his shame to it. To Paulina's praise of the carver's excellence which "makes her / As she lived now," Leontes returns to what might have been but is not: "as now she might have done / So much to my good comfort as it is / Piercing to my soul" (5.3.32–34). Returned to a vision of her self when first he wooed her, he declares his remorse: "I am asham'd" (5.3.37). It is clear from the words of Camillo and Polixenes at this point that Leontes is crying. Camillo's logic, though motivated by pity and not by politics, uses the same logic of accounting. There is, he claims, no sorrow that could possibly be so great as not to be blown away by sixteen winters. ("My Lord, your sorrow was too sore laid on / Which sixteen winters cannot blow away / So many summers dry" {5.3.49–51}). He has understood that forgiveness is aporetic.[38] For how can Hermione forgive him? She is dead. And there is nothing he can do that might count as reparation in this instance. The encounter with Paulina after the oracle's declamation has indicated that nothing can come from him that might make any difference, no way of being led away from his sorrows. It is only by fully acknowledging the absolute lucidity of Leontes' remorse that we can credit the final resurrection of his hopes and loves. He lives now fully unprotected by his own fantasies and denials, quite naked before his own terrible actions. The statue gives him a view of Hermione, but it is in the felt presence conjured by her likeness, in the sheer promise and gratuity of her return, in the self-forgetful yearning and love conjured into being by the statue, that he can also bear the thought of being seen by her, and so bear his shame. His remorse, as I have been arguing, has awakened him to the reality of Hermione. In being able to see her, he must be able to bear being seen by her such that both can be brought to new life through this new presencing. His shame and his repentance are then the very substance of the grace he is in the process of receiving, and there can be no separation between the two movements.

Cleomenes' discourse has been continued in the interventions of Polixenes and Camillo as they attempt to assume the agency of absolution again and to assuage his penitential tears. Yet the logic of the scene does not lie with their comfort; it stakes itself exclusively on the mutuality of response between Hermione and Leontes. Leontes' remorse has awoken him to her reality. But her agency is crucial here. (That is why it is a conscious rejection rather than an enaction of Ovid's Pygmalion: she is decidedly not his creation, his fantasy, though Paulina offers that as a teasing possibility.)[39] I imagine that quite what she will do in the chapel when Paulina has drawn the curtain *must* be open. None of the responses can be predicted, they can only be risked. Were Leontes to revert to fantasy, would she hold still? Could she hold still? The demands of human nature would militate against that. Realizing that she is alive is part of the mesmerizing power of this moment, and she will have to move sooner or later because she is woman, not stone. But if his responses proved disappointing she cannot, being living, avoid acknowledging him, even if such an acknowledgment takes the form of rebuff. (It does take such form in some stagings, and no staging can erase the absent presence of Mamillius in this scene or the weight and waste of time, the pointless, corrosive destruction of love and life.) If she is to remarry him, if he is now to take her hand in his, it must be that in being warm, it *can* go cold.[40]

Leontes is transformed in his understanding of himself—sinful and redeemed from sin in one and the same moment, as the past is carried into a redeemed memory. And so a new present and a new presence is made possible. "This is my body," we might understand Hermione as saying, through which you both remember me and acknowledge me. This is sacramental theater. For in it "how we present ourselves to each other (the classical domain of theater) and how we are present to each other (the domain of the sacrament)" have once again become both theological and theatrical resources, and the Pauline tropes of mortification and vivification are both figurative and actual.[41] Here is Donne glossing Shakespeare's play (as I like to think) in his 1626 sermon on 1 Cor. 15.29:

> But this death of desperation, or diffidence in God's mercy, by God's mercy hath swallowed all of us, but the death of sinne hath swallowed us all, and for oure customary sinnes we need a resurrection; And what is that? *Resurrectio a peccato, & cessatio a peccato, non est idem;* every cessation from sin is not a resurrection from sinne. A man may discontinue a sinne, intermit the practice of a sin by infirmity of the body, or by satiety in the sinne, or by the absence of that person, with whom he hath used to communicate in that sin. But *Resurrectio, est secunda ejus, quod interrit station.* A resurrection, is such an abstinence from the practice of the sin, as is grounded upon a repentance, and a detestation of the sin, and then it is a setting and an establishment of the soule in that state, and disposition: it is not a sudden and transitory remorse, nor onely a reparation of that which was ruined, and demolished, but it is a building up of habits contrary to former habits, and customes, in actions contrary to that sin, that we have been accustomed to. Else it is but an Intermission, not a Resurrection, but a starting, not a waking; but an apparition, not a living body; but a cessation, not a peace of conscience.[42]

In many of the scenes of return and recollection that I alluded to earlier, there comes a moment when the sudden apparition of the returning figure hovers between the insubstantial and the substantial. So the king in *All's Well* will wonder if Helena is real, and Pericles will wonder whether Marina is flesh and blood and not an angel or a blessed spirit. These meanings hover between a gift so wonderful it cannot be of this world, and a sense of imminent haunting loss—and they might say, as the resurrected Christ does: "for a spirit hath not flesh and bones as you see me here" (Luke 24.39).

Perhaps the most extended trope of this kind of encounter is the one between the twins, Sebastian and Viola in *Twelfth Night*. Viola is in man's clothing, so she mirrors Sebastian exactly. This time the question is not: are you flesh and blood? But are you a spirit? Yes, says Sebastian, "but am in that dimension grossly clad / Which from the womb I did participate" (5.1.237–38). He could have said—no, I am flesh and blood. But he chooses to animate the other meaning of ghost—not a spirit from the dead but that which gives life to mortal bodies. Do we need the Lutheran joke on ubiquity to see how this figure is borrowing a sacramental affect, a sacramental effect?[43] This is recognition as realization, a recognition that slowly grants the reality of the other's ensouled body, which loss has made so precious.

But Sebastian's eucharistic language is not just a localized joke of here and there, hic et ubique, a joke repeated in *Hamlet* as Stephen Greenblatt has reminded us.[44] When Calvin in the *Institutes* pours scorn on this same Lutheran doctrine, he says that Luther renders Christ into a "phantasm." And his subsequent discussion of Christ's resurrected body coheres with exactly the kind of exploration of faith and credence, of realization, that occurs in this same statute scene. In Book IV of the *Institutes* Calvin discusses the appearances of the resurrected Christ in a eucharistic idiom. He is here concerned to distinguish his views, on the one hand, from the gross absurdity of the papist view of the sacrament, and conversely from the view that envisages faith itself as a "mere imagining," one that therefore has no reality,[45] and again from the view that sees participation in Christ as the product of an intellectual understanding only (therefore purely cognitive). The paradigm of participation is, of course, the eucharist, the "sacred supper" and he proceeds to a dense commentary on John 6. It is here that he reserves his greatest scorn for Luther's idea. The Lutheran doctrine of ubiquity, he claims, opens the door to Marcionism.[46] In so doing it makes the body of Christ a "phantom or apparition."[47] In Calvin's insistence that faith in the body of Christ operates *effectually* and in a realm distinct both from "merely human imagining" (in which case it is subjective and in the domain of human fantasy) and from the reach of epistemology (mere knowledge), the resurrection appearances are intrinsically linked to faith's reality. This is what is at stake in the fleshliness of Christ and the fleshliness of Hermione. What Shakespeare adds to Calvin is the beauty and the miracle of what Calvin might call the "merely human." Shakespeare utterly abjures the eradication of the human in reformed versions of grace. For it was axiomatic to reformed grace that as God-given, and to be God-given, it must be free of all human words and deeds. It is human response that is, for him, rather the medium of grace.

"It is required / You do awake your faith": Shakespeare's Theater of Faith

So how could it not be the case that all who attend these mysteries—the audience on the stage and the audience off it—must awake their faith? The Johannine resurrection narrative takes it as axiomatic that the resurrected Christ appears only to those who believe. Indeed John never uses a noun for the term "faith," but only a verb: faith is not something that you have but something you do. Of the other disciple who reached the empty tomb before Peter, the author of the fourth gospel says: "Then went in also that other disciple which came first to the sepulcher, and hee saw, and believed."[48] We are not told that these disciples believed because they remembered the scriptural predictions of resurrection.[49] The risen lord appears only to those who believe in him. It is just such a distinction that Augustine is at pains to make in his commentary on John 6: "that you should believe in him; not that you should believe things about him (Ut credatis in eum, non, ut credatis ei)." He goes on to say: "But if you believe in him, that is because you believe what you have heard about him, whereas whoever believes things about him does not by that fact believe in him; for the demons too believe truths about him but still do not believe in him."[50]

In Augustine's vital distinction between belief in a person and belief about that person, we might discern how the prevailing cognitivist models that inform so much of the discourse on religion in the current academy understand belief in terms of "about," not "in." And for the statue scene we don't need to believe any set of precepts at all to have the experience available to us. But we do have to trust Paulina's authority. Both John and Paulina understand that the credibility of the resurrection is bound to the credence of believers. Indeed this is simply a tautology. So Paulina's banishment of all those unwilling to awaken their faith is an impeccably orthodox statement, a philosophical and theological tautology, one might say. And it is vital that what she says is that what is required is that you awake your faith, not that you willingly suspend your disbelief. The latter notion is in contemporary usage, at least, tutored in cognitivist (and in the end, I think, incoherent) models.[51] The condition of wonder that the scene seeks to cultivate is not at all attendant upon belief but rather of immediate attunements and attitudes.[52] The statue scene, one might say following Altieri, rests on commitments, not opinions.[53] We do not need to rely on notions of make-believe.[54] The primacy of belief-based modes of analysis then only obscures the working of this scene and its modes of recovery precisely from the epistemic modes of understanding. So it is also vital that Leontes' faith is as foundationless as his doubt has been. This is what makes it, and the new community founded on it, so fragile and so central. *The Winter's Tale* has been called a miracle play. But the miracle is only ordinary just as another human life is both miraculous and ordinary. It is as if theater requires the resources of both art and religion because credit and trust have come to seem not so much the ground of our intelligibility to each other, as phenomena that require nothing short of a miracle.

In an astonishingly prescient series of reflections in the *Dialogue Concerning Heresies,* Thomas More's narrator argues with a figure called "the messenger" who, having been infected with Lutheran heresy, comes to argue the position of *sola scriptura* and *sola fide.* What emerges in his pressingly skeptical inquiries is that nothing will lay to rest his doubts and fears. The dialogue simply breaks off in a shared meal. But at one point in the dialogue, the narrator compares the messenger to someone who is trying to prove that his father is really his. If you needed proof of everything, he suggests, you would constantly doubt your own origins and legitimacy. The whole proof would rest on one woman, and she would have the most cause to lie:

> Let the knowledge of the father alone therefore amonge our wittys mysteryes. And let us se yf we byleue nothynge but that we se our selfe who can reken hymmselfe sure of his owne mother for possible it were that he were changed in the cradell....[55]

More's fundamental point is that the messenger is simply unanswerable on his own terms and that he has forgotten the most fundamental forms of trust on which our everyday relations are habitually based. Such skepticism is, he implies, both completely compelling and utterly corrosive for its practitioners' most basic relations, and therefore self-understandings. You cannot prove who you are. He could be describing Leontes, who doubts not his father's paternity, but his own. More's casting of this fundamental problem—in 1529—shows that a man's fears about paternity and the most divisive religious issues of his culture can feed off the same world and soul-destroying perspective, whose attempted cure will only push him more deeply into the disease of doubt. Wittgenstein says, "The child learns by believing the adult. Doubt comes *after* belief."[56]

MAKING GOOD IN *THE TEMPEST*

A person is a person through other persons.
DESMOND TUTU, *NO FUTURE WITHOUT FORGIVENESS*

Hasn't anyone who has been hurt wished above all that the one who harmed him could come to understand the measure of the hurt? This desire is informed by a longing for justice, but also a hunger for recognition as an aspect, even a condition of it. There are dangers in this. For in entertaining the idea that the person who hurt us will acknowledge the full dimensions of that hurt, we may forget that we must in this case see ourselves as the one so nearly crushed or defeated by that hurt, see ourselves as his victim when it might seem as if our very survival might depend on overcoming this fact.

This is Prospero's dilemma. Why does Prospero appear before the conspirators dressed as the Duke of Milan? So that they might recognize him? So that the long time between might vanish? Or so that he does not have to see himself in their eyes as a mere man, and one brought low by their successes at that? If *The Winter's Tale* through the figure of Leontes explored the contours of remorse in the mind of the harmer, *The Tempest* examines the hold of the past over the one who has been harmed, and the means by which the present can make its peace with the past. The possibility and resources of forgiveness can, after all, be fully grasped only if the mutuality of harmer and harmed, caught in the same act, can be mutually recognized. *The Tempest* explores the difficulties of such acknowledgments.

It was the practices of restitution as part of the sacrament of penance that had traditionally throughout the Middle Ages underwritten justice as a component part of charity. Justice entailed rendering to everyone his own.[1] Yet such justice is inevitably concerned with the capacities for acknowledgment of the parties involved. It is with such complexities that *The Tempest* is concerned. Once again, we will find the play plumbing the resources, structures, and inherited languages of penance. Penance is after all traditionally understood as the "second plank after shipwreck," an image repertoire Shakespeare consciously exploits in developing the supra-individual agency of the metamorphic sea.[2]

The languages of penance emerge most clearly in the play, first, through the exploration of the project of restitution, and second, through a eucharistic language of feast and participation. Like *The Winter's Tale,* this play strives toward a recovery of memory from private language and private possession, and stages forms of public enactments that work as recoveries of self, language, and society at one and the same time.

At the beginning of the last act of *The Tempest,* Ariel gives Prospero a description of Alonso, Sebastian, and Antonio and their followers. They are:

> Confin'd together
> In the same fashion as you gave in charge,
> Just as you left them; all prisoners, sir,
> In the line-grove which weather-fends your cell;
> They cannot boudge till your release.
> (5.1.7–11)

The men are brought to "sorrow and dismay" (5.1.14). Some are distracted and the others mourn around them. Gonzalo is crying. They lie in Prospero's mercy.

Prospero does not characteristically ask questions. His language is almost invariably in the imperative mood. He issues commands, requests, orders, and demands. He also *tells* people things, or rather, he reminds people of things and these reminders (of which more later) are an integral part of the play's exploration of the grammar of remembrance and its task in forgiveness. But here Ariel's description elicits one of Prospero's first genuine questions. Ariel has depicted the King and his companions in such a way as to arouse pity. But in case his description is not sufficient, he makes a suggestion:

> Your charm so strongly works 'em
> That if you now beheld them, your affections
> Would become tender.
>
> (5.1.17–19)

It is here that Prospero is prompted to ask: "Dost thou think so, spirit?" (5.1.20). Unlike his other questions this one requires no missing information to be supplied; nor is it about the execution of an order. Rather, Prospero wonders about an appropriate response of tender affections. He is, for the first time, curious and attentive to the workings of another mind—call it a not-yet-free spirit. What might it take for Prospero to be able to behold the "men of sin" (3.3.53) with tender affections? Ariel tutors Prospero in how to be human, how to be kind. Whatever his project has been, he makes the decisive move from vengeance to virtue.[3] It is the work of the rest of the play to parse out the complexity of "They cannot boudge till your release." "Your release" might be an echo of the Prosperian imperative, a reiteration that release is in his command. They can't move until you release them. But the grammar reveals the release as fully reciprocal. They won't be able to move until you yourself are released. The release of Prospero works as an objective and subjective genitive.

The release will unleash the past's hold only if it is fully mutual. And this release for Prospero will involve learning to accept his humanity, becoming kind, inhabiting his kind. This mutuality is *hard;* it is hard because it depends on unreliable, recalcitrant others. If it turns out that becoming human is a task, a project, a goal that is never definitively accomplished, but that has to be endlessly begun, then it is also clearer than ever why it might be so tempting, so plausible and compelling to evade that task and its disappointments. Indeed the mood of disappointment that hangs over the end of this play can be seen to be not so much a despair rooted in Shakespearean biography, as many Shakespeare critics once held, but rather a logical consequence of the picture of language it enacts.

The Tempest is a play that has been fully bent on the project of making good. The "tempest" is itself the name for the action of the past in the present; it is what raises and allays passions of the mind. The project of making amends will involve the restitution of a usurped kingdom, but in the process of the profound exploration of memory that ensues, it becomes clear that there can be no such perfect exchange as that envisaged in restitution. In the confrontation with the irrevocable nature of the past's losses, memory comes to be seen not as the private possession of Prospero's imagining, but as fully intersubjective, incorrigibly temporal, utterly social. The hope of restitution will lie in a transformation by love, and the future such love might hold. In sounding the resources of the language of forgiveness *in time,* the play is making an argument for, and enacting a form of theater that will address our freedom, not our confinement. It will seek its redress in the risky, terrifying forms of mutual address, not the enactment of one person's "present fancies."[4] In this activity it takes up crucial aspects of the work of penance: amendment, including restitution, and the ethical self-accounting this entails; the role of memory in confession, and as in *Cymbeline* and *The Winter's Tale,* an exploration of the agencies of forgiveness. But, as in those plays, it places the penitential work of forgiveness in the entire community of speakers.

It is conventional to see in *The Tempest* a revenge plot that overcomes revenge.[5] Yet, in the exploration of redress in the play, the role of restitution has been overlooked. In this chapter I show how the possibilities of communion and a eucharistic language of real-ization are explored through restitution. This project comes to be reimagined through the work of theater as a time-bound, linguistic medium. Finally, I show the play's investment and enactment of such participation as a linguistic community and the paths taken to surpass or overcome that inescapable horizon in forms of magic and the autonomizing of language.

The Quaint Device

One of the central images in the exhortations to Holy Communion in the *Book of Common Prayer* and also in the "Homily of the Worthy Reception" is the image of the heavenly banquet where all must be guests "and not gazers, eaters and not lookers."[6] The great suggestiveness and longevity of this idea can be seen from the use Shakespeare makes of it in *The Tempest.*

In act 3, scene 3 of *The Tempest,* several "strange shapes" bring in a banquet, on which Alonso and his companions propose to feed.[7] But Ariel, by means of a "quaint device," causes it to vanish and confronts them with their own sin: "But remember / (For that's my business to you) that you three / From Milan did supplant good Prospero" (3.3.68–70). The prospective feast becomes an act of remembrance of past selves that prevents participation until that memory has restored them to repentance. The feast depends on being in "charity"—and this will mean avowals, "heart's sorrow" (3.3.81), a relinquishment of the usurped fruits of past ill deeds, and a restoration of the relations such acts have damaged through forgiveness. In the *Book of Common Prayer,* the minister could at his discretion "call and advertise" any "open and notorious evil livers" from communion, and the service for Holy Communion contains a number of exhortations to encourage and educate parishioners about worthy reception of the sacrament.[8] These use the imagery of St. Luke's banquet and St. Matthew's wedding feast (Luke 14.15–24; Matthew 22.1–14) as well as the Pauline injunction of 1 Cor. 11.28–29: "But let a man examine himself. And so let him eat of that bread and drink of that cup. For he that eateth and drinketh unworthily, eateth and drinketh damnation to himself, not discerning the Lord's body."[9] Here the work of theater echoes the work of the mass in a substitution of haunting power and equivocation—for the feast can be realized only in those relations of charity.[10] Without them it is insubstantial. Here we have finally moved away from the Aristotelian language of substance that had controlled eucharistic discussion for so long, to a language of participation. Shakespeare is taking up a dense source of controversy and allusion here.

In the eucharistic debates of the 1560s, John Jewel, Bishop of Salisbury, and Thomas Harding rehearse exactly this theme. Their debate shows the stakes of making the presence real in languages that echo in the airy nothings of the play, and help us to see how the island substantiates the desires and memories of each of the protagonists.[11] Taking up the central idea that the eucharist is a "supper," they both wonder: who can eat at the feast? For John Jewel the Roman Catholic mass is a meal for one, because the congregation does not partake of the bread or the cup. What kind of a meal is it when the cup is withdrawn from the guests, when the guests are invited to watch one man eat his solitary feast? Can it be a feast at all when only one person eats and the others watch?

> To such a banquet Pasetes the juggler used sometimes to call his friends. There was a great shew of vanity, and plenty of all manner of meats and drinks, the table full: but, when any of the guests would have touched anything, it vanished suddenly away and was turned to nothing; and so, when their eyes were full, they put up their knives, and rose a hungred. Even thus Mr Harding feedeth and feasteth the people of God with shews and ceremonies, and suffereth them in the mean while to starve for hunger.[12]

The spectators of the feast are not participants at all according to Jewel; they "heareth nothing, understandeth nothing, eateth nothing, drinketh nothing, tasteth nothing."[13] This is feast theatricalized, and the spectators long for substance as they gaze on at the priest's greedy and selfish plenitude.[14]

But for Harding it is precisely Jewel's denial of transubstantiation that renders the feast a nullity. At Jewel's feast, says Harding, there are only signs and figures, for no matter how strong the imagination of the participant, the body of Christ is merely bread and wine. So he asks:

> whether of those two is the colder ceremony, and more simple supper, to have bread and wine, with a sign only of flesh and blood, or to have real flesh and blood, with such form of bread and wine as by the power of God do no less bodily nourish us than the substance would have done, we doubt not of men's wise judgment. Ye have your carnal banquests fat and full enough of the best flesh, and it is with you superstitious to eat dry and Lenten meats. But ye will have your spiritual banquets so lean and carrion as a man may well discern whether ye have more fantasy to your flesh or to your spirit.[15]

It will be apparent how each man wishes to hold onto a version of real presence but understands that we arrive at it in different ways. And each man abhors the other's view, imagining that it nullifies the very source and means of salvation and makes hungry where it should satisfy.

In the mass, as in the communion, the eucharist is judge as well as redeemer. It is diagnostic. What it shows is the shape of sin. That is why Ariel's business is a reminder to the sinners of what they are. In *The Tempest* the possibilities of sitting down and eating together are going to depend on the art of memory in the activity of forgiveness.[16] Indeed the fundamental

premise of this play is that memory is communal, that it cannot be the possession of any one person alone.

How can they eat at the feast? How can the nothing of the feast become
substantial and real for them? What will substantiate the body of Christ,
make it actual as a people who might come to "the peace of the present"?
The play goes on to explore the fully traditional project of restitution as a
prerequisite for such a communion.

Making Good: The Project of Restitution

In this book I have been concerned with exploring the sea-changes entailed in the continuities and discontinuities in the reform of the sacrament
of penance. I have examined the notion of sufficiency and satisfaction, the
question about what is "enough" in the explorations of remorse in *The
Winter's Tale* and *Cymbeline*. Yet the precise relation between satisfaction
and restitution remained a controversial part of reformed discussions of
penance, as of medieval discussions. An under-remarked aspect of these
transitions is the continuity in the practice of restitution. *The Tempest* addresses the afterlives of the sacrament of penance, and the grammar of
forgiveness and acknowledgment, through a contemplation of restitution.
The Tempest also turns out to be an exploration of the resources of theater
in the work of penitence.

It is hard to get a grip on Prospero's project, for the details about the
execution of his plan are as precise as the project itself is vague. It is clear
that "bountiful Fortune," "a most auspicious star" (1.2.178, 182) has created
an opportunity for him to encounter his enemies again, and his response to
Ferdinand and Miranda's courtship indicates that their love is something
he desires, but cannot compel ("Heaven rains grace / On that which breeds
between 'em" [3.1.75–76]). The only overt declaration of his purpose is
strangely (and importantly) retrospective, coming after Ariel's invitation
to feel his common humanity with those confined, which seems to prompt
a turn from vengeance to virtue:

> They being penitent,
> The sole drift of my purpose doth extend
> Not a frown further.
>
> (5.1.28–29)

Vengeance or virtue, wild justice or penitential justice: both require the restoration of a kingdom:

> I do forgive
> Thy rankest fault—all of them; and require
> My dukedom of thee, which perforce, I know
> Thou must restore.
>
> (5.1.131–34)

Prospero declares that his sole purpose lies in producing the penitence in his aggressors, but penitence would properly and naturally have entailed the restoration of what had been unjustly seized.

For all the radical changes in the theology of repentance and the liturgical enactment of it, there was, in fact, remarkable continuity in the extra-liturgical rites of reconciliation.[17] It was still regarded as the preserve of the parish priest to ensure not just reconciliation, but, if necessary, restitution as an aspect of the preparation for communion. Being in charity with others entailed justice; justice was a component part of charity. To participate in the eucharist, to sit at the common table with one whom you had wronged was to take the sacrament to your damnation. It was this concern with unworthy reception of the sacrament that indicated that it was not a mere symbol of love but an actual embodiment of forgiveness.[18] To understand the exploration of the losses and returns enacted in restitution, and to explore its failures and successes, I will need to say something more about this practice and its history.

A distinction between satisfaction and restitution was quite commonplace in the sacramental literature of the Middle Ages.[19] Restitution was owed whenever justice had been violated, and justice could be violated when something proper to a person was taken away.[20] This might entail damage to reputation as well as to property. Indeed Thomas Aquinas understood the sin of detraction to be accounted worse than theft, though not on the scale of homicide or adultery.[21] The idea here is that something essential, yet intangible, had been violated: reputation, honor, identity. Restitution was therefore essential to any sense of tangible, visible justice. It is this aspect of justice as a component part of penance that has been psychologized away in the broadly pelagianizing framework of modern thought.[22] But it is still very much available to Shakespeare.

What vitiates Claudius's prayer in *Hamlet* is his unwillingness to restore the crown he has stolen: "May one be pardon'd and retain th'offense?"

(3.3.47). He himself recognizes that this renders his attempted act of re-pentance utterly hollow.[23] Restitution is understood as the prerequisite of a proper contrition for an act that has involved theft, or any wrongful or unlawful possession. Restitution is then bound up with the first part of the medieval tripartite component of penance: contrition rendering it actual rather than hollow. But it is also bound up with the third part of penance: satisfaction, and indeed sometimes dangerously confused with it.[24] The ne-cessity of restitution is a commonplace of medieval literature.

In that long and great tradition of scholastic commentary, the Commen-taries on Peter Lombard's *Sentences,* restitution takes up the lion's share of discussions of penance in several treatments.[25] Although conventionally un-derstood to be the "satisfaction" owed to man, rather than to God, and not, in many senses, a formal part of the sacrament of penance, it was in practice a prerequisite for worthy reception of the sacrament, part of the prepara-tion for annual or (in the case of the post-Reformation), tri-annual commu-nion. It is fascinating to observe that the practice appears to be a continuous part of the role of the parish priest in the reconciliation of his parishioners. Medieval discussion of restitution is apparent, for example, in such pastoral manuals as *Speculum Sacerdotale* or *Pupilla Oculi.* Lyndwood's *Provinciale* insists on the fact that restitution is a prerequisite for satisfaction.[26] The at-tacks on friars for not insisting on it are a stock trope of anti-fraternalism, and the mode and method of restitution, as well as complaints about the evasion of it, are a central part of medieval penitential discourse.[27]

George Herbert in his *A Priest to the Temple or, The Country Parson* opens the first chapter with the pastoral "work of conciliation," and goes on to exemplify the pastor on Sundays spending his time "in reconciling neighbours that are at variance or visiting the sick."[28] The pastor, says Her-bert, is a lawyer and a physician as well as shepherd, and he wants his flock to resort to him as a judge before they go to law.[29]

Restitution remains an ideal and a pastoral practice, and is itself a tes-timony to some remarkable continuities in pre- and post-Reformation England. In the exhortation that precedes the order for communion in the first *Book of Common Prayer,* restitution is mandated as a requirement of worthy reception:

> And yf any man have doen wrong to any other: let him make satisfaction,
> and due restitution of all landes and goodes, wrongfully taken away or with-
> holden, before he come to Goddes borde, or at the least be in ful minde and

purpose so to do, as sone as he is able, or els let him not come to this holy table, thinking to deceyue God, who seeth all menes hartes.[30]

The 1552 version of this exhortation is changed to emphasize the contexts of the great feast of communion. Those who refuse to participate in communion are like those who refuse to come to a great feast:

> And wheras ye offend god so sore in refusing this holy Banquet, I admonishe, exhort, and beseche you, that unto this unkindnes ye wyll not adde any more. Which thing ye shal doe, if ye stande by as gazers and lokers on them that doe communicate, and be no partakers of the same yourselues.[31]

The language about restitution has somewhat changed, however. After encouraging an examination and lamentation of sins, the curate is to return to the language of reconciliation and restitution:

> And yf ye shal perceiue your senses to be such, as be not only against god, but also againste your neighbours: then ye shal reconcile your selues unto them, ready to make restitucion and satisfaccion according to the uttermost of your powers, for all injuries and wronges done by you to any other; and likewise beeyng ready to forgeue other that have offended you, as you would have forgeuenesse of your offences at gods hande.... [32]

The language has again been changed. Notice that there is a subtle psychologization of harm-doing. The court of judgment is now the self-perception of the wrong-doer: "yf ye shal perceiue your senses to be such...." In addition there is the idea that there is a separation of sin against God and neighbor. This would have been quite alien to Thomas Aquinas, for example, who said that love of God includes love of neighbor because "it is specifically the same act whereby we love God, and whereby we love our neighbour."[33]

In the *Book of Common Prayer* of 1559 the language has yet again changed. Now "open and notorious evil livers" who have offended the congregation or done wrong to a neighbor are to be called and advertised by the curate not to "presume to the Lord's table" until they have repented, made amends so that the congregation are "satisfied," and "recompensed the parties he hath done wrong unto, or at least declare himself to be in full purpose to do so, as soon as he conveniently may."[34] The word "restitution" has been removed completely, and though the language of amends and recompense is still very much present, the specification of "open and notorious evil livers" speaks the language of public scandal rather than harm and wrong-doing. This kind of a distinction between sins known, say, only to the priest, and those that are openly known and that have therefore brought public scandal onto the church, is a commonplace distinction in medieval commentaries. It is also a distinction maintained in the Genevan context of the consistory where the question of public scandal is as much a question of the pollution of a church as private sin.[35] It is almost as if the ecclesiological implications have trumped the questions of sinfulness themselves so that it is the purity and pollution of the church that is at stake, as against the reform and repentance of the wrong-doers as component parts of that body.

In commenting on the language of the exhortation, Rowan Williams has maintained that the removal of the very specific and straightforward requirement for restitution from the 1549 prayer book "tells us...a good deal about what could or could not be said against the background of the later years of King Edward VI's reign, when social rapacity had reached an unprecedented pitch."[36] That social rapacity was certainly part of the discussions about dominion as the old world encountered the new. I have tried to chart these changes to give some indication of the way in which, in giving up on the more straightforward injunction to restitution, a whole understanding of communion as a relation to justice, and justice as an aspect of charity, is lost.[37] This is a very consequential loss. We are on the way to the psychologization of forgiveness that is a feature of the modern world and the kinds of splittings I outlined in part 1 of this book.[38]

In most of the treatments of restitution, it is understood as a practice organized around tangible things, possessions and property, as in clear cases of theft, robbery, and wrongful possession, but medieval handbooks as often meditate on intangible things that are harder, not to say impossible to give back.[39] For example in the *Fasciculus Morum,* a fourteenth-century preacher's handbook, restitution is treated in the section dealing with charity as the remedy for envy. In a commentary on the text: "This is my commandment that you love one another," under the heading love of neighbor, there ensues the following discussion:

> And notice: Let us assume you took some worldly goods from your neighbour. I ask you: who would absolve you without your making restitution?

> Indeed, no one alive, if you have the means. But ruining your good name is a
> greater harm than taking his worldly goods for according to the Wise Man,
> "a good name is better than many riches." Therefore no one can absolve him
> unless he brings back his good name. But this cannot be done in any way; for
> when you began to defame your neighbour you added things that were not
> there in the first place, and the person who hears you has added more when
> he told this to someone else, and the third even more, and so on ad infinitum.
> How will you manage to revoke all these things, as you are required to do?[40]

It is fascinating in this reflection to see how quickly the preacher moves
from the necessity of restitution for absolution to the impossibility of restitution in the realm of reputation when it is words, not goods, at stake.
Words, it seems, cannot be taken back; they cannot be rendered back to
their "owner." They exist in a different medium of temporal and linguistic
exchange, and their damages are thus irrevocable.

It is not just the *Fasciculus Morum* that concentrates on the difficulty of
"giving back." This is a leitmotif in many of the treatments in the Commentaries which discuss the obstacles to proper rendition. And, of course, in
Piers Plowman, it is a moment of horrifying crisis in this great poem that explores pardon, in at least two points. The first is when Covetousness comes
to realize that he will not be able to return what he's taken: Repentance's
words to him: "Thow art an unkynde creature—I can thee noght assoille /
Til thow make restiucion" drive him to despair; and the second moment
is the moment when the Barn of Unity, which represents the Church and
all of Christian society, is destroyed when the people decide that they will
not practice restitution.[41] It is evident that there is a very long literary life in
these complex notions for it is also a major preoccupation of George Eliot's
Adam Bede. When Arthur Donnithorne realizes that his seduction of Hetty
Sorrel has created the conditions for her infanticide, despair, and depor-
tation, and ruined the courtship of the honorable Adam, a courtship that
might have prevented Hetty's delusive misconceptions about her role in
Arthur's future, it is the temporality of amends-making that is the theme:

> if there had been any possibility of making Adam tenfold amends—if deeds
> of gift, or any other deeds, could have restored Adam's contentment and re-
> gard for him as a benefactor, Arthur would not only have executed them all
> without hesitation, but would have felt bound all the more closely to Adam,
> and would never have been weary of making retribution. But Adam could

receive no amends, his suffering could not be cancelled; his respect and affection could not be recovered by any prompt deeds of atonement. He stood
like an immovable obstacle against which no pressure could avail; an embodiment of what Arthur most shrank from believing in—the irrevocable-
ness of his own wrong-doing.[42]

Restitution can never restore, not only because of the very logic of human
action, but because of its remorseless temporality. As the *Fasciculus* author
knows, one saying sets in train another, which sets in train another, in such
a way that it can never be recalled. In the context of this remark we might
see *The Tempest* as exploring the problems that arise when time is taken
into account in restitution, restoring the past's losses. Perhaps Prospero's
hope is for a full restitution of his lands, an open acknowledgment of the
harm done to him, and the full penitence of the wronged parties. In desiring this he would be desiring no more than the requirements of justice as
it had been historically understood in the penitential system, but the play
explores the precise ways in which such a hope might be disappointed by
registering the social contexts of loss, possession, and restitution in the context of a fully temporal order. Involved in this fantasy is a spatialization of
time: the island is the place where a variety of temporal fantasies coexist
and must be made to become aware of each other.[43] What *The Tempest* will
end up suggesting is that our best hope lies in new beginnings disclosed by
love. This is the example provided by Ferdinand and Miranda. This form
of new beginning is completely different from the language of renovation
offered in contemporary Calvinist discourses of the self, whose model of
conversion is atemporal in that it insists on the complete death of the old
self, and the complete and utter novelty of the new self. The older model of
sin as habit had, on the contrary, worked with the logic of time's passing.[44]

In *The Tempest* restitution is inextricably intertwined with recall, with
memory. The place of putative reconciliation becomes the place for further
greedy and murderous fantasies. Prospero's remembrance of the conspirators interrupts the masque's idealist theater, but the larger point here is
that the greed and hatred that inspire such conspiracies will never be apoc-
alyptically overcome, but will rather be encountered again and again.

To recall something is to perceive that it is utterly bound up with the
minds and thoughts of others, their histories and their logics. This, in turn,
means that there can be no absolute renovation, no brave new beginnings,

just the fragile, precious and tenacious hope of starting over. The world can only seem brave and new on the basis of innocence rather than experience. If Prospero's project of restitution, then, is utterly tied up with the question of recall and memory it is also, as the example from the *Fasciculus* poignantly reminds us, bound up with a relation to language. Prospero tries to enact a fantasy of restitution that can bypass the circuit of other minds, and the work of language.

The Grammar of Remembrance

The mood of remembrance in *The Tempest* is overwhelmingly imperative at the beginning of the play.

> But remember
> (For that's my business to you)....
> (3.3.68)
> Remember
> First to possess his books.
> (3.2.91–2)
> Remember I have done thee worthy service.
> (1.2.247)

Characters implore, demand, entreat, and variously command each other to remember. They remind each other of pasts they have forgotten:

> Dost thou forget
> From what torment I did free thee?
> (1.2.250–51)

Prospero in particular supplies the histories that are supposed to explain and justify the current state of relations on the island, relations that underwrite his mastery and the servitude of the island's others. Prospero's reminders tend to turn to a piece of history, supply a necessary piece of information that needs to be brought to the fore, as if he can fill the gaps of the other's recalcitrantly wandering mind. His memory is used in these conversations to bring people back to heel, whether it is Ariel to his bonded service, Caliban to his interminable servitude, or Miranda to her father's precepts. But memory cannot be supplied like a possession from one person to another. It is not in the definition of any one person, however powerful, however authoritative. So the imperative mood of remembrance is radically undercut by a competing sense of the complex interdependency of memory in the relations of each to each.

This complex interdependency emerges as early as the second scene of the first act, structured around Prospero's three encounters with Miranda, Ariel, and Caliban. It is Prospero's conversation with Miranda I will analyze here to pursue the question of the grammar of remembrance. Prospero supplies both Miranda and the spectators of *The Tempest* with a narrative about their arrival on the island. This story releases him from the present's confinement, and makes him "more better / Than Prospero, master of a full poor cell" (1.2.19–20). Miranda is ignorant, he declares, not simply of the history of their arrival, but of "what thou art." In supplying a narrative about their arrival he hopes to tell her who and what she is, and Miranda initially appears to accept his terms: "You have often / Begun to tell me what I am, but stopped / And left me to a bootless inquisition" (1.2.34–35). Prospero imagines that she is a blank slate unable to remember anything because she was only three when she came to the island: "Canst thou remember / A time before we came to this cell?" (1.2.38–39). But he answers his own question before she has a chance to do so: "I do not think thou canst. For then thou wast not / Out three years old" (1.2.40–41).

And yet her clear response is that she can indeed remember the four or five women who tended her. This memory is much more like a dream than an assurance (1.2.45). It cannot provide any "warrant," yet it is here to work as a testimony that she cannot be the blank slate that Prospero imagines she is. Miranda's response to Prospero is not so much a statement as a question: "Had I not / four or five women once, that tended me?" It affirms that their memories are shared, parsed out together.

What we find throughout this scene is that Prospero's notion that he can supply Miranda's memory entirely from his own, as the donation of his history, is economically and beautifully short-circuited. Miranda, child of the father, turns out to be the subtlest of tutors. When she hears the story of their shared history, of their exile in the ship, their vulnerability to the seas, she twice supplies the response she was too young to give then: "O my heart bleeds / to think o'th' teen I have turn'd you to, / Which is from my remembrance!" (1.2.63–64). Prospero is not yet ready to hear this, but she repeats a similar sentiment several lines later: "Alack, for pity! / I, not rememb'ring how I cried out then, / Will cry it o'er again" (1.2.132–34).

The present, not just the past, has become newly available to her. Out of that new present, Miranda gives Prospero succor in the form of sympathy, so that he will not feel so alone. Memory here is put into the context of our deepest dependencies. Miranda, or so Prospero thinks, must learn who she is at his hands. Yet, giving her fresh response, she thinks of the trouble she must have been for him, and learns that she was so far from a trouble as the creature who preserved him.

Prospero imagines that he can grant her permission to remember as if the discourse of remembrance is in his control: "If thou rememb'rest aught ere thou cam'st here / How thou cam'st here thou may'st" (1.1.51–52). But the deeper implications of this encounter concern the subtle, pervasive interdependencies of memory. Miranda is a child; her history will indeed be given to her from the language of the elders in her life: where else can it come from? Yet she has imagined a past that he cannot conceive she has. This makes memory something shared in language, and something through which new feelings may emerge of love, care, and tenderness, of a father and infant oddly protecting each other from the unruly, violent betrayals of history, and the pain and terrible vicissitudes of the sea. Memory is not a private possession; it cannot be passed on intact from one to the other. The story, once told, provides new contexts for sharing, and this turns out to change the felt sense of the story, to transform both the past and the present.

The grammar of remembrance is, of course, also related to the grammar of forgetting, and here the question of the control of memory and the ownership of it become even more pointed. If characters in the play are continuously being enjoined to remember their histories, histories supplied to them by powerful others, then it turns out that characters also forget at the most crucial moments of action. Miranda thankfully "forgets" her father's precepts about Ferdinand to such an extent that she is able to conduct a clandestine marriage with him (3.1.58–59, 85–90). Her forgetting is in the most significant way tied up with her freedom and her desires. Forgetting is involuntary; it reveals the limits of the human will.

This same logic of forgetting also applies to Prospero, who has arranged a masque to celebrate the wedding of his children. The masque, as many critics have noted, is the perfect piece of idealist theater.[45] Its underlying ideology is neoplatonic, in which courtiers body forth the perfection of heavenly essence, all designed to help construct a sovereign viewpoint. It is a familiar point that this piece of idealist theater is interrupted by

Prospero's memory of the "foul conspiracy," and is thereby aborted. Prospero's lapse of memory is something he has failed to do rather than something he does. His involuntary forgetting shows that his "present fancies" are not transparently available to him.[46] They are radically distended and extended, suborned not just by the conspirators, but by his own forgetting of them, an involuntary gap in his mind that threatens to repeat the neglect of political affairs in the past that spawned the new creatures who displaced him. Prospero's forgettings are a testimony to time's dark abysm. They also pay witness to the limitations of any pelagian philosophy and its investments in the autonomous choices of a sovereign will.[47]

It is for this very reason that it is, in my view, a mistake to stage *The Tempest* as entirely internal to the imaginings of Prospero. There have been many contemporary versions of this reading, especially Peter Greenaway's film *Prospero's Books*. Perhaps the most extreme stage version of this was Tim Carroll's 2005 Globe production in which three actors, Mark Rylance, Alex Hassell, and Edward Hogg, aided by six dancers, played all the roles. Rylance, as Prospero, began alone on stage with a toy ship which he moved around as if the toy was in a tempestuous sea, while miming all the other speaking parts. He thus set up the shipwreck as a revengeful fantasy that emerged entirely out of his own longings and desires. Yet the action of the play is emphatically not confined to Prospero's mind. It is not an internal psychodrama. While Prospero's desires are indeed highly pertinent and material to the working through of the plot of *The Tempest,* this staging subverts the logic of the play which seeks to bring Prospero to an encounter with those whose otherness he might learn to recognize. If the other characters are merely extensions of his own psyche, then the work of the play in exploring precisely the painful relinquishment of this fantasy, the painful realization of others, is all undone. It is true that all the different parts of the play are welded together not through the normal theatrical mechanisms of dialogue and encounter, but because they are part of Prospero's "project." "Their association," says Anne Barton, "depends firstly upon the fact that all of them meet in the consciousness of Prospero."[48] The various groups on the island—the court party of Antonio, Sebastian, Alonso, and Gonzalo, the new lovers, Ferdinand and Miranda, and the conspirators Stephano, Trinculo, and Caliban, have been ignorant of each other's existence until the last scene. Yet the drive of the play is to bring their separate fantasies and conversations—about marriage, about conspiracy, about grief and guilt—into relation. For all of them this will involve the encounter with others and the reality of others' thoughts, feelings, and utterances. It is to Prospero's crucial encounters with the minds of others that I now turn. This can be understood only by addressing Prospero's relation to language.

Prospero, Language, and Other Minds

Critics have debated at length the nature of Prospero's magic arts. Counterpointed with Sycorax, yet using the words of Ovid's Medea, Prospero's secret studies have nurtured the political ambitions of those around him and away from prudential rulership. It is clear, then, that the magic arts are linked to a conversation about rule: service, servitude, and lordship, instruction and education, the idealist neoplatonizing vision of masque, and the ambitions of empire as Shakespeare alludes to Virgilian Rome, and the widow Dido left behind at its founding (2.1.77–86).[49] Yet the most important dimension of Prospero's relation to magic is its relation to language. Above all, what Prospero's magic gives him is a way of autonomizing language, and so of relating to others in such a way that he does not have to be exposed in language. Above all, this power is predicated on avoiding his own exposure in language. To become too obsessed about the exact nature of Prospero's magic (John Dee, Marcilio Ficino, etc.) is, then, to miss the more central point about language itself.

It is clear enough that his magic gives him power over others. He can send them into a stupefied sleep at any point; he can prevent Ferdinand, for example, from drawing his sword, and he can put to sleep and awake the courtly party at will. He can also render himself invisible so that he can watch others without their seeing that he is watching them. Thus, he watches over the supposedly clandestine betrothal of Ferdinand and Miranda, and he watches over the eucharistic banquet brought and removed by Ariel to bring the guilty men to penitence. "My high charms work," he says,

> And these, mine enemies, are all knit up
> In their distractions. They are now in my pow'r
> And in these fits I leave them.
>
> (3.3.88–91)

Prospero's charms are a kind of speech act that exercise a hypnotic effect over their victims; they are not words addressed to the freedom of the other, but rather treat that other as the mere instrument of a predetermined will. They require no response that might surprise the charmer. And so the charmer never has to be singled out or exposed in his own responses. So this use of language gives him a full exposure to others without ever exposing himself in any way.

His magic is thus a way of imagining that he can overcome or supersede the damages and dangers of the past without acknowledgment. Or rather, it allows him to imagine that he can be acknowledged on his terms alone. Since acknowledgment must be mutual, this is no acknowledgment at all. He imagines recovering his kingdom with an accusation only. In confronting the conspirators he hopes and expects not only restitution, but their remorse. But he bypasses the necessity for expression in this endeavor; he bypasses any mutuality of response in his dealings with others. Why would he want to do this?

It will be impossible to motivate this question, at least to give it a non-moralistic answer, without thinking about the central discourse about "becoming human" in the play. I have suggested that Ariel tutors Prospero in an appropriate response of pity rather than vengeance, one which seems to motivate Prospero's relinquishment of magic, which means in the play his relinquishment over a certain kind of instrumentalizing language. To relinquish such language is to put yourself on the same ground as the others; it is to risk your own expression and response, your own legibility, and hence vulnerability, to others. *The Tempest* turns out to be a play about the task and difficulty of "becoming human."

Becoming Human

Surely being human is not a task; is it not just a fact of our biology? Caliban is clearly a man; we are told he has a human shape. Yet, taking cues from the various ascriptions of him by other characters, he has been variously portrayed as a fish, a dog with one or two heads, a lizard, a monkey, a snake, half-ape, half-man with fins for arms, the missing link, and even a tortoise.[50] In fact, the stage history of Caliban, including his description by Prospero as a "savage and deformed slave" and his racialization, is itself testimony that to see someone as human is a task. We characteristically say in our criticisms of the deadening cruelties of slave societies, that slave-owners treated their slaves like animals; that they do not see slaves as human beings. In *The Claim of Reason,* Stanley Cavell argues that this phrase cannot be meant:

> When he wants to be served at table by a black hand, he would not be satisfied to be served by a black paw. When he rapes a slave or takes her as concubine, he does not feel he has, by that fact itself, embraced sodomy. . . . He does not go to great length to convert his horses to Christianity or to prevent their getting wind of it. Everything in his relation to his slaves shows that he treats them as more or less human—his humiliations of them, his disappointments, his jealousies, his fears, his punishments, his attachments.[51]

Slave-owners, he suggests, are not missing a piece of information—that slaves are, after all, human beings. What, then, are slave-owners missing? Cavell suggests that the slave-owner takes himself to be "private in respect to them, unknowable to them." As well as power over the slaves, he thus has "power over his experience in relation to them." For Cavell, this means that he has placed the slaves outside the circle of linguistic mutuality and therefore justice. Should he stop seeing himself as having that power, or they find the power to acknowledge him in terms other than his mastery, he might see himself through their eyes and know that they had seen themselves through his.[52] Another way of putting this might be: he can speak for the slave, but the slave cannot speak for him.

Prospero regards himself as the sole authority, if you like, on himself, but the result is that he remains unknown, unimplicated in the lives of others. Cavell's assessment here is reliant on his reading of Wittgenstein's "private language argument" in the *Philosophical Investigations.* Most commentators read Wittgenstein's remarks here as an *argument* about the impossibility of the private linguist's attempts. Language is public and shared. The private linguist cannot do what he wants to do and, when we try to imagine this, we fail. Cavell, however, reads the moral of the argument less as a thesis than as the release of a fantasy of a desire to be inexpressive. If we have a picture of language in which we are the sole authority on the inner objects in our own minds and in which we *cannot* make these known to others, then we are released from the responsibility of making ourselves known to others. So the fantasy expresses the extent to which language is shared and why we might seek to deny or evade this fact. Here our expressiveness becomes a burden we cannot escape. The fantasy gives us an escape route at the price of our own immense loneliness and isolation. This too has been Prospero's fantasy; the play gives it expression and release.[53]

This is essentially Prospero's predicament in *The Tempest,* and it is why I insist on the island as the place of necessary expression and encounter, not a place fully internal to the workings of Prospero's mind. To conceive it in this way is to extend the hold of this fantasy and the loneliness and isolation it ensures.

Prospero's harnessing of the power of magic is a wish to escape his terrible vulnerability as he confronts the murderous conspirators. In his case, as in so many others, nothing is more human than the desire to escape being human. Prospero's relation to language, his charms, his spells, his aspirations to be more than human are both an attempt to escape his vulnerabilities to others, and his exposure to them. This attempt involves a theatricalization of others, and this is why the play is also an exploration of the resources of theater in the task of acknowledgment.

It is the last scene which gives us the clearest way of seeing both the models of theater at work here, and the difficulty of acknowledgment, and its relation to the task of becoming human.

They cannot boudge till your release

Prospero vows to relinquish his charms and magic; this means that he will relinquish, as I have argued, a particular relation to language. Is this borne out by the last scene? What versions of theater and theatricality does the last scene offer?

The island is the place, as Simon Palfrey has phrased it, of "perilous repentance, projection and self-rehearsal."[54] It is a place which each of the characters imagines he can create in his own image: a place where one might make oneself a fortune, gain a kingdom, imagine a perfect social order, restore all that was once taken from you. In the final scene it is as if all these individual psyches and groups are to meet together, to be confronted with each other in such a way as to place limits on each other's projections. So the language of "coming to the senses," of materializing, is the language of giving form and shape to a new community of memory, one in communion with others. Is there to be a brave new world? Can it be founded in the renovation of forgiveness? What forms of acknowledgment are entailed in such a project?

What seems most striking in the careful orchestration of this last scene is the way in which mutuality of response is still pointedly averted. The men of sin are brought in and stand within a charmed circle. The spell that has kept them in wonder and amazement, and immobilized their bodies and their minds, is about to wear off. The recognitions and realizations of the last scene await. In the last three great scenes of recognition we have explored in *Pericles, Cymbeline,* and *The Winter's Tale,* it is the mutuality of response that is lovingly evoked in scenes that extend the vocabulary of theater. Here, it seems that mutuality is at first avoided. Let us first examine some of these avoidances and what is at stake in them.

Prospero's first words address the "solemn air" that accompanies the entrance of Ariel escorting the men of sin to the charmed circle:

> A solemn air, and the best comforter
> To an unsettled fancy, cure thy brains.
> (5.1.58)

Is "cure thy brains" a command, an entreaty, a prayer, an invocation? Any decision we make about this is an assessment of Prospero's new relation to language and the extent of his "reformation." If this is not yet clear, it is at least clear that none of those who stand charmed are capable of a response until line 106. For nearly fifty lines he talks at them, not to them, veering between direct apostrophe and third-person speech in a highly unstable combination. If he is intensely aware of their presence, they are not aware of his presence at all. He cries when he sees Gonzalo "falls fellowly drops" (l. 64), and the implicit stage directions we can read from his speech tells us that they are beginning to stir. At this point he addresses Gonzalo and speaks to him, but it is clear that Gonzalo and Alonso cannot at this point respond to him, so his own words, his expression of fellow-feeling, his accusation of Alonso, and his deep sense of betrayal by Sebastian—including the words of forgiveness—are uttered in the absence of any possible response. "I do forgive thee / Unnatural though thou art" (5.2.78–79) precedes "Their understanding / Begins to swell" (5.1.79–80). Here is the crucial line: "Not one of them / That yet looks on me or would know me." This implies they are looking at him but without any recognition. It is at this point that Ariel fetches the hat and rapier in his cell, and he now presents himself as the former Milan. But he is playing fancy dress. He is no longer or not yet Milan. He is staging himself for them. If they recognize him as the former Milan, they will not see what they have reduced him to, and he might hope to elicit their awe, but not their compassion. After he is reclothed in these new garments, Gonzalo begins to stir, and after this Prospero announces himself. This is not quite "It is I, Hamlet the Dane," but a kind of self-conjuring: "Behold, sir King / The wronged Duke of Milan, Prospero" (5.2.107–8). When Alonso begins to come to a realization of something outside of his own dazed senses, Prospero replies to Gonzalo, and then when he tries to embrace him, Gonzalo replies, not to Prospero but to Alonso—"whether this be or be not, I'll not swear" (5.2.123–24). Prospero then addresses them all, singling out Sebastian and Antonio in an aside. Sebastian assumes that he is the devil or someone bewitched, and so that he is not seeing a human being at all.

Prospero then appears to speak directly to Antonio—first forgiving not him, but his rankest fault, and then demanding the restoration of his kingdom. There is, of course, no spoken response from Antonio. Then he embarks on the last round of his working on them—his last piece of theater—saying to Alonso he has lost his daughter, and collapsing the two tempests—"in this last tempest" (5.1.153). Then he unfolds another spectacle as he discloses Ferdinand and Miranda playing chess: "I will requite you with as good a thing / At least bring forth a wonder to content ye / As much as me my dukedom." Antonio never responds to him, but he has in fact carefully calculated all his words to them as words to which they *cannot* respond. When they come to, he has had the chance to re-present himself as one-time Milan, and he can produce the two lovers as a *fait accompli*—the future unfolded in an instant.

It is as if he can reveal himself in his vulnerability as the one wronged only when they cannot see him, when they cannot therefore acknowledge him as the one they have wronged. So this freezing has the effect of being able to isolate out in time the reactions first, of the wronged to the wrongers, and then, of the wrongers to the wronged. And perhaps this is part of the point of this temporal delay. The response will not be simultaneous. This is crucial. Prospero has always tried to protect himself from the responses of others. He wants to see them but not be seen. In this way he withholds himself from any just response. His is a flight from the particularity of relationship, and the doubleness, the essential mutuality of acknowledgment. When I acknowledge, I am exposed to the other and to my concept of the other. (We don't know when we have reached the limits of acknowledgment, and therefore when and whether we are avoiding it.) Acknowledgment singles out the knower and the known.

The play has offered us a series of ways of thinking about theater, and its powers and limits: the masque and the feast are opposed images of spectatorship and participation that themselves compose meta-theatrical spectacles of gazing and looking on. In this last scene we are offered a different model of theater and theatricalization. This scene explores and exposes a fantasy of nonreciprocal response. And this of course is a model of theater. In theater, as Stanley Cavell has discussed, the characters we see before us are in our presence. That is part of our task in theater—to make them present to us. This means responding to them with all our powers of empathic projection. But we are not in their presence. To be in their presence would simply mean to dissolve the show. The conditions of theater itself relieve us from the perennially endless task of our own expressiveness in respect of others, of our perpetual response to others.[55] Because we are not present to them, we do not have to *do* anything in relation to our own responses; we *can't* do anything. We are enjoined to "suffer with those we see suffer," but relieved of the responsibility of having to act on the basis of our felt responses. In everyday life we are never relieved of this burden of response and responsibility.

Prospero relinquishes his charms; he begins therefore to place himself as a man among men; but he still wishes to evade his own legibility to others. He theatricalizes himself, withholding himself from others until the last. Theatricalization is here understood as any act that makes my face or yours a mask.[56] If I withhold my emotions from my face, and from my language, I am presenting you with a role. If I also refuse to grant that your expressions are yours, I do the same thing, make a role for you.

Miranda can brave a response of wonder and of warmth, but her exemplary empathic projections, her capacity for compassion and wonder are, we are informed, based on her innocence, an innocence which must nevertheless be cherished, for the future will depend upon it. Can wonder and pity survive experience, betrayal, irreparable loss, powerlessness?

Prospero has tried to be beyond the human and has therefore rendered himself inhuman, and nothing is more human than this. The brave new world discovered in *The Tempest* abjures the Pauline language of putting on the new man, for the new can only be patiently made out of the old and the fallen. The projects of any total renovation are empty, as in Gonzalo's utopian fantasies.

It is not therefore surprising that an air of disappointment hangs over the ending of this play. Scholars have often read a Shakespearean biography in this ending. It is Shakespeare's last singly authored play; so it is his farewell to the stage and its limits before he crawls toward death in Stratford upon Avon.[57] But there is no need to posit a Shakespearean biography for this disappointment. Perhaps if we make the disappointment a part of the story of Shakespeare's life, we will not have to make it part of our own story.

The ending of this play is not disappointing simply because it is so unresolved: the silent Antonio, the ambiguous response of Sebastian, the premature consolation of Gonzalo which does not seem to sum up the play we ourselves have seen, all these make any definitive closure impossible. It is disappointing because it returns us to inescapably human horizons, and we long for more than those. To return to those merely human horizons is to return to the circuits of linguistic exchange and the limits of our own desire to express ourselves, and read each other's expressions. The disappointments of the ending turn out to be fully internal to the view of language Shakespeare has been intent on articulating. The conclusion of this great play is, it turns out, the unsurpassable horizon of our mutual responses to others. This is what forms and founds community; not the epic Virgilian drives of Aeneas in his founding of Rome, nor the ceaseless counter-epic transformations that inform the Ovidian unpicking of that epic in Medean witchcraft and its powers. Nothing underwrites this community, or can act as its guarantor; it can come to no final resolution, but only commit itself to future conversations that cannot supersede the horizons of our agreements *in* language.[58]

In the last few sublime lines of the play, actor, character and audience meet in the speech act of prayer.

> Now I want
> Spirits to enforce, art to enchant;
> And my ending is despair,
> Unless I be reliev'd by prayer,

> Which pierces so, that it assaults
> Mercy itself, and frees all faults.
> As you from crimes would pardon'd be
> Let your indulgence set me free.
>   (Epilogue 13–20).

The words of the actor pass over to the prayers of the audience and the mutual longing for a mercy necessary to all. Pardon comes not from a sovereign will but is granted from sinner to sinner in mutual acknowledgment, forgiving as we are forgiven. Only in this way, without enforcement, without enchantment, can art yield its good works.

NOTES

Introduction

1. Hannah Arendt, *The Human Condition* (Chicago: University of Chicago Press, 1958), 237.

2. In Arendt's striking phrase: "The possible redemption from the predicament of irreversibility...is the faculty of forgiving" (ibid.).

3. A point well made in David Hirst, *The Tempest* (Houndmills, Basingstoke: Macmillan, 1984). Of course, the profoundly recursive *Cymbeline* and *Winter's Tale* are patently rewritings of *Othello,* but I hope the choice of *King Lear* as central to all four romances will become clear as this book progresses. See especially chapter 4. For two studies of Shakespeare's treatment of forgiveness, see the suggestive book by Robert Grams Hunter, *Shakespeare and the Comedy of Forgiveness* (New York: Columbia University Press, 1965), and Michael D. Friedman, *The World Must Be Peopled: Shakespeare's Comedies of Forgiveness* (Cranbury, NJ: Associated University Presses, 2002).

4. Medieval orthodoxy taught that sacramental confession and absolution canceled the *culpa* or guilt of sin; the *poena,* punishment or penalty, incurred by the sin could be canceled through pardons and indulgences but also of course by performing the penance set by the priest in confession. Stephen Greenblatt's *Hamlet in Purgatory* (Princeton: Princeton University Press, 2001) makes a compelling argument about the loss of purgatory and a theater of remembrance haunted by purgatorial spirits who could no longer be helped by the actions of those on earth. In so far as he investigates penance, it is exclusively through the investigation of purgatory, pardons, and indulgences. For insightful comments on the exclusion of questions of justice from questions of remembrance in this model, see Lorna Hutson, *The Invention of Suspicion: Law and Mimesis in Shakespeare and Renaissance Drama* (Oxford: Oxford University Press, 2007), 265. My book is

concerned with the legacies of *sacramental* penance, confession, and absolution by a priest, rather than the pardon or the indulgence.

5. David Steinmetz in "Reformation and Grace," in *Grace upon Grace: Essays in Honor of Thomas A. Langford,* ed. Robert K. Johnston, L. Gregory Jones, and Jonathan R. Wilson (Nashville: Abingdon Press, 1999).

6. "An Homily of Repentance and of True Reconciliation unto God," in *The Homilies Appointed to Be Read in Churches,* the edition of John Griffiths revised by Ian Robinson (Bishopstone, Hertfortshire: Brynmill Press, 2006), 385.

7. "When our Lord and Master Jesus Christ said, 'repent' [Matt. 4:17], he willed the entire life of believers to be one of repentance," in *Ninety Five Theses or Disputations on the Power and Efficacy of Indulgences,* in *LW,* vol. 31, *The Career of a Reformer,* ed. Harold T. Grimm and Helmut T. Lehmann (Philadelphia: Muehlenberg and Fortress, and St. Louis: Concordia, 1957).

8. That is why this book does not alone trace local moments or statements of forgiveness in Shakespeare's plays but charts the implication of forgiveness in patterns of recognition and acknowledgment, and the history of acknowledgment in the sacrament of penance and reconciliation. Forgiving does not always require using the actual words of forgiveness. Indeed, Cordelia's forgiveness of King Lear ("No cause, no cause" [4.6.75]) refuses all language of blame and responsibility, and the most overt words of forgiveness uttered by Prospero to Sebastian ("For you, most wicked sir, whom to call brother / Would even infect my mouth, I do forgive / Thy rankest fault" [5.1.130–32]) are spat out between clenched teeth. I owe this point to Marianne Novy. For her own exploration of patterns of recognition, see *Love's Argument: Gender Relations in Shakespeare* (Chapel Hill: University of North Carolina Press, 1984).

9. Stanley Cavell, "Performative and Passionate Utterance," in *Philosophy the Day after Tomorrow* (Cambridge, Mass: Harvard University Press, 2005), 155–91. I discuss this terminology in more detail in chapters 2 and 5.

10. In a brilliant discussion of *Cymbeline,* Tony Tanner has talked of "the coming in to existence of an un-customed world or de-customed world—a chaos of blighted and bloodily broken bonds," and this is a wonderful description of the world of the tragedies and the limits and possibilities of repair in the post-tragic plays. See Tony Tanner, *Adultery in the Novel: Contract and Transgression* (Baltimore: Johns Hopkins University Press, 1979), 47. See also Sandra Laugier, "Wittgenstein and Cavell: Anthropology, Skepticism, and Politics," in *The Claim to Community: Essays on Stanley Cavell and Political Philosophy,* ed. Andrew Norris (Stanford: Stanford University Press, 2006), 19–37, for a precise rendering of versions of community in the work of Cavell and Wittgenstein, which distinguishes Cavell's understanding from the one more common in communitarian thought.

11. This is a central dimension of Cavell's unique exploration of Wittgenstein's private language argument in the extraordinary part 4 of *The Claim of Reason: Wittgenstein, Skepticism, Morality, and Tragedy* (New York: Oxford University Press, 1979, 2nd ed., 1999), especially, 348–70. See especially page 343: "The dependence of reference upon expression in naming our states of consciousness is, I believe, the specific moral of Wittgenstein's inventions containing the so-called private language argument."

12. Cavell treats Macbeth as melodrama rather than tragedy in *Disowning Knowledge in Seven Plays of Shakespeare* (Cambridge: Cambridge University Press, 1987, new ed., 2003). For some engagements with Cavell's work on Shakespeare, see Harry Berger, *Making Trifles of Terrors: Redistributing Complicities in Shakespeare* (Stanford: Stanford University Press, 1997); Richard Wheeler, "Acknowledging Shakespeare: Cavell and the Claim of the Human," in *The Senses of Stanley Cavell,* ed. Richard Fleming and Michael Payne (Lewisburg, PA: Bucknell University Press, 1989), and Lawrence F. Rhu, *Stanley Cavell's American Dream: Shakespeare, Philosophy, and Hollywood Movies* (New York: Fordham University Press, 2006). I have also profited from Richard Halpern's unpublished paper on Stanley Cavell, "Intimate Histories: Stanley Cavell on, and as, King Lear," and thank him for allowing me to read it in manuscript.

13. This book is therefore offered as a contribution to the history of skepticism as it is conceived by Stanley Cavell, and the "convulsion of sensibility we call the rise of Protestantism" in *The Claim of Reason,* 470, and in the introduction to *Disowning Knowledge in Seven Plays of Shakespeare.* Cavell has described skepticism as "a kind of argument of language with itself" in *In Quest of the Ordinary: Lines of Skepticism and Romanticism* (Chicago: University of Chicago Press, 1988), 5, and I have come to find that the kinds of disappointments endemic to the way we possess language (*In Quest,* 5) are lived through in particular and intense ways in the Reformation.

14. Ludwig Wittgenstein, *Philosophical Investigations,* trans. G.E.M. Anscombe, Remark 373. See also Remark 371: "Essence is expressed by grammar."

15. J. L. Austin, "A Plea for Excuses," in *Philosophical Papers,* ed. J. O. Urmson and G. J. Warnock (Oxford: Oxford University Press, 1961, 3rd ed., 1979), 182–83.

16. Ibid., 182.

17. "I'll teach you differences" was the rejected epigraph to the *Investigations.*

18. It is for this reason that ordinary language philosophy insists on bringing words home from their metaphysical to their ordinary use, and it explores the profound resistances to that activity in the temptation to imagine that words will speak for us independently of our investments. Thus Wittgenstein in the *Philosophical Investigations* says: "What *we* do is to bring words back from their metaphysical to their everyday use" (Remark 116).

19. A point made by Richard Fleming in *First Word Philosophy: Wittgenstein-Austin-Cavell, Writings on Ordinary Language Philosophy* (Lewisburg, PA: Bucknell University Press, 2004), 79.

20. Timothy Gould, *Hearing Things: Voice and Method in the Writing of Stanley Cavell* (Chicago: University of Chicago Press, 1998), 96.

21. Duncan's monarchical confidence makes him obtuse to the implications of his own remark; he is hardly disturbed at all by the split he talks about, yet the phrase is haunting for the way in which it expresses a central Shakespearean preoccupation. I owe this point to Heather Hirschfeld.

22. This is sensibly discussed in John Cox, "Was Shakespeare a Christian, and If So, What Kind of a Christian Was He?" in *Christianity and Literature* 55.4 (2006): 539–66.

1. The Mind's Retreat from the Face

1. Fergus Kerr, *Theology after Wittgenstein* (Melksham, UK: Cromwell Press, 1997), 46.

2. Ibid.

3. "I must finally conclude that this proposition, *I am, I exist,* is necessarily true whenever it is put forward by me or conceived in my mind" and "I am a mind, or intelligence, or intellect, or reason…a thinking thing." René Descartes, *Philosophical Writings,* trans. J. Cottingham, R. Stoothoff and D. Murdoch, 2 vols. (Cambridge: Cambridge University Press, 1985), 1:15, 17.

4. See for example, Katherine Eisaman Maus, *Inwardness and Theater in the English Renaissance* (Chicago: University of Chicago Press, 1995), and David Hillman, *Shakespeare's Entrails: Belief, Skepticism, and the Interior of the Body* (Basingstoke: Palgrave Macmillan, 2007).

5. Gertrude could, of course, have said, "Why *is* it so particular with thee?" This would certainly make her appear more overtly callous, and it would remove the implication that she perceives a showiness in Hamlet's mourning, a sense that in so mourning he is drawing attention to himself.

6. Stanley Cavell, *The Claim of Reason: Wittgenstein, Skepticism, Morality, and Tragedy* (New York: Oxford University Press, 1979, 2nd ed., 1999), 376.

7. Ibid., 357.

8. Stanley Cavell, *Philosophy the Day after Tomorrow* (Cambridge: Harvard University Press, 2005), 20.

9. Cavell, *The Claim of Reason,* 470. See also Fergus Kerr's comments on these passages in *Work on Oneself: Wittgenstein's Philosophical Psychology* (Arlington, VA: Institute for the Psychological Sciences Press, 2008), 102.

10. David Martin Jones, *Conscience and Allegiance in Seventeenth Century England: The Political Significance of Oaths and Engagements* (Rochester: University of Rochester Press, 1999), 15.

11. Edward Vallance, *Revolutionary England and the National Covenant: State Oaths, Protestantism, and the Political Nation, 1553–1682* (Woodbridge, Suffolk: Boydell Press, 2005), 27.

12. Susan Brigden, *London and the Reformation* (Oxford: Clarendon Press, 1989), 223; and see also Geoffrey Elton, *Policy and Police: The Enforcement of the Reformation in the Age of Thomas Cromwell* (Cambridge: Cambridge University Press, 1972).

13. Michael Questier, "Loyalty, Religion, and State Power in Early Modern England: English Romanism and the Jacobean Oath of Allegiance," in *The Historical Journal* 40.2 (1997): 312.

14. Brigden, *London and the Reformation,* 226, fol. 73v.

15. Excerpted in *A Treatise of Equivocation c. 1598,* in Robert Miola, ed., *Early Modern Catholicism: An Anthology of Primary Sources* (Oxford: Oxford University Press, 2007), 86.

16. For an exploration of casuistry, see Lowell Gallagher, *Medusa's Gaze: Casuistry and Conscience in the Renaissance* (Stanford: Stanford University Press, 1991).

17. John Baxter, *A Toile for Two-Legged Foxes,* cited in Julian Yates, *Error, Misuse, Failure: Object Lessons from the English Renaissance* (Minneapolis: University of Minnesota Press, 2002), 156.

18. Francis Bacon, *Certain Observations Made Upon A Libel Published this Present Year, 1592,* in James Spedding, *Letters and Life of Francis Bacon,* 7 vols. (London: Longmans, Green, 1890), 1:178.

19. Yet it was the oath that was developed as the political instrument precisely to ensure a window into the soul of the subject. In his recent discussion of the notorious *ex officio mero* oath, by which men were compelled to swear to tell the truth to magistrates before they even knew what crime they were being charged with, Ethan Shagan says that oaths were "a point where people were required by law to align their words with their thoughts, potentially giving the courts direct access to their consciences." Ethan Shagan, "The English Inquisition: Constitutional Conflict and Ecclesiastical Law in the 1590s," *The Historical Journal* 47.3 (2004): 543.

20. Michael Questier, *Conversion, Politics, and Religion in England, 1580–1625* (Cambridge: Cambridge University Press, 1996), 104.

21. Ibid., 105, Statutes, IV, 1071.

22. Ibid., 124.

23. Ibid., 124ff.

24. *Religion and Society in Early Modern England: A Sourcebook,* ed. David Cressy and Lori Anne Ferrell (London: Routledge, 1996), 130.

25. Peter Lake, "Religious Identities in Shakespeare's England," in *A Companion to Shakespeare,* ed. David Scott Kastan (Oxford: Blackwell, 1999), 64.

26. *Myroure of Oure Lady,* ed. J. H. Blunt (London: Kegan, Paul, Trench, Trubner, 1989), *EETS* e.s. 19, 54.

27. Nicholas Ridley, "A Piteous Lamentation of the Miserable State of the Church of England in the Time of the Revolt from the Gospel," in *The Works of Nicholas Ridley,* ed. Rev. Henry Christmas for the Parker Society (Cambridge: The University Press, 1941), 50.

28. *An Answer to Thomas More's Dialogue,* ed. Rev. Henry Walter, 3 vols. (Cambridge: The University Press, 1850), 1:9.

29. *An Answer to Thomas More's Dialogue,* in *Works of the English and Scottish Reformers,* ed. Thomas Russell (London: Ebenezer Palmer, 1828), 3:11.

30. *The Book of Common Prayer 1559,* ed. John Booty (Charlottesville: University of Virginia Press, 2005), 20.

31. I deal with this at length in chapter 7 of *Signifying God: Social Act and Symbolic Relation in The York Corpus Christi Play* (Chicago: University of Chicago Press, 2001).

32. Quoted in Heiko Oberman, *Luther: Between God and the Devil,* trans. Eileen Walliser-Schwarzbart (New York: Doubleday, 1989), 240.

33. *The Defence of the Apology of the Church of England,* in *The Works of John Jewel, Bishop of Salisbury,* ed. John Ayre for the Parker Society, 4 vols. (Cambridge: The University Press, 1850), 3:444.

34. Diarmaid MacCulloch, *Thomas Cranmer: A Life* (New Haven: Yale University Press, 1996), 430. The Christmas game analogy might have been suggested by the habit of men and women dividing up into groups on opposite sides of the chancel to receive communion. This might have reminded the rebels of a feast-day dance.

35. *The Remains of Thomas Cranmer, Archbishop of Canterbury,* 4 vols. (Oxford: The University Press, 1833), 2:214.

36. Edward Muir, *Ritual in Early Modern Europe* (Cambridge: Cambridge University Press, 1997), 7.

37. Thomas Becon, *The Catechism of Thomas Becon With Other Pieces Written by Him in the Reign of King Edward the Sixth,* ed. John Ayre for the Parker Society, vol. 2 (Cambridge: The University Press, 1844).

38. Parker Society, 1, 357.

39. *The Obedience of a Christian Man,* ed. David Daniell (London: Penguin, 2000), 115.

40. *A Dialogue Concerning Heresies,* ed. T.M.C. Lawler, Germain Marc'hadour, and Richard Marius, 2 parts, in *The Complete Works of St. Thomas More,* 6 vols. (New Haven: Yale University Press, 1981), 1:58.

41. Martin Luther, *De abroganda missa privata,* in *D. Martin Luthers Werke: Kritische Gesamtausgabe,* 127 vols. (Weimar: H. Böhlau, 1883–2009), henceforth abbreviated as WA, Weimarer Ausgabe, 8:419.

42. Luther, WA, 42:334, cited in Jaroslav Pelikan, *The Reformation of the Church, 1300–1700* (Chicago: University of Chicago Press, 1984), 174.

43. This citation and the following one are from William Flesch, *Generosity and the Limits of Authority: Shakespeare, Herbert, Milton* (Ithaca: Cornell University Press, 1992), 1: "Skepticism offers the ego confronted with contingency a choice of alternatives, and the choice it offers is one by which the ego can't lose."

44. Luther, WA, 40–41:590.

45. Timothy McDermott, ed., *Summa Theologiae: A Concise Translation* (Notre Dame, IN: Christian Classics, 1989), 559.

46. J. L. Austin, *How to Do Things with Words* 2nd ed., ed. J. O. Urmson and Marina Sbisa (Cambridge: Harvard University Press, 1975), 10.

47. Roy Rappaport, *Ritual and Religion in the Making of Humanity* (Cambridge: Cambridge University Press, 1999), 122. See also J. L. Austin, *Philosophical Papers* (Oxford: Oxford University Press, 1979), 236.

48. Kerr, *Theology after Wittgenstein,* 172.

49. "Homily on Repentance and True Reconciliation unto God," in *The Homilies Appointed to Be Read in Churches* (Brynmill: Preservation Press, 2006), 385.

50. Cavell, *The Claim of Reason,* 125.

51. Ibid., 121.

52. Bernard Beckerman, *Shakespeare at the Globe, 1599–1609* (New York: Macmillan, 1962), 35.

53. Ibid.

2. Rites of Forgiveness

1. Anthony Dawson and Paul Yachnin, *The Culture of Playgoing in Shakespeare's London: A Collaborative Debate* (Cambridge: Cambridge University Press, 2001).

2. Jeffrey Knapp, *Shakespeare's Tribe: Church, Nation, and Theater in Renaissance England* (Chicago: University of Chicago Press, 2002), 120. See also 16–17.

3. T. G. Bishop, *Shakespeare and the Theater of Wonder* (Cambridge: Cambridge University Press, 1996), 73.

4. Regina Schwartz, *Sacramental Poetics at the Dawn of Secularism: When God Left the World* (Stanford: Stanford University Press, 2008). Other work on Shakespeare and sacraments includes Stephen Greenblatt, "The Mousetrap," in *Practicing New Historicism,* by Catherine Gallagher and Stephen Greenblatt (Chicago: University of Chicago Press, 2000), 136–62; David Coleman, *Drama and the Sacraments in Sixteenth Century England: Indelible Characters* (Houndmills: Palgrave, 2007); Huston Diehl, *Staging Reform, Reforming the Stage: Protestantism and Popular Theater in Early Modern England* (Ithaca: Cornell University Press, 1997); Joel Altman, "'Vile Participation': The Amplification of Violence in the Theater of Henry V," *Shakespeare Quarterly* 42 (1991): 1–32; and C. L. Barber, *Creating Elizabethan Tragedy: The Theater of Marlowe and Kyd,* ed. Richard Wheeler (Chicago: University of Chicago Press, 1988). The previous works are largely focused on the eucharist. Two excellent recent analyses of *The Merchant of Venice* examine the legacies of penance. See Heather Hirschfeld, "'And he hath enough': The Penitential Economies of *The Merchant of Venice,"* in a special issue of *JMEMS* on *Premodern Shakespeare,* ed. Sarah Beckwith and James Simpson, 40.1 (Winter 2010): 89–117, and Elizabeth Fowler, "Towards a History of Performativity: Sacrament, Social Contract, and *The Merchant of Venice,"* in *Shakespeare and the Middle Ages,* ed. John Watkins and Curtis Perry (Oxford: Oxford University Press, 2010), 68–77.

5. The inseparability of penance and eucharist is a major theme of my book *Signifying God: Social Act and Symbolic Relation in the York Corpus Christi Plays* (Chicago: University of Chicago Press, 2001).

6. The Forgiveness Project is "a charity which explores forgiveness through the stories of real people." See https:/www.theforgivenessproject.com/. The stories cited here were accessed on January 29, 2009. They can be found on the website under "Stories." The centrality of storytelling to reconciliation is explored in chapter 5.

7. Avishai Margalit, *The Ethics of Memory* (Cambridge: Cambridge University Press, 2002), 203.

8. *ST* 2.2.23.2.ad 1. (I use the standard conventions for citing from the *Summa* in which reference is made first to the part, next to the quaestio, then to the article, then subsequently to the reply to the objections in the articles.)

9. *ST* 3.90.2.

10. *Institutes* 3.4.2. All citations from Calvin's *Institutes* are taken from *Calvin: Institutes of the Christian Religion,* 2 vols., trans. Ford Lewis Battles, ed. John T. McNeill (Louisville: Westminster John Knox Press, 1960).

11. Quoted in David Steinmetz, *Luther in Context* (Grand Rapids, MI: Baker Academic, 2002), 110.

12. Gerald Bray, ed., *Documents of the English Reformation 1526–1701* (Cambridge: James Clarke, 1994, rpt. 2004), 291. The italics represent the 1571 additions to the 1563 articles, themselves a revision of Edward VI's Forty-Two Articles (1553).

13. In chapter 11, part 3 of *The Claim of Reason,* Stanley Cavell takes issue with John Rawls's understanding that promise is an "institution." I take these issues up again in chapter 5, "Acknowledgment and Confession in Cymbeline."

14. Geneva Bible, Matt. 16.18–19. All citations from the Geneva Bible are from *The Geneva Bible: A Facsimile of the 1560 Edition,* with an introduction by Lloyd Berry (Madison: University of Wisconsin Press, 1969).

15. Peter Lombard provides the first account of orders as a sacrament as "a certain sign, that is, something sacred, by which a spiritual power and office is given to the one ordained. Therefore a spiritual character is called an *ordo* or grade, where the promotion to power occurs" (Book 4, dist. 24, c.13, *Sententiae* 2:405), *Sententiae in IV Libris Distinctae,* ed. Ignatius Brady, 3rd ed. (Grottaferrata: Editiones Collegii S. Bonaventurae ad Claras Aquas, 1971 and 1981), cited in Gary Macy, *The Hidden History of Women's Ordination* (Oxford: Oxford

University Press, 2008), where he comments that this is a decisive break in the history of ordination, wherein it becomes "tied securely to power rather than to vocation" (106). Scholars of the late twelfth and early thirteenth centuries would go on to ally the sacrament of orders tightly with the sacrament of the altar and the ability to make Christ present in the eucharist.

16. For an account of the theology of "in persona Christi" and "in persona ecclesiae," see B-D. Marliangeas, *Clés pour une théologie du ministère* (Paris: Editions Beauchesne, 1978).

17. E.g. Peter Lombard, *Sententiae* IV. d.5. c.1.1. The idea is traditional and is repeated for example in Richard Hooker, *Of the Laws of Ecclesiastical Polity*, vol. 2 (Cambridge: Harvard University Press, 1977), Book 5, 77.8, p. 430: "whether wee preach, pray, baptize, communicate, condemne, give absolution, or whatsoever, as disposers of Gods misteries, our wordes, judgments, actes and deedes, are not oures but the holie Ghostes."

18. For the two forums see, for example, James A. Brundage, *Medieval Canon Law* (London: Longman, 1995); R. H. Helmholz, *The Spirit of the Classical Canon Law* (Athens: University of Georgia Press, 1996), and F. D. Logan, *Excommunication and the Secular Arm in Medieval England* (Toronto: Institute for Medieval Studies, 1968).

19. Hooker, *Lawes,* Book 6, 5.4, p. 11. See also Thomas Aquinas, *ST* 3.80.6: a priest should not expose a person's sins by denying him the sacrament of the altar.

20. See John Bossy, "Practices of Satisfaction," in *Retribution, Repentance, and Reconciliation: Papers Read at the 2002 Summer and 2003 Winter Meeting of the Ecclesiastical History Society* (Woodbridge, Suffolk: Boydell Press, 2004), 108. See also Deborah Shuger, *Censorship and Cultural Change: The Regulation of Language in Tudor-Stuart England* (Philadelphia: University of Pennsylvania Press, 2006), 147–48, 155.

21. T. W. Drury, *Confession and Absolution: The Teaching of the Church of England as Interpreted and Illustrated by the Writings of the Reformers of the Sixteenth Century* (London: Chas. J. Thynne, 1903), 260.

22. *ST* 3.84.3.

23. Canon 9 of Trent: "If anyone shall say that the priest's sacramental absolution is not a judicial act, but the mere ministry of pronouncing and declaring that sins are forgiven the one who confesses, so long as he believes that he has been absolved and this even though the priest does not absolve seriously but in jest, or shall say that confession is not required of the penitent that the priest may absolve him, anathema sit." Cited in Kenan Osborne, *Reconciliation and Justification* (New York: Paulist Press, 1990), 178.

24. Hugh of St. Victor, *De sacramentis 1, ix, 2, On the Sacraments of the Christian Faith* (Cambridge, MA: Medieval Academy of America, 1951). Hugh's work noticeably precedes the influence of Aristotle on theories of transubstantiation.

25. Alister E. McGrath, *Iustitia Dei: A History of the Christian Doctrine of Justification* (Cambridge: Cambridge University Press, 1986).

26. Thomas Becon, *The Castle of Comfort* in *The Early Works of Thomas Becon,* ed. John Ayre, vol. 3 (Cambridge: The University Press, 1843), 556.

27. Ibid., 558.

28. Ibid., 566.

29. John Jewel, *The Defence of the Apology of the Church of England,* in *The Works of John Jewel, Bishop of Salisbury,* ed. John Ayre for the Parker Society, 4 vols. (Cambridge: The University Press, 1845), 3:381.

30. *LW,* 40:373.

31. See Gerald Bray, ed., *The Anglican Canons, 1529–1947* (Woodbridge, Suffolk: Boydell Press, 1998), lxxv.

32. Jewel, *Defence,* 378.

33. Peter Lombard, *Sentences,* Book 4, dist. XVI, 1.

34. Gordon J. Spykman, *Attrition and Contrition at the Council of Trent* (Kampen: Kok, 1955), 6.

35. *ST* 1.2.112.5.

36. "An Homily of the Worthy Reception and Reverent Esteeming of the Sacrament of the Body and Blood of Christ," in *The Homilies Appointed to Be Read in Churches* (Brynmill: Preservation Press, 2006), 321.

37. Ibid., 322.

38. Ibid.

39. Ibid., 325 from the Second Part of the Homily.

40. Ibid., 323.

41. Ibid., 324.

42. John Stachniewski, *The Persecutory Imagination: English Puritanism and the Literature of Religious Despair* (Oxford: Oxford University Press, 1991); see too David Como, *Blown by the Spirit: Puritanism and the Emergence of an Antinomian Underground in Pre–Civil War England* (Stanford: Stanford University Press, 2004).

43. See Kenneth Fincham and Nicholas Tyacke, *Altars Restored: The Changing Face of English Religious Worship 1547–c. 1700* (Oxford: Oxford University Press, 2007); Peter Lake, "Lancelot Andrewes, John Buckeridge, and Avant-Garde Conformity at the Court of James I," in *The Mental World of the Jacobean Court*, ed. Linda Peck (Cambridge: Cambridge University Press, 1991), 113–53, H. C. Porter, *Reformation and Reaction in Tudor Cambridge* (Cambridge: Cambridge University Press, 1958).

44. *Institutes* 3.4.2, p. 625.

45. The history of this phrase and the theology behind it is discussed in Artur Landgraf, *Dogmengeschichte der Fruhscholastik*, pt. 1, vol. 1 (Regensburg: Pustet, 1952), 249–64; Heiko A. Oberman, "Facientibus quod in se est Deus non denegat gratiam: Robert Holcot, O.P., and the Beginnings of Luther's Theology," *Harvard Theological Review* 55 (1962): 317–42, and now David Aers, *Salvation and Sin: Augustine, Langland, and Fourteenth Century Theology* (Notre Dame: University of Notre Dame Press, 2009), 34–35. For Luther's disgust at the "faciendi" see *Heidelberg Disputation* (1518) in *LW,* 31:40: "The person who believes that he can obtain grace by doing what is in him adds sin to sin so that he becomes doubly guilty."

46. *Institutes* 3.4.2, p. 625.

47. *Institutes* 3.4.17, p. 642.

48. *Institutes* 3.4.18, p. 644: "The whole reckoning of absolution depends upon faith and repentance. And these two things elude the knowledge of man when he has to pass sentence upon another man. Therefore it follows that certainty of binding and loosing does not lie within the competence of earthly judgment."

49. *Institutes* 3.4.18, pp. 644–45.

50. *Institutes* 3.4.21, p. 647.

51. Ibid.

52. *Institutes* 3.4.27, pp. 653–54.

53. *Luther and Erasmus: Free Will and Salvation,* ed. E. Gordon Rupp and Philip S. Watson (Philadelphia: Westminster Press, 1969).

54. Lee Wandell Palmer, *The Eucharist in the Reformation: Incarnation and Liturgy* (Cambridge: Cambridge University Press, 2006), 108.

55. *On the Bondage of the Will,* in *Luther And Erasmus: Free Will and Salvation,* p. 134.

56. *Institutes* 1.14.22, p. 182.

57. Jennifer Herdt, *Putting on Virtue: The Legacy of the Splendid Vices* (Chicago: University of Chicago Press, 2006), 175.

58. Steinmetz, *Luther in Context,* 7.

59. Bray, *Anglican Canons,* 125.

60. Berndt Hamm, *The Reformation of Faith in the Context of Late Medieval Theology and Piety: Essays by Berndt Hamm* (Leiden: Brill, 2004), 166.

61. Ibid., 167.

62. Ibid., 193.

63. Diarmaid MacCulloch, *The Reformation* (New York: Viking, 2003), 574–75.

64. Margo Todd, *The Culture of Protestantism in Early Modern Scotland* (New Haven: Yale University Press, 2002), 130.

65. Ibid., 254.

66. *The Book of Common Prayer 1559,* ed. John Booty (Charlottesville: University of Virginia Press, 1976), 316.

67. Peter Lake, *The Boxmaker's Revenge: 'Orthodoxy,' 'Heterodoxy,' and the Politics of the Parish in Early Stuart London* (Stanford: Stanford University Press, 2001), 74.

68. Edmund Grindal drew up directions for Public Penance. First there should be a sermon exhorting the penitents to repentance. Penitents should stand bare-headed "with the sheet" on a raised platform before the congregation. They should be publicly questioned so as to evoke a public confession leading up to a prayer for pardon. "The Archbishop's Directions for Penance" in William Nicholson, *The Remains of Edmund Grindal: Successively Bishop of London and Archbishop of York and Canterbury* (Cambridge: University Press, 1843), 455.

69. F. G. Emmison, *Elizabethan Life: Morals and the Church Courts* (Colchester: Benham, 1973), 282.

70. Ibid., 290.

71. Ibid., 287. Some inventive penances and the equally inventive responses to them on the part of the penitents are described in Christopher Haigh, *The Plain Man's Pathway to Heaven: Kinds of Christianity in Post-Reformation England, 1570–1640* (Oxford: Oxford University Press, 2007).

72. The Order of Communion later included in the Edwardian Prayerbook (1549) is marked by a sense of the altogether different speech acts of individual and general confession, and makes allowances that "such that be satisfied with a general confession, not to be offended with them that do use, to their further satisfying, the auricular and secret confession to the priest; nor those also which think needful or convenient, for the quietness of their consciences particularly to open their sins to the priest: to be offended with them that are satisfied with their humble confession to God, and the general confession to the church," *The First and Second Prayerbooks of Edward VI* (1910), 217. In the Elizabethan prayerbook of 1559, something of the unfinished matter of the reform of church government enters the language introducing the "commination" with its regret for the practice of open penance and the anticipation of a future "restoration" of the "said discipline."

73. Hooker, *Lawes,* Book 6, p. 48.

74. See James Sharpe, "Last Dying Speeches: Religion, Ideology, and Public Execution in Seventeenth Century England," *Past and Present* 107 (1985): 144–67, and Peter Lake and Michael Questier, chaps. 6 and 7 in *The Anti-Christ's Lewd Hat: Protestants, Papists, and Players in Post-Reformation England* (New Haven: Yale University Press, 2002).

75. Patrick Collinson, "Shepherds, Sheepdogs, and Hirelings: The Pastoral Ministry in Post-Reformation England," in *The Ministry, Studies in Church History,* ed. W. Sheils and Diana Wood (Oxford: Blackwell, 1989), 216.

76. Yet R. H. Helmholz, the foremost authority on canon law in England, suggests that this did not end the study of canon law at Oxford and Cambridge; see Helmholz, *Roman Canon Law in Reformation England* (Cambridge: Cambridge University Press, 1990), 152.

77. Legislation both in 1536 and subsequently in 1544 authorized a commission to reform canon law, but it was not until Edward VI's first Parliament that canon law revision began. The resulting *Reformatio* was published by John Foxe in 1571, but it was never enacted in Parliament despite several abortive attempts. The document and the attempts to legislate it are given in Gerard Bray, ed., *Tudor Church Reform: The Henrician Canons of 1535 and the Reformatio Legum Ecclesiasticarum* (Bury St. Edmunds, Suffolk: Boydell Press, 2000), for the Church Record Society.

78. Hooker, *Lawes,* Book 6, p. 48.

79. Ibid., p. 47

80. Drury, *Confession and Absolution*, 255.

81. *The First and Second Prayer Books of Edward VI*, 217, 385; *The Book of Common Prayer 1559*, 257.

82. *The Book of Common Prayer 1559*, 303.

83. Thomas Aquinas, *ST* 3.84.3.

84. Elizabeth Fowler, *Literary Character: The Human Figure in Early English Writing* (Ithaca: Cornell University Press, 2003), especially chap. 4. See also her more recent "Towards a History of Performativity: Sacrament, Social Contract, and *The Merchant of Venice*," in *Shakespeare and the Middle Ages*, ed. John Watkins and Curtis Perry (Oxford: Oxford University Press, 2009), 68–77, for a perspective very consonant with this book: "penitential literature," she suggests, "is a hotbed of thought about intention and recognition" (75).

85. For a particularly lucid account of Austin's work in distinguishing illocutionary force and perlocutionary effect, see Alice Crary, *Beyond Moral Judgment* (Cambridge: Harvard University Press, 2007), especially p. 65, and Timothy Gould's important essay "The Unhappy Performative," in *Performativity and Performance*, ed. Andrew Parker and Eve Kosofsky Sedgwick (New York: Routledge, 1995), 19–44. For Cavell's elucidation of the deepest implications of Austin's legacy, see "Counter-Philosophy and the Pawn of Voice," in *A Pitch of Philosophy: Autobiographical Exercises* (Cambridge: Harvard University Press, 1996), and his foreword to *The Literary Speech Act: Don Juan with J. L. Austin, or Seduction in Two Languages* by Shoshana Felman (Stanford: Stanford University Press, 2003).

86. This analysis is dependent on Stanley Cavell's thought and examples in his essay "Performative and Passionate Utterance," in *Philosophy the Day after Tomorrow* (Cambridge: Harvard University Press, 2005), 152–91. The phrase "recovery of speech" is taken from Cavell's responses to the essays collected in *The Claims to Community: Essays on Stanley Cavell and Political Philosophy*, ed. Andrew Norris (Stanford: Stanford University Press, 2006), 269.

87. On problems with functionalism and ritual, see chap. 2 of *Signifying God*.

88. J. L. Austin, *How to Do Things with Words*, ed. J. O. Urmson and Marina Sbisa (Cambridge: Harvard University Press, 1962), 148.

89. On "sensitivity to occasions" see Crary, *Beyond Moral Judgment*, 71. It is the aim of this book to show how "learning to speak is inseparable from development of a moral outlook" (43).

3. Repairs in the Dark

1. Anne Barton, introduction to *Measure for Measure*, in *The Riverside Shakespeare* (Boston: Houghton Mifflin, 1997), 2nd ed., 579.

2. On the large literature on marriage contracts in *Measure for Measure*, see E. Schanzer, "The Marriage Contracts in *Measure for Measure*," *Shakespeare Survey* 13 (1960): 81–89, and Victoria Hayne, "Performing Social Practice: The Example of *Measure for Measure*," *Shakespeare Quarterly* 44.1 (Spring 1993): 1–29. For the background on reformed views of marriage, see E. Carlson, *Marriage and the English Reformation* (Oxford: Wiley-Blackwell, 1994), and David Cressy, *Birth, Marriage, and Death: Ritual, Religion and the Life-Cycle in Tudor and Stuart England* (Oxford: Oxford University Press, 1997).

3. Peter Lake with Michael Questier, *The Anti-Christ's Lewd Hat: Protestants, Papists, and Players in Post-Reformation England* (New Haven: Yale University Press, 2002), 626; for anti-Calvinism, 656.

4. Ibid., 628, 648, 652. For the change from a preoccupation with sins of aversion to one with sins of concupiscence, see John Bossy, *Christianity in the West, 1400–1700* (Oxford: Oxford University Press, 1985), 38.

5. *The Book of Common Prayer 1559*, ed. John E. Booty (Charlottesville: University of Virginia Press, 2005; 1st ed., 1975), 290.

6. Frederick J. Furnivall, ed., *Handlyng Synne, EETS* o.s. 119 (London: K. Paul, Trench, Trubner, 1901). The manual was translated by Robert Mannyng of Brynne from William of Waddington's *Manuel des Péchiez.*

7. For a famous instance that collapses penitential and physical groping, see Chaucer's *Summoner's Tale,* Fragment 3 of *The Canterbury Tales,* l. 1816: "thise curatz been ful necligent and slowe / To grope tenderly a conscience / In shrift." See *The Riverside Chaucer,* ed. Larry Benson (Boston: Houghton Mifflin, 1987).

8. From the introduction to the Blackfriars edition of the *Summa,* edited by Thomas Gilbey and T. C. O'Brien, 61 vols. (London: Blackfriars, 1964–1973), vol. 1.

9. *ST* 1.2.1.1.

10. *ST* 1.2.85.2.ad 3.

11. *On the Bondage of the Will,* trans. Philip S. Watson and Benjamin Drewery, *LW,* 33:226. See Quentin Skinner, *The Foundations of Modern Political Thought,* 3 vols., vol. 2, *The Age of Reformation* (Cambridge: Cambridge University Press, 1978), 6.

12. For illuminating comments on sin and Langland's allegorical figure of "Semyuief," see David Aers, "Remembering the Samaritan, Remembering Semyuief," chap. 4 of *Salvation and Sin: Augustine, Langland, and Fourteenth-Century Theology* (Notre Dame: University of Notre Dame Press, 2009), 83–132.

13. *Institutes* 2.1.8, p. 251.

14. *Institutes* 2.1.9, p. 252.

15. *Institutes* 2.1.8, p. 251.

16. Cited in John Witte, *Law and Protestantism: The Legal Teachings of the Lutheran Reformation* (Cambridge: Cambridge University Press, 2002), 2, from *LW,* 36:70.

17. Skinner, *The Age of Reformation,* 14.

18. Ibid., 14–15.

19. *Luther and Calvin: On Secular Authority,* ed. Harro Höpfl, Cambridge Texts in the History of Political Thought (Cambridge: Cambridge University Press, 1991), 12.

20. Ibid., 9.

21. Ibid., p. xvi. Luther pointedly omits Matthew 26.52, Isaiah 2.4, and Luke 22.38 from his scriptural citations about the sword. Says Höpfl: "there is no question that Luther meant the 'sword' reference most literally: it is not the judge, but the Executioner who epitomized ruling for Luther" (xvi).

22. Ibid., 15.

23. Ibid., 30.

24. The Geneva Bible, Matt. 5.38–39. The Rheims Bible annotates this passage with a reference to Anabaptism, and Anabaptism is also a spectre for Calvin in his commentary on the Sermon.

25. *LW,* vol. 21, *The Sermon on the Mount and The Magnificat,* ed. Jaroslav Pelikan, 108: on Matt. 5.38–42, Luther says: "Christ is talking about a spiritual existence and life and He is addressing Himself to his Christians. He is telling them to live and behave before God and in the world with heart dependent upon God and uninterested in things like secular rule or government, power or punishment, anger or revenge."

26. Ibid., 113.

27. Ibid.

28. Ibid., 210.

29. Cited by William Cavanaugh, *Torture and Eucharist: Theology, Politics, and the Body of Christ* (Oxford: Wiley-Blackwell, 1998), 5.

30. Jennifer A. Herdt, *Putting on Virtue: The Legacy of the Splendid Vices* (Chicago: University of Chicago Press, 2008), 174.

31. For example, in his long debate on church government with John Whitgift, Thomas Cartwright calls the archbishop's court a "filthy quave-mire and poisoned plash of all abhominations

that do infect the whole realm," quoted in *The Defence of the Answer to the Admonition, against the Reply of Thomas Cartwright* in *The Works of John Whitgift,* part 3, ed. by Rev. John Ayre for the Parker Society (Cambridge: The University Press, 1853).

32. See R. H. Helmholz, *Roman Canon Law in Reformation England,* 113: "Conduct that had once been sorted out privately now gave rise to public controversy."

33. Ibid., 114.

34. George Herbert, *A Priest to the Temple or The Country Parson, His Character and Rule of Holy Life,* in *George Herbert: The Complete English Poems,* ed. John Tobin (London: Penguin, 1991), 260.

35. Conor McCarthy, *Marriage in Medieval England: Law, Literature and Practice* (Woodbridge, Suffolk: Boydell Press, 2004), 22.

36. Ibid., 23.

37. On lay authority and the sacrament of marriage, see Emma Lipton, *Affections of the Mind: The Politics of Sacramental Marriage in Late Medieval English Literature* (Notre Dame: University of Notre Dame Press, 2007).

38. John Mirk, *Instructions for Parish Priests,* ed. Gillis Kristensson (Lund: C. W. K. Gleerup, 1974), 182, cited in Liana Farber, *An Anatomy of Trade in Medieval Writing: Value, Consent, and Community* (Ithaca: Cornell University Press, 2006), 113.

39. Farber, *Anatomy of Trade,* 127.

40. Alastair Minnis, *Fallible Authors: Chaucer's Pardoner and the Wife of Bath* (Philadelphia: University of Pennsylvania Press, 2008), 275.

41. See ibid., 274. Netter perceives that such an attack on the sacrament of marriage is effectively an attack on all the sacraments. Thomas Netter, *Doctrinale* 2.766–67.

42. Pollock and Maitland, *History of English Law,* 2:368–69, cited in Farber, *Anatomy of Trade,* 114.

43. Brian Tierney, "Canon Law and Institutions," in *Proceedings of the Seventh International Congress of Medieval Canon Law,* ed. Peter Lineham (Vatican City: Bibliotheca Apostolica Vatican, 1988), 67. Says Tierney: "canonists had invented a form of marriage which by its nature could not be proved."

44. Shannon McSheffrey, *Marriage, Sex, and Civic Culture in Late Medieval London* (Philadelphia: University of Pennsylvania Press, 2006), 25.

45. Ibid., 27.

46. Ibid., 31.

47. Witte, *Law and Protestantism,* 294.

48. Marjorie Keniston McIntosh, *Controlling Misbehaviour in England, 1370–1600* (Cambridge: Cambridge University Press, 1998).

49. Ralph Houlbrooke, *Death, Religion and the Family in England, 1480–1750* (Oxford: Oxford University Press, 1998), 110.

50. Julia Reinhard Lupton, *Citizen-Saints: Shakespeare and Political Theology* (Chicago: University of Chicago Press, 2005), 145.

51. Ibid., 149.

52. The great purchase of this idea is thoroughly explored in Wendy Doniger, *The Bedtrick: Tales of Sex and Masquerade* (Chicago: University of Chicago Press, 2000), and Janet Adelman, "Bed Tricks: On Marriage as the End of Comedy in *All's Well That Ends Well* and *Measure for Measure,*" in *Shakespeare's Personality,* ed. Norman N. Holland, Sidney Homan, and Bernard J. Paris (Berkeley: University of California Press, 1989), 151–74.

53. *ST.* 1.2.19.6, vol. 18, p. 67, of Blackfriars edition.

54. See *The Phoenix* (first performance, 1604), in *Thomas Middleton: The Collected Works,* general editors, Gary Taylor and John Lavagnino (Oxford: Clarendon Press, 2007). *The Phoenix* is edited by Lawrence Danson and Ivo Kamps, pp. 91–127. John Marston, *The Fawn* (first performance, 1604) (Lincoln: University of Nebraska Press, 1965), and *The Malcontent* (1603; revised

version performed by the King's Men, 1604), ed. M. L. Wine (Lincoln: University of Nebraska Press, 1965).

55. It is fascinating to see Gabriel Biel spell out penance and matrimony as the two sacraments where the words of the lay participant make up the matter of the sacrament: "Alia sunt sacramenta, quae requirunt per se et essentialiter, hoc est necessario, ut sit verum sacramentum, actum eius qui sacramentum recipit; ut in paenitentia et matrimonio," in Gabrielis Biel, *Collectorium circa quattuor libros Sententiarum,* Libri quarti pars prima, ed. Wilfridus Werbeck and Udo Hofmann (Tubingen: J. C. B. Mohr, 1975), Dist. 14, Quaestio 2, p. 447. Interestingly, in twelfth-century sacramental theology, the role of consent in valid marriage parallels the debates on contrition in valid confession; see Robert Shaffern, *The Penitent's Treasury: Indulgences in Latin Christendom, 1175–1375* (Scranton: University of Scranton Press, 2007), 95.

56. For *King John,* see *The Complete Plays of John Bale,* 2 vols., ed. Peter Happe (Woodbridge, Suffolk: D. S. Brewer, 1985–86), vol. 2. For the relations between anti-theatricality and anti-catholicism in relation to Bale and the reformation of Catholic ritual, see Sarah Beckwith, *Signifying God: Social Relation and Symbolic Act in the York Corpus Christi Plays* (Chicago: University of Chicago Press, 2001), especially chap. 7, "Theaters of Signs and Disguises," 121–57.

57. See Penn Szittya, *The Anti-Fraternal Tradition in Medieval Literature* (Cambridge: Cambridge University Press, 1989).

58. On the "jurisprudential topoi" by which sexual vows are used to explore dominion, see Elizabeth Fowler, "Chaucer's Hard Cases," in *Medieval Crime and Social Control,* ed. Barbara Hanawalt and David Wallace (Minneapolis: University of Minnesota Press, 1999), 124–42. On the question of consent in marriage as modeling social justice, see Stanley Cavell, "The Conversation of Justice: Rawls and the Drama of Consent," in *Conditions Handsome and Unhandsome: The Constitution of Emersonian Perfectionism* (Chicago: University of Chicago Press, 1988), 101–26.

59. Gordon Kipling, *Enter the King: Theatre, Liturgy, and Ritual in the Medieval Civic Triumph* (Oxford: Clarendon Press, 1998).

60. Ernst Hertwig Kantorowicz, *The King's Two Bodies: A Study in Medieval Political Theology* (Princeton: Princeton University Press, 1957).

61. The speech is printed in Charles Howard McIlwain, ed., *The Political Works of James I* (Cambridge: Harvard University Press, 1918), 272.

62. Thomas Becon, *The Castle of Comfort,* in *The Early Works of Thomas Becon,* vol. 3, ed. John Ayre (Cambridge: The University Press, 1843), 562.

4. The Recovery of Voice in Shakespeare's *Pericles*

1. *The Faerie Queene,* ed. A. C. Hamilton (Padstow: Longman, 2001), book 1, canto 9, stanza 48. The words of Romans 6.23 hang over the Red Cross knight: "the wages of sinne is death": "And to his fresh remembraunce did reuerse / The ugly view of his deformed crimes, / That all his manly powers it did disperse, / As he were charmed with inchaunted rimes / That oftentimes he quakt, and fainted oftentime."

2. For Stephen Greenblatt's famous account of exorcisms as stage plays, see "Shakespeare and the Exorcists," in *Shakespearean Negotiations* (Berkeley: University of California Press, 1988), 94–128. For a beautiful reading of this scene, see Thomas Bishop, "Shakespeare's Theatre Games," in "Premodern Shakespeare," *JMEMS* 40.1 (Winter 2010), ed. James Simpson and Sarah Beckwith, 65–88.

3. Stanley Cavell asks and answers the question why Edgar fails to reveal himself to his father in compelling and consequential ways in "The Avoidance of Love," in *Must We Mean What We Say?* (Cambridge: Cambridge University Press, 2002), 282–85. He returns to this scene again in "The Interminable Shakespeare Text," in *Philosophy the Day after Tomorrow* (Cambridge: Harvard University Press, 2005), 56, where he comments that Edgar has avoided using words "in his own voice."

4. See Robert Bartlett, *Trial by Fire and Water: The Medieval Judicial Ordeal* (Oxford: Clarendon Press, 1986), and Lorna Hutson, *The Invention of Suspicion: Law and Mimesis in Shakespeare and Renaissance Drama* (Oxford: Oxford University Press, 2007).

5. This is the burden of Stanley Cavell's profoundly influential essay, "The Avoidance of Love," and part 4 of *The Claim of Reason*.

6. Frank Kermode, *Shakespeare's Language* (London: Allen Lane, 2000), 257: "one feels the whole of Shakespeare's enterprise was to see what could be made of the recognition scene, how it could be drawn out, given the greatest possible emotional force."

7. Peter Brook, *Bodywork: Objects of Desire in Modern Narrative* (Cambridge: Harvard University Press, 1993), and Terence Cave, *Recognitions* (Oxford: Clarendon Press, 1988).

8. Cavell, "The Interminable Shakespeare Text," 56.

9. See especially Michael Neill's superb *Issues of Death: Mortality and Identity in English Renaissance Tragedy* (Oxford: Oxford University Press, 1997).

10. This is partly a problem, of course, produced by the periodization of modernity; see James Simpson, "Diachronic History and the Shortcomings of Medieval Studies," in *Reading the Medieval in Early Modern England*, ed. David Matthews and Gordon McMullan (Cambridge: Cambridge University Press, 2007), 17–30, and the introduction to "Premodern Shakespeare," *JMEMS* 40.1 (Winter 2010), ed. James Simpson and Sarah Beckwith, 65–88. See the pioneering work of Louis Montrose, *The Purpose of Playing: Shakespeare and the Cultural Politics of Elizabethan Theatre* (Chicago: University of Chicago Press, 1996), and for the astonishingly influential argument about the role of theater in evacuating ritual, Greenblatt, "Shakespeare and the Exorcists." For a criticism of this view see Cavell, "The Interminable Shakespeare Text," and Jeffrey Knapp, *Shakespeare's Tribe: Church, Nation, and Theater in Renaissance England* (Chicago: University of Chicago Press, 2002), 8.

11. For *Mucedorus*, see Arvin H. Jupin, ed., *A Contextual Study and Modern Spelling Edition of Mucedorus*, The Renaissance Imagination (New York: Garland, 1987); for romance, see Patricia Parker, *Inescapable Romance: Studies in the Poetics of a Mode* (Princeton: Princeton University Press, 1979); and for a comprehensive treatment of the transformation of medieval romance, see Helen Cooper, *The English Romance in Time: Transforming Motifs from Geoffrey of Monmouth to the Death of Shakespeare* (Oxford: Oxford University Press, 2004), especially pp. 406–7 on *Leir* and *Lear*.

12. Francis Beaumont, *The Knight of the Burning Pestle*, ed. Sheldon P. Zitner (Manchester: Manchester University Press, 2004).

13. For a comprehensive discussion of the canon and chronology of the plays see Stanley Wells and Gary Taylor, *William Shakespeare: A Textual Companion* (New York: W. W. Norton, 1997), 69–144, especially pp. 128–31. See also p. 530: F Lear should probably be placed between *The Winter's Tale* and *Cymbeline*. For the relation of the Lear texts, see Gary Taylor and Michael Warren, eds., *The Division of the Kingdoms: Shakespeare's Two Versions of King Lear* (Oxford: Clarendon Press, 1983).

14. For a brilliant analysis of such effects and techniques, see T. G. Bishop, *Shakespeare and the Theater of Wonder* (Cambridge: Cambridge University Press, 1996), 93–124.

15. My citations from the *Confessio Amantis* are from the edition by Russell A. Peck, published for TEAMS (Western Michigan University, Medieval Institute Publications, 2000–2004), 3 vols., vol. 1. All references are given parenthetically by line.

16. Philip Edwards, "Shakespeare's Romances: 1900–1957," *Shakespeare Survey* 11 (1958): 1–18, 5.

17. Roger Warren, ed., *Pericles* (Oxford: Oxford University Press, 2003), 8.

18. Helen Cooper, "'This worthy olde writer': *Pericles* and Other Gowers, 1592–1640," in *A Companion to Gower*, ed. Sian Echard (Cambridge: D. S. Brewer, 2004), 105.

19. Ibid., 109.

20. *Middle English Dictionary*, ed. Hans Kurath (Ann Arbor: University of Michigan Press, 1952–2001).

21. The complexity of this word is usefully explored in relation to Langland's complex sense of "kynde knowing" by Sister Clemente Davlin in "'Kynde Knowing' as a Middle English Equivalent for 'Wisdom' in Piers Plowman B," in *Medium Aevum* (1981), 5–15; Teresa Tavormina, *Kindly Similitude: Marriage and Family in Piers Plowman* (Cambridge: D. S. Brewer, 1995); James Simpson, *Piers Plowman: An Introduction* (Exeter: University of Exeter Press, 2007); and Nicolette Zeeman, *Piers Plowman and the Medieval Discourse of Desire* (Cambridge: Cambridge University Press, 2006).

22. Terence Cave, *Recognitions: A Study in Poetics* (Oxford: Oxford University Press, 1988), 290. In his stunning chapter on *Pericles,* Thomas Bishop has extended this perception: Marina and not just her virginity is a glass reflecting back images of her clients: "Marina can be taken as an emblem of Shakespearean representation itself, at least in one of its aspects," *Shakespeare and the Theater of Wonder,* 111.

23. William Robbins, "Romance, Exemplum, and the Subject of the *Confessio Amantis,*" in *Studies in the Age of Chaucer* 19 (1997): 157–81.

24. Jonathan Bate, *Shakespeare and Ovid* (Oxford: Clarendon Press, 1993), 220.

25. Lawrence Twine, *The Patterne of Painefull Adventures,* in *Narrative and Dramatic Sources of Shakespeare,* ed. Geoffrey Bullough, vol. 6 (London: Routledge and Kegan Paul, 1966), 457.

26. The production took place in the summer of 2003. It had been preceded by a small-scale one-hour-long version with five actors, which played to refugee groups around the country. "We told the story of Pericles and they told us stories back, by turns amazing, shocking, unbelievable, painful, normal," www.cardboardcitizens.org.uk/index.php?pid=2&subid=25, accessed June 6, 2009.

27. Stanley Cavell, *The Claim of Reason* (Oxford: Oxford University Press, 1979), see especially chaps. 4 and 7.

28. Steven Affeldt has some very helpful comments in his essay "The Ground of Mutuality: Criteria, Judgment, and Intelligibility," in *European Journal of Philosophy* 6 (1998): 1–31.

29. For a fine analysis of this exquisite scene, see Inga-Stina Ewbank, "'My Name is Marina': The Language of Recognition," in *Shakespeare's Styles: Essays in Honour of Kenneth Muir,* ed. Philip Edwards, Inga-Stina Ewbank, and G. K. Hunter (Cambridge: Cambridge University Press, 2004), 126, where she notes that three times in this scene speaking is identified with delivering: "The miracle lies latent in what is happening, but it is born to us through what is spoken." See also C. L. Barber, "'Thou that beget'st him that did thee beget': Transformation in *Pericles* and *The Winter's Tale,*" *Shakespeare Survey* 22 (1969): 59–67. See also Marianne Novy, *Reading Adoption: Family and Difference in Fiction and Drama* (Ann Arbor: University of Michigan Press, 2008), chap. 3 on recognition in Shakespearean families.

30. Or: "my fader, ho so that it stoned, / Your tale is herd and understonde, / As thing which worthi is to hiere / Of gret ensaunple and matiere / Wherof, my fader, god you quyte. / Bot in this point myself acquite / I mai riht wel, that nevere yit / I was assoted in my wit / But only in that worthi place / Wher alle lust and alle grace / Is set, if that danger ne were" (*CA* 8. 2029–39).

31. Here I respectfully disagree with Steven Mullaney's understanding of Shakespeare's Gower. Mullaney claims that Gower for Shakespeare is a "unique figure," not "the voice of history" or of time but rather representing timeless authority. See "'All That Monarchs Do': The Obscured Stages of Authority in *Pericles,*" from *The Place of the Stage* (Chicago: University of Chicago Press, 1988), 135–53, reprinted in *Pericles: Critical Essays,* ed. David Skeele (New York: Garland, 2000), 179. On the contrary, it was Shakespeare's careful reading of Gower, who turns out to have been a version of the lover all along, that informs his invocation of Gower's "authority," which is not timeless at all but utterly time-bound—tied to an incarnate body, resurrected in the conditions of theater, which may or may not be able to receive his story. Gower, as it were, outs himself as an old man ill suited to love but told by Venus to write edifying poetry.

32. Bishop, *Shakespeare and the Theater of Wonder,* 94.

33. I am not of the opinion that Pericles is atoning for anything in this play. Some stagings have Pericles' failure to rescue Antiochus's daughter as the crime/sin which demands atonement

through suffering. This seems to me a fundamental misreading of the first scene. Difficult as it is to parse out from the incredibly corrupt text, the first scene suggests to me that Pericles has knowledge (he works out the riddle of incest) which precisely cannot be acknowledged or expressed. So I am not arguing that *Pericles* is a play about forgiveness in the same way as *Cymbeline, The Winter's Tale,* and *The Tempest*. But I am suggesting that the play stages the restoration of self and community through expression, restoring the world through language. This is to grant the expressiveness that is obviated in the private language fantasy, a fantasy that has taken even deeper hold in the pervasive notion of a "gap" between inner and outer, between mind and world, which is a major (and understandable) form of retreat from the coercive public forms of a culture that definitely wanted to make windows into the souls of its subjects.

5. Acknowledgment and Confession in *Cymbeline*

1. This is important in Aquinas's unfinished treatment of penance in the *Summa Theologiae*. Aquinas tells us that repentance is a virtue which he has previously defined, after Aristotle in the Nicomachean Ethics, as "a habit of choosing according to right reason," *ST* 3.85.1. He explains that penitence grieves when there is good reason to grieve in proportion to the magnitude of the sins and with the full intention to get rid of them. He further argues that it is a virtue or a virtuous act, not just an emotion. He has previously explained that the *actions* pertaining to penance are performed "both on the part of the penitent sinner, and on the part of the priest absolving" that signify something holy, *ST* 3.85.1. ad.1. He goes on to give a description of penance in terms of the familiar scholastic vocabulary of form and matter. What the penitent says gives material for the sacrament and what the priest says gives it form. In fact, "the matter of penance is not God, but human acts," *ST* 3.85.2.ad 2.

2. See Timothy Gould, *Hearing Things: Voice and Method in the Writing of Stanley Cavell* (Chicago: University of Chicago Press, 1998), 70: "An unexpressed confession (which is not the same as a tacit, or unspoken, confession) is not a confession. The act of *making* a confession is indispensable to the existence of the confession." My chapter on *Pericles,* I hope, will have brought out one dimension of the fact or act of speaking, and this chapter shows the centrality of confession to *Cymbeline*. That confession must be performed might well strike one as being obvious, but the commitments secured through the act of confession are obscured by a long and still tenacious history by which thoughts are depicted as mental objects accessible only to the one whose mind they are in. The history of confession is then treated as part of the history and growth of an interiority. In the *Trialogus,* for example, Wyclif had declared that true penance exists in the mind, an assertion whose implications are well understood by Thomas Netter in his refutation of the epistemological implications of such a view. See *Doctrinale* 2.766–72 and the discussion in Alistair Minnis, *Fallible Authors: Chaucer's Pardoner and the Wife of Bath* (Philadelphia: University of Pennsylvania Press, 2008), 274ff. Wittgenstein contends with confession in relation to the "hidden internal" in part II of the *Philosophical Investigations,* section xi, p. 222. The criteria for the truthfulness of a confession as understood by Wittgenstein is not that it describes inner events, but that it is taken up by others; see Richard Eldridge, *Leading a Human Life: Wittgenstein, Intentionality, and Romanticism* (Chicago: University of Chicago Press, 1997), 131.

3. Wittgenstein, *Philosophical Investigations,* 3rd ed., trans. G.E.M. Anscombe (Oxford: Wiley—Blackwell, 1991) from Remark 546: "And words can be wrung from us—like a cry. Words can be *hard* to say: such for example, as can be used to effect a renunciation, or to confess a weakness: Words are also deeds."

4. Though it is important, as I will go on to show, that the king's pardon comes after the spontaneous confessions of the community created through their acts of speech.

5. Raimond Gaita, *Good and Evil: An Absolute Conception* (London: Routledge, 2004, 1st ed., 1991), 52, and for further reflections, see chapter 6, "Shakespeare's Resurrections."

6. James Wetzel, "Wittgenstein's Augustine: The Inauguration of the Later Philosophy," in *Polygraph* 19/20, ed. Russ Leo, special issue, *Cities of Men, Cities of God: Augustine and Late Secularism.* This excellent essay addresses the whole question of the secularization of confession in fascinating ways.

7. See Augustine's *Confession,* trans. Henry Chadwick (Oxford: Oxford University Press, 1991), book 10, chapter 3, where Augustine contemplates the audience for confession.

8. Peter Lombard, *Sententiae in IV libris* distinctae, 4.171.13; Duns Scotus, *Oxford Commentary on the Sentences,* 4.16.1.7.

9. It is fascinating to see that this image of the soul likened to a coin with the king's stamp on it has an important history in accounts of human and divine agency. David Aers has recently argued that it is a central image for Ockham's thoroughly extrinsicist account of the workings of divine grace. Ockham's image for the grace at work in the sacraments is a leaden denarius bestowed by a sovereign will. He contrasts this with Aquinas's model of grace patterned on the human voice, for him an indication that spiritual powers can be in a body instrumentally (*ST* 3.62.4ad.1). For Ockham's image see his commentary on the fourth book of Peter Lombard's *Sentences: Scriptum super libros sententiarum, VI. 6.* See David Aers, *Salvation and Sin: Augustine, Langland and Fourteenth-Centry Theology* (Notre Dame: University of Notre Dame Press, 2009), 51. Aers's illuminating commentary on different models of human and divine agency as competitive or cooperative is highly relevant to Shakespeare's late work. The extremely theatrical forms of intervention in the late plays—oracle, heavenly music, Jupiter on his eagle—are the frame for what I have termed Shakespeare's miracles of the ordinary.

10. For this beautiful formulation, see Gaita's chapter 4, "Remorse and Its Lessons," *Good and Evil,* 49. The entire rich chapter is a deep meditation on the ethics of remorse and the philosophical tradition of thought about it.

11. Martin Butler, ed., *Cymbeline* (Cambridge: Cambridge University Press, 2005), notes to 5.3.122, p. 216; Roger Warren, ed., *Cymbeline* (Oxford: Oxford University Press, 1998), 232. Greenblat, Cohen, Howard, and Maus, eds., *Cymbeline* in the *Norton Shakespeare* (New York: Norton, 1997) interestingly does not mention sin but glosses "bonds" as "these old legal agreements; these cruel links with life; these harsh fetters," 3029, fn. 5. The language of bonds is also invoked in the exchange of tokens that precedes Posthumus's banishment from Cymbeline's court. The bracelet that Posthumus gives Imogen is "a manacle of love," and with it Imogen becomes his "fairest prisoner" (1.1.123–24). I return to this idea later on in this chapter.

12. Bishop's Bible, in *The New Testament Octapla: Early English Versions of the New Testament in the Tyndale–King James Tradition* (Edinburgh: Thomas Nelson & Sons, 1946), 97.

13. Thomas Becon, *The Castle of Comfort,* in *The Early Works Of Thomas Becon,* vol. 3, ed. John Ayre (Cambridge: The University Press, 1843), 556; John Jewel, *The Defence of the Apology of the Church of England* in *The Works of John Jewel, Bishop of Salisbury,* ed. John Ayre for the Parker Society, 4 vols. (Cambridge: The University Press, 1845–50), 3:369. Hooker explores the issue in Book 6 of *Of the Lawes of Ecclesiastical Polity* (Cambridge: Harvard University Press, 1981), vol. 3, ed. P. G. Stanwood, 14: "Our lord and Saviour in the 16th of St. Matthewes Ghospell giveth his Apostles regiment in generall, over God's Church. For they that have the keyes of the Kingdome of heaven are thereby signified to be stewards of the house of god, under whom they guide, command, judge and correct the family."

14. I don't have time in this chapter to explore the way the providential plot of *Cymbeline* ("the more delayed delighted") negates every effort made by Posthumus to run his own fate and the questions of grace and agency this raises.

15. On the keys see chapter 2.

16. *Institutes* 3.3.10.

17. Lancelot Andrewes, from *Ninety Six Sermons by the Right Honourable and Reverend Father in God, Lancelot Andrewes, Sometime Bishop of Winchester,* vol. 5 (Oxford: John Henry Parker,

1843; New York: AMS Press, 1967). Andrewes's sermon defends the work of the ministry in the act of absolution.

18. When Lancelot Andrewes was appointed to the parish of St. Giles Cripplegate, he sought to revive the practice of Lenten confession; see *Lancelot Andrewes: Selected Sermons and Lectures,* ed. Peter McCullough (Oxford: Oxford University Press, 2005), xviii. For "avant-garde conformity" see Peter Lake, "Lancelot Andrewes, John Buckeridge, and Avant-Garde Conformity at the Court of James I," in *The Mental World of the Court of James I,* ed. Linda Levy Peck (Cambridge: Cambridge University Press, 1991), 113–33.

19. H. J. Schroeder, ed., *Disciplinary Decrees of the General Councils* (St. Louis: B. Herder, 1937), 259–60.

20. William Tyndale, *The Obedience of a Christian Man,* 117: "Shrift in the ear is verily a work of Satan." Repentance obviates confession for Tyndale: "When a man feeleth that his hert consenteth to the law of God, and feeleth himself meek, patient, courteous and merciful to his neighbour, altered and fashioned like to Christ, why should he doubt but that God hath forgiven him and chosen him and put his spirit in him, though he never cram his sin into the priest's ear?" (118). Tyndale's question—"Why should he doubt?"—was not met with the same blithe confidence that he expresses here by the many thousands for whom it would become the key pastoral problem, the central question of practical divinity, and the main cause of a rash of suicides in the early seventeenth century. This is the territory explored in John Stachniewski, *The Persecutory Imagination: English Puritanism and the Literature of Religious Despair* (Oxford: Clarendon Press, 1991).

21. *The Book of Common Prayer 1559: The Elizabethan Prayer Book,* ed. John Booty (Charlottesville: University of Virginia Press, 1976), 257. See now also Timothy Rosendale, *Liturgy and Literature in the Making of Protestant England* (Cambridge: Cambridge University Press, 2007), especially p. 94, for the "attenuation of sacerdotal and institutional significance" regarding confession and absolution in the 1549 prayerbook.

22. Patrick Collinson, *From Cranmer to Sancroft* (London: M.P.G. Books Ltd., 2006), 72.

23. See Debora Shugar, "The Reformation of Penance" in *Huntington Library Quarterly* 71.4 (2008): 557–73, especially p. 569 for the carry-over from medieval practices of the extra-liturgical rites of reconciliation. See also John Bossy, *Peace in the Post-Reformation* (Cambridge: Cambridge University Press, 1998), and my chapter 7. I am grateful to Deborah Shugar for conversation on this point.

24. Morning Prayer, in *The Book of Common Prayer 1559,* ed. Booty, 50.

25. Ibid., 357.

26. The "commonality" of common prayer is a central point in Ramie Targoff, *Common Prayer: The Language of Public Devotion in Early Modern England* (Chicago: University of Chicago Press, 2001), 28–35.

27. Morning Prayer, in *The Book of Common Prayer 1559,* ed. Booty, 50.

28. Ibid., 259.

29. "And there shall be no celebration of the Lord's Supper except there be a good number to communicate with the priest, according to his discretion," ibid., 267.

30. The impossibility of separating out abuses from ceremony is addressed in the preface to the BCP, "Of Ceremonies, Why some be abolished and Some retained," 20.

31. Quoted in Antjie Krog, *Country of My Skull: Guilt, Sorrow, and the Limits of Forgiveness in the New South Africa* (New York: Random House, 1998), 23.

32. It is fascinating to see how Richard Greenham addressed the question of a sense of generalized depravity, as opposed to the (more humbling) specifications of particular sins: "He told me…when any came with a troubled conscience for syn, wisely to discern whither they bee meanly greeved, with a general and roving sight of ther sins, or whither they bee extreamly throughn down, with the burden of particular sins; if so they bee, then it is good at the first to shew that noe syn is so great, but in christ it is pardonable, and that ther is mercy with god that hee might bee

feared. Soe on the one side shewing mercy to come from god, but soe as they are nothing fit to re-
ceiv mercy, unless they feel ther particular and prockt sins. But if ther sorrow bee more confused
in general things, then it is good to humble them more and more, to give them a terror of gods justice, for particular sins. For experience doth teach us, that this is the best way to see sin and to bee
humbled to see sin, because often men wil acknowledge greater sins they have been in, then that
little (sin) they presently ly in": *"Practical Divinity": The Works and Life of Revd Richard Greenham,*
ed. Kenneth L. Parker and Eric J. Carlson (Aldershot: Ashgate, 1998), 161. For a map of the very
numerous "pastoralia" sponsored by the legislation of the Fourth Lateran, see Leonard E. Boyle,
"The Fourth Lateran Council and the Manuals of Popular Theology," in *The Popular Literature
of Medieval England,* ed. Thomas J. Heffernan (Knoxville: University of Tennessee Press, 1985),
30–43; the essays in Boyle, *Pastoral Care, Clerical Education and Canon Law, 1200–1400* (London:
Varorium Reprints, 1981); Pierre Michaud-Quantin, *Sommes de casuistique et manuels de confession
au moyen âge (XII–XVI siècles)* (Louvain: Analecta mediaevalia Namurcensia, 1962); and Joseph
Goering, "The Internal Forum and the Literature of Penance and Confession," in *History of Medieval Canon Law,* ed. W. Hartmann and K. Pennington (Washington, DC: Catholic University
Press of America, 2001), 1–75.

    33. George Eliot, *Middlemarch* (Oxford: Oxford University Press, 1996), 493.

    34. Ibid., 492. See here also Michael Neill, "'The Language of the Heart': Confession, Meta-
phor, and Grace in J. M. Coetzee's *Age of Iron,*" in *New Windows on a Woman's World: Scholarly
Writing in Honour of Jocelyn Harris,* ed. Colin Gibson and Lisa Marr (Dunedin: University of
Otago Press, 2005), 515–43. I am grateful to Michael Neill for sending me a copy of this essay in
advance of publication. See also Coetzee's essay "Confession and Double Thoughts: Tolstoy, Dos-
toyevsky, and Rousseau," in *Comparative Literature* 37 (1985): 193–232.

    35. John Field and Thomas Wilcox's "Admonition to Parliament" is published in *Puritan
Manifestoes: A Study of the Origins of Puritan Revolt,* ed. Walter Howard Frere (London: S.P.C.K.,
1954). The long debate on "the discipline" is conducted across a range of voluminous texts including those of Walter Travers and Cartwright and Whitgift's responses to Cartwright in the 1570s,
and of course in the works of Richard Hooker. See John Whitgift, *Works,* ed. John Ayre (Cambridge: The University Press, 1851–53), published for the Parker Society, vols. 46–48.

    36. The "discipline" was to locate church elders as having power to be judges in all cases of
conscience, and to have authority to excommunicate, suspend from the church, and absolve. They
were to have the power to choose and depose officers in the church. Moreover this institution was
an essential: it would involve the abolition of the bishopric, the ecclesiastical courts, and the dis-
mantling of the current relations between church and commonwealth. For an exploration of the
literature of discipline, especially in the works of George Herbert, see Kenneth Graham, "George
Herbert and the Discipline of History," in *JMEMS* 31.2 (2001): 349–78.

    37. J. L. Austin, *How to Do Things with Words,* 2nd ed., ed. J. O. Urmson and Marina Sbisa
(Cambridge: Harvard University Press, 1975), 110.

    38. Stanley Cavell, "Performative and Passionate Utterance," in *Philosophy the Day after To-
morrow* (Cambridge: Harvard University Press, 2005), 172–73.

    39. For Austin as "skittish about emotion," see ibid., 156. The reasons for that skittishness are
spelled out with extraordinary acumen in the essential companion essay to "Performative and Passionate Utterance," "Counter-Philosophy and the Pawn of Voice," in *A Pitch of Philosophy: Autobiographical Exercises* (Cambridge: Harvard University Press, 1996).

    40. "Perlocutionary verbs not only do not name what they do (as to say the illocution-
ary 'I promise, beseech, order, banish…you' *is* to promise, beseech, order, banish you), they can
not…unprotectedly be said at all: to utter, "I seduce, alarm, amuse…you," is not only not to *do*
anything, it is in an obvious sense not so much as to *say* anything (yet)," "Performative and Passionate Utterance,'" 171. Cavell prefers to say: "the illocutionary act is, we might say, built into the
verb that names it" (172).

41. Ibid., 172.

42. Ibid., 189 for the "you" coming into the picture; and for Cavell's examples, see p. 173.

43. Ibid., 173.

44. Such as, for example, the one in *Monumenta Ritualia Ecclesiae Anglicanae,* ed. William Maskell, 3 vols. (Oxford: Clarendon Press, 1882), 3:293–303, or among myriad examples, Jean Gerson, *On the Art of Hearing Confession,* in P. Glorieux, ed., *Oeuvres complètes* (Paris: Desclée, 1960–), vol. 7, section 11.

45. See, for example, John Mirk, *Instructions for Parish Priests,* lines 923ff.

46. For an excellent analysis of the circumstances and causes of sin in the confessional, see Dallas G. Denerey II, *Seeing and Being Seen in the Later Medieval World: Optics, Theology, and Religious Life* (Cambridge: Cambridge University Press, 2005), chap. 2, "The Devil in Human Form: Confession, Deception, and Self-Knowledge," 39–74.

47. Or to a lay person *in extremis.*

48. On the completeness of confession, see the illuminating words of David Myers, *"Poor Sinning Folk": Confession and Conscience in Counter-Reformation Germany* (Ithaca: Cornell University Press, 1996), 165.

49. From the succinct summary in Stanley Cavell, "The Incessance and the Absence of the Political," in *The Claim to Community: Essays on Stanley Cavell and Political Philosophy,* ed. Andrew Norris (Stanford: Stanford University Press, 2006), 272.

50. See Julie Paulson, "A Theater of the Soul's Interior: Contemplative Literature and Penitential Education in the Morality Play *Wisdom,*" in *JMEMS* 38.2 (2008): 253–84.

51. All quotations from *The Castle of Perseverance* and from *Mankind* are taken from the editions in *The Macro Plays, EETS* 262, ed. Mark Eccles (Oxford: Oxford University Press, 1969).

52. The main trouble in *The Castle* is the ubiquitous, pervasive nature of Covetousness. Covetousness is the very mechanism of worldliness in the play, and constantly obstructs the performance of the works of mercy.

53. The Parson's Tale, in *The Riverside Chaucer,* 3rd ed., general editor, Larry D. Benson (Boston: Houghton Mifflin, 1987), l. 696.

54. Much of the criticism of the morality play tradition confuses naming and calling. It understands the dramatis personae as abstractions, not people, and tends to confuse examples with generalizations. The difference here, as Toril Moi has taught us, is that it is possible to generalize from a particular case without putting one's subjectivity on the line. But it is impossible to see one's own experience as an instance of a more general cause without staking oneself in one's claims. Essential here is Stanley Cavell's seminal essay "Must We Mean What We Say?" in *Must We Mean What We Say?* (Cambridge: Cambridge University Press, 1969, updated ed., 2002), 19, and see also Toril Moi's admirably lucid explication in *What Is a Woman? and Other Essays* (Oxford: Oxford University Press, 1999).

55. Cavell, *The Claim of Reason,* 206ff.

56. For this important distinction see David Schalwyck, *Speech and Performance in Shakespeare's Sonnets and Plays* (Cambridge: Cambridge University Press, 2002), p. 15–16. See also the same author's "Shakespeare's Speech," *JMEMS* 40.2 (Spring 2010): 373–400.

57. See chapter 6 on *The Winter's Tale* and also Cavell, "Counter-Philosophy and the Pawn of Voice," 115.

58. *Philosophical Investigations,* Remark 432: "Every sign *by itself* seems dead. *What* gives it life?—In use it is alive. Is life breathed into it there? Or is the *use* its life?"

59. Raimond Gaita, *A Common Humanity: Thinking about Love and Truth and Justice* (London: Routledge, 1998), 221.

60. Lewis Hyde, *The Gift: How the Creative Spirit Transforms the World* (Edinburgh: Canongate, 2006), first published 1979. He goes on to say: "It is true that when a gift enhances our life, or even saves it, gratitude will bind us to the donor. Until it is expressed that is. Gratitude, acted

upon or simply spoken, releases the gift and lightens the obligations of affection between lovers, family, and comrades.... It is not for a theory of gift exchange to explain why we so often enter and maintain relationships that have in them no life to offer" (73). One might also here think of the many commentaries that draw attention to the "as" in "Forgive us as we are forgiven" in the Lord's Prayer.

61. I am indebted to both Nancy Bauer and Richard Fleming for their comments and readings of Austin and Wittgenstein in a series of workshops held at Duke University on Ordinary Language Philosophy in 2007–2009. See Cavell's fascinating and important comments on Austin's idea of "our word is our bond" in "Counter-Philosophy and the Pawn of Voice," 101, 120.

62. A remark of Cavell's is also relevant here: "And confession, unlike dogma, is not to be believed but tested, and accepted or rejected. Nor is it the occasion for accusation, except of yourself, and by implication those who find themselves in you," "The Availability of Wittgenstein's Later Philosophy," in *Must We Mean What We Say?*, 71. The distinction between this understanding of confession and the new sense of confession as a (dogmatic) declaration of faith as, for example, in the Augsburg Confession, should now be apparent. Indeed it is this sense of confession that determines the historiographical paradigm of confessionalization as it is developed from the work of Heinz Schilling and Wolfgang Reinhard. See Heinz Schilling, *Die Konfessionkonflict und Staatsbildung* (Gütersloh: Gütersloher Verlagshaus, 1981), and Wolfgang Reinhard, "Zwang zur Konfessionalisierung? Prologemena zu einer Theorie des konsfessionellen Zeitalters," in *Zeitschrift für historische Forschung* 10 (1983): 257–77. In this paradigm, confession is the declaration of an allegiance, an allegiance closely connected with the articulation of dogmatic or doctrinal difference.

63. This is explored most profoundly in Book 10 of Augustine's *Confessions.* I owe this formulation and this analysis to Paul Griffith in his excellent book *Lying: An Augustinian Theology of Duplicity* (Grand Rapids, MI: Brazos Press, 2004), 92–93. Griffith's book is an exploration of Augustine's exceptionless ban on the lie. A lie "grasps the gift, owning it in imagination, and, so, sinning." For Augustine, according to Griffiths, it is therefore performatively incoherent because: "Speech is a gift given, and a condition of its use is that it is received as such" (93).

64. For a fascinating analysis of recognition as gift, see Mark Rogin Anspach, *A charge de revanche: Figures élémentaires de la réciprocité* (Paris: Seuil, 2002), and Paul Ricoeur, *The Course of Recognition,* trans. David Pellauer (Cambridge: Cambridge University Press, 2005), especially, chap. 3.

6. Shakespeare's Resurrections

1. I don't have time in this essay to pursue the Shakespearean "resurrections" of the late plays as conscious reworkings of the earlier spectres, but for a beginning, see Richard Kearney's helpful recent assessment of readings of Hamlet's ghost, "Spectres of *Hamlet,*" in *Spiritual Shakespeares,* ed. Ewan Fernie (London: Routledge, 2005), 157–85.

2. See Elizabeth Williamson, "Things Newly Performed: The Resurrection Tradition in Shakespeare's Plays," in *Shakespeare and Religious Change,* ed. Kenneth J. E. Graham and Philip D. Collington (Houndmills: Palgrave Macmillan, 2009), 110–32; Karen Marsalek, "Marvels and Counterfeits: False Resurrections in the Chester *Antichrist* and *I Henry IV,*" in *Shakespeare and the Middle Ages,* ed. Curtis Perry and John Watkins (Oxford: Oxford University Press, 2009), 217–40; and Sean Benson, *Shakespearean Resurrection: The Art of Almost Raising the Dead* (Pittsburgh: Duquesne University Press, 2009), which all came to my attention as I completed a draft of this book.

3. This is beautifully explored by Piero Boitani, "To Recognize Is a God: Helen, Mary Magdalene, Marina-Menuchim," chap. 5 of his *The Bible and Its Rewritings* (Oxford: Oxford University Press, 1999), 130–81.

4. *Measure for Measure,* 3.1.148–51: "Thy sin's not accidental, but a trade. Mercy to thee would prove itself a bawd. / 'Tis best that thou diest quickly."

5. *Much Ado about Nothing,* 5.4.66–67, best encapsulates the movement from funeral to wedding: to Don Pedro's amazed response—"the former Hero, Hero that is dead!"—Leonato replies: "She died, my lord, but whiles her slander lived," anticipating Leontes' brutal, petrifying slandering of Hermione.

6. *Pericles,* 5.1.

7. It is just these transformations worked through the grace of forgiveness that allow for a future at all, that allow for the possibility that the sinner can recognize his victim as his hope: Rowan Williams, *Resurrection: Interpreting the Easter Gospel* (Harrisburg, PA: Morehouse, 1982), 11.

8. Such resurrections may be the vehicles of mortifying shame, a shame that nevertheless is a reminder of a fundamental connectedness with others. In his chapter "Remorse" in *Lost Icon: Reflections on Cultural Bereavement* (Edinburgh: T. & T. Clark, 2000), Rowan Williams reflects that remorse, honor, and shame are "areas of our human experience and discourse" that "are unintelligible except on the assumption that my past, my publicly identifiable history, the story that can be told of me, does not *belong* exclusively to me" (104). The deeply Wittgensteinian reflections in this work on remorse are a guiding influence on this chapter, as are those of Raimond Gaita (see below). For a further meditation on the challenge presented by shame and remorse to the liberal discourse of rights, see W. James Booth, *Communities of Memory: On Witness, Identity, and Justice* (Ithaca: Cornell University Press, 2006), 40, 67.

9. This is of course the burden of Stanley Cavell's brilliant analysis of Leontes as skeptic in his essay "Recounting Gains, Showing Losses: Reading *The Winter's Tale,*" reprinted in his *Disowning Knowledge in Seven Plays of Shakespeare* (Cambridge: Cambridge University Press, 2003; 1st ed., 1987). Cavell's analysis of Shakespearean tragedy is part of his profound redefinition of skepticism in *The Claim of Reason: Wittgenstein, Skepticism, Morality, and Tragedy* (Oxford: Oxford University Press, 1979, updated ed., 1999). See also "Knowing and Acknowledging" and "The Avoidance of Love: A Reading of King Lear" in *Must We Mean What We Say?* (Cambridge: Cambridge University Press, 1976, rpt. 2002). I analyze the language of acknowledgment in Cavell's sense in "The Play of Voice: Acknowledgment, Knowledge, and Self-Knowledge in *Measure for Measure,*" in *Spectacle and Public Performance in the Late Middle Ages and the Renaissance,* ed. Robert E. Stillman (Leiden: Brill, 2006), 121–44.

10. Nashe is here talking about atheists in *Christ's Tears over Jerusalem* in *The Unfortunate Traveller and Other Works,* ed. J. B. Steane (Harmondsworth: Penguin, 1972, rpt. 1982), 479: "most of them, because they cannot grossly palpabrize or feel God with their bodily fingers, confidently and grossly discard Him."

11. By this I mean that Christians know Christian truths only by virtue of being transformed by the Christian story. See, for example, Stanley Hauerwas, *Performing the Faith: Bonhoeffer and the Practice of Nonviolence* (Grand Rapids, MI: Brazos Press, 2004), esp. part 11; William T. Cavanaugh, *Torture and Eucharist: Theology, Politics, and the Body of Christ* (Oxford: Blackwell, 1998), and Sarah Beckwith, *Signifying God: Symbolic Act in the York Corpus Christi Plays* (Chicago: University of Chicago Press, 2001).

12. David Steinmetz in "Reformation and Grace," in *Grace upon Grace: Essays in Honor of Thomas A. Langford,* ed. Robert K. Johnston, L. Gregory Jones, and Jonathan R. Wilson (Nashville: Abingdon Press, 1999), 75.

13. Ibid.: "Reformers were convinced that only those who love God hate sin. Thoroughly unconverted sinners are perfect children in their knowledge of sin" (83).

14. Richard Hooker, *Of the Laws of Ecclesiastical Polity: Books VI, VII, VIII,* ed. Peter Stanwood (Cambridge: Harvard University Press, 1981), book VI, chap. 6, 97, vol. 3 of *The Folger Library Edition of the Works of Richard Hooker,* ed. W. Speed Hill, 7 vols. (Cambridge: Harvard University Press, 1977–1998). Book VI was not printed until 1648. See Peter Stanwood's introduction for the complex textual history of this book.

15. J. L. Austin, *How to Do Things with Words* (Cambridge: Harvard University Press), 151.

16. Hooker, *Of the Laws,* book VI, 97.

17. See chapter 3.

18. Rowan Williams, *Lost Icons: Reflections on Cultural Bereavement* (Edinburgh: T. & T. Clark, 2000), 104.

19. Hannah Arendt, *The Human Condition* (Chicago: University of Chicago Press, 1998, 1st ed., 1958), 243.

20. Raimond Gaita, *Good and Evil: An Absolute Conception* (London: Routledge, 2004, 1st ed., 1991), xxi.

21. Ibid., 52.

22. The imbrication of church and theater, as of the sacraments of penance and eucharist, especially as they are understood in the "sacramental theater" of the mystery cycles, is the topic of my book *Signifying God.*

23. Arendt, *The Human Condition,* 237.

24. John 21.9, *The Bishop's Bible in The New Testament Octapla: Eight English Versions of the New Testament in the Tyndale–King James Tradition,* ed. Luther A. Weigle (Edinburgh: Thomas Nelson & Sons, 1946).

25. Williams, *Resurrection,* 118: "If…[the apparitions] were fundamentally experiences of restoring grace, they take their places in a concrete, shared human history of hope, betrayal, violence and guilt, and are evidenced *not* by individual report but by the continuing existence of the community in which this history is caught up and redeemed."

26. For some lovely reflections on Robert Southwell's *Saint Peter's Complaint* and Peter's remorse, see Brian Cummings, *The Literary Culture of the Reformation: Grammar and Grace* (Oxford: Oxford University Press, 2002), 246ff.

27. *The Towneley Plays,* 2 vols., ed. Martin Stevens and A. C. Cawley (Oxford: Oxford University Press, 1994), *EETS* s.s. 13, vol. 1, *Thomas of India,* Play 28, ll. 8, 29–30.

28. *The Resurrection,* Play 18, ll. 402ff., 414–18, in *The Chester Mystery Cycle,* 2 vols., vol. 1, ed. R. M. Lumiansky and David Mills (Oxford: Oxford University Press, 1974), *EETS* s.s. 3.

29. *Christ's Resurrection,* in *The Late Medieval Religious Plays of Bodleian MSS. Digby 133 and E Museo 160,* ed. Donald C. Baker, John L. Murphy, and Louis B. Hall Jr. (Oxford: Oxford University Press, 1982), 287.

30. *Resurrection,* ll. 343–48, Play 26 of *The Towneley Plays.*

31. Thomas in Towneley's *Thomas of India,* ll. 405, 494, Peter at l. 8 and Jesus' response at 135. Peter in Chester's *Christ on the Road to Emmaus,* l. 175, and again in *The Ascension,* l. 18.

32. *OED.*

33. Robert Stanley Forsyth, in *The Relation of Shirley's Plays to the Elizabethan Drama* (New York, 1914), 89, cited in B. J. Sokol, *Art and Illusion in The Winter's Tale* (Manchester: Manchester University Press, 1994), 239, fn. 72, lists over a hundred uses of this motif.

34. Peter Womack, *English Renaissance Drama* (Oxford: Blackwell, 2006), 303.

35. This play, formerly known as *The Second Maiden's Tragedy* (provisionally so titled by the Master of the Revels), has recently been decisively attributed to Middleton and is edited by Julia Briggs in *Thomas Middleton: Collected Works,* ed. Gary Taylor and John Lavagnino (Oxford: Clarendon Press, 2007). All citations from this path-breaking and exciting new edition of the collected works are from the left-hand text column, which is as close as possible to Middleton's original composition.

36. *The Lady's Tragedy,* 4.4.43. See Beckwith, *Signifying God,* chap. 5, for more on Easter Rites in relation to tropes of resurrection.

37. Womack, *English Renaissance Drama,* 303.

38. For reflection on the aporias of forgiveness, see John Milbank, *Being Reconciled: Ontology and Pardon* (London: Routledge, 2003), and for some thoughts on *The Winter's Tale* in the same book, see "Grace: The Midwinter Sacrifice," chap. 8.

39. For Ovid, Pygmalion, and *The Winter's Tale,* see Leonard Barkan, *The Gods Made Flesh: Metamorphosis and the Pursuit of Paganism* (New Haven: Yale University Press, 1986), 283–87.

40. For Stanley Cavell's idea of *The Winter's Tale* as remarriage comedy, see Cavell, *The Pursuits of Happiness: The Hollywood Comedy of Remarriage* (Cambridge: Harvard University Press, 1981), 19.

41. From my *Signifying God,* xv.

42. *The Sermons of John Donne,* ed. George R. Potter and Evelyn Simpson, 10 vols. (Berkeley: University of California Press, 1953–62), 7:216.

43. *Twelfth Night,* 5.1.226–29: "I never had a brother / Nor can there be that deity in my nature / Of here and everywhere."

44. Stephen Greenblatt, *Hamlet in Purgatory* (Princeton: Princeton University Press, 2001), 307.

45. *Calvin: Institutes of the Christian Religion,* 2 vols. (Louisville: Westminster John Knox Press, 1960), 1.4.17.6, p. 1366.

46. Marcion was a mid-second-century Christian thinker who maintained that the God of the Jews was not the God of Jesus, and that Christ was a phantom.

47. *Institutes* 4.17.17, p. 1380.

48. John 20.8–9, *Bishop's Bible.*

49. A point made in Rowan A. Greer, *Christian Life and Christian Hope: Raids on the Inarticulate* (New York: Crossroad, 2001).

50. In Joannem, tract 29, no. 6. For vital commentary on the distinction between *credere Deum, credere Deo,* and *credere in Deum,* see Henri de Lubac, *The Christian Faith: An Essay on the Apostle's Creed* (San Francisco: Ignatius Press, 1986), 141. I am most grateful to David Aers for pointing me toward de Lubac here.

51. See Wilfred Cantwell Smith, *Believing: A Historical Perspective* (Oxford: One World, 1977). Cantwell Smith charts the modernizing tendency to make "belief" propositional and its ancient and medieval use as predominantly part of a "credo." He observes that Shakespeare's use of "belief" is nearly always in the form of a verb, not a noun, and furthermore that the first- and second-person uses of that verb outnumber the third-person uses by a ratio of nine to one. This observation rests on the crucial distinction between "I believe" and "he believes." "I believe" is not only self-engaging but descriptive of the external world, but "he believes" is descriptive only of his state of mind. For example, "I believe that it is raining" is a statement about the weather. "He believes that it is raining" is not.

52. This is importantly explored in Charles Altieri, *The Particulars of Rapture: An Aesthetics of the Affects* (Ithaca: Cornell University Press, 2003), 122. See also, T. G. Bishop, *Shakespeare and the Theater of Wonder* (Cambridge: Cambridge University Press, 1996), 17–41, 125–75, for the best account of wonder in Shakespeare's work and for a fine reading of *The Winter's Tale.*

53. Altieri, *Particulars of Rapture,* 125.

54. See Richard Moran, "The Expression of Feeling in Imagination," *Philosophical Review* 101 (1994): 75–106.

55. Thomas More, *A Dialogue Concerning Heresies,* ed. T.M.C. Lawler, Germain Marc'hadour, and Richard Marius, 2 parts, in *The Complete Works of Thomas More,* 6 vols. (New Haven: Yale University Press, 1981), 1:64.

56. Ludwig Wittgenstein, *On Certainty,* ed. G.E.M. Anscombe and G. H. von Wright (New York: Harper and Row, 1969).

7. Making Good in *The Tempest*

1. *ST* 2.2.58. The quaestio is: "Whether Justice is Fittingly Defined as Being the Perpetual and Constant Will to Render to Each One His Right." And in the Reply to the 6th objection, Aquinas states: "Just as love of God includes love of our neighbour, as stated above (*ST* 2.2.25.1), so too the service of God includes rendering to each one his due."

2. Peter Lombard describes penance as "secunda tabula post naufragium": *Sententiae.* Dist. XIV. xxii. The first plank is of course baptism.

3. This is a key moment in Hank Rogerson's superb film about Curt Toftland's production of *The Tempest* and his work with prisoners at the Luther Luckett Correctional Complex in LaGrange, Kentucky, in the brilliant documentary *Shakespeare Behind Bars* (2005). As I shall discuss below, it is clear that being human is a task. Leonard Ford says: "As a prisoner, it's something I have to check everyday: to look at myself and say, 'No, I am going to be human,'" cited at www.csmonitor.com/specials/shakespeare/index.html. See also Niels Herold's insightful essay "Movers and Losers: *Shakespeare in Charge* and *Shakespeare Behind Bars,"* in *Native Shakespeares: Indigenous Appropriations on a Global Stage,* ed. Craig Dionne and Parmita Kapadia (Aldershot: Ashgate, 2008), 153: "Just as characters within *The Tempest* are individuated by the sufferings Prospero causes them, so this core group of actors is driven through theatrical playing enactively to acknowledge the tragedy that put them behind bars."

4. The phrase is from 4.1. Ferdinand asks whether he may think that the masquers—Iris, Juno, and Ceres—are "spirits." Prospero responds: "Spirits, which by mine art / I have from their confines called to enact / My present fancies" (4.1.120–21).

5. For two fine treatments see Michael Neill, "Remembrance and Revenge: *Hamlet, Macbeth,* and *The Tempest,"* in *Jonson and Shakespeare,* ed. Ian Donaldson (Atlantic Highlands, NJ: Humanities Press, 1983), 35–56, and John Kerrigan, *Revenge Tragedy: Aeschylus to Armageddon* (Oxford: Oxford University Press, 1996), 194, 211–16.

6. *Homilies* (London: The Prayer Book and Homily Society, 1852), p. 413; *BCP,* 256.

7. The scene is an allusion to *Aeneid* 3.225–57. For the pattern of Virgilian echoes in *The Tempest,* see Donna Hamilton, *Virgil and The Tempest: The Politics of Imitation* (Columbus: Ohio State University Press, 1990), and Heather James, *Shakespeare's Troy: Drama, Politics, and the Translation of Empire* (Cambridge: Cambridge University Press, 1997), chap. 6.

8. *BCP,* 1559, 247. This was reinforced in the 1604 canons; see Canon 26, reprinted in Gerald Bray, ed., *The Anglican Canons 1529–1947,* Church of England Record Society, vol. 6 (Woodbridge, Suffolk: Boydell Press, 1998), 297.

9. For further comments on this practice and its implications, see David Aers and Sarah Beckwith, "The Eucharist," in *Cultural Reformations: Medieval and Renaissance in Literary Histories,* ed. Brian Cummings and James Simpson, Oxford Twenty-First Century Approaches to Literature, vol. 2 (Oxford: Oxford University Press, 2010). See also Christopher Marsh, "'Common Prayer' in England 1560–1640: The View from the Pew," *Past and Present* 171 (2001): 75; J. P. Boulton, "The Limits of Formal Religion: The Administration of Holy Communion in Late Elizabethan and Early Stuart London," *London Journal* 10.2 (1984): 135–54, especially p. 140, and now Kenneth Fincham and Nicholas Tyacke, *Altars of Power: The Changing Face of English Religious Worship, c. 1547–c. 1700* (Oxford: Oxford University Press, 2007), 26, where they cite Thomas Cranmer on "spiritual eating" of the eucharist.

10. Michael Neill makes the strongest claim for this scene as central to the poetics of remembrance in the play: "In *The Tempest* memory becomes re-membering, re-jointing the divided self, re-incorporating it in the membership of the community; and the theatre, for its part, becomes Communion," "Remembrance and Revenge," 49. As will become apparent later, I regard the question of membership of this communion as more fragile and risky, less achieved, than Michael Neill—the goal rather than the achievement of both the represented and performed actions.

11. A table of the rather complex chronology of the debate between Jewel and Harding is given in *The Works of John Jewel,* ed. Richard William Jelf, 8 vols., vol. 1 (Oxford: The University Press, 1848), xiv–xv. Thomas Harding, writing from his exile in Louvain, published *A Confutation of a Booke Intituled An Apologie of the Church of England* in 1565 in response to Lady Bacon's 1564 English translation of the *Apologia Ecclesiae Anglicanae,* 1562. Jewel had initiated the controversy in his Challenge Sermon, inviting Catholics to publicly defend their religion with

scriptural proofs. For a fruitful analysis of the controversy see Marcy L. North, *The Anonymous Renaissance: Cultures of Discretion in Tudor-Stuart England* (Chicago: University of Chicago Press, 2003), 120–27.

12. *The Defence of the Apology of the Church of England,* in *The Works of John Jewel, Bishop of Salisbury,* ed. John Ayre for the Parker Society, 4 vols. (Cambridge: The University Press, 1854–50), 3:474.

13. Ibid.

14. In *A Reply unto M. Harding's Answer* (1565) there is a protracted discussion of "private masses" which bears on the discussion here. Against Harding's assertion that the priest communicated on behalf of the church and that every mass is "common," not private, Jewel reverts to the logic of the feast: "for if it be a feast, how is it received by one alone?" *The Works of John Jewel,* ed. Jelf, vol. 1, 158. The imagery of the feast is one place where the logic of inclusion and exclusion is debated, and this goes to the heart of a chief distinction between Jewel and Harding: the logic of transubstantiation makes it possible for those who receive unworthily to receive the sacrament along with the worthy. For Jewel's Calvinist thinking, this was a pollution of the body of Christ, a terrible profanation of a church attempting to fashion itself in the image of the savior. In *A Confutation of a Book,* Harding had said that those who felt themselves to be not ready to receive communion, but who "for the loue of it desire to be present and behold at that table, and spiritually to taste of that helthfull dish by faith, charitie, prayer and fervent devotion, wherin they do not wholly absteine from the holy communion: such are not to be condemned as idle lookers on, for so ye make them, nor to be driven out of the church": *A Confutation of a Booke* (Ilkley, Yorkshire: Scolar Press, 1976), English Recusant Literature 1558–1640, selected and ed. D. M. Rogers, vol. 310, 92.

15. *The Defence,* 523–24. Harding makes this good point: "If I can receive Christ in my house at home by faith and spirit, how is that work proper to his supper which may be brought without his supper?" (524). I am citing Harding from Jewel's citations, which are both extensive and accurate.

16. As David Aers pointed out to me, having a memory of one's deeds does not commit the doer to repentance. Perhaps a memory of the deed would commit hard-hearted persons to do it all over again. This time they might cut the throats of Prospero and Miranda for good measure. This is an important point. The appropriate form of memory is, of course, contrition, which entails an acknowledgment of one's actions under the name of sin, and acknowledgment of those harmed as remorse. Contrition relies on the voluntary movement of the heart activated by grace, and the further conspiracy of Sebastian and Antonio (2.1) and Stephano, Trinculo, and Caliban might be subject to control and discovery in the conditions of the island, but not necessarily the grace of contrition. Here human agency reaches its limit.

17. I am indebted to Deborah Shuger for this point. See John Bossy's analysis of what he calls "the moral tradition" in *Peace in the Post-Reformation* (Cambridge: Cambridge University Press, 1998). The rites of peace-making and the role of the church in them are also explored in Bossy's series of articles: "Blood and Baptism: Kinship, Community and Christianity in Western Europe from the Fourteenth to the Seventeenth Centuries," *Studies in Church History* 10, *Sanctity and Secularity,* ed. D. Baker (1973): 129–43; "The Mass as a Social Institution, 1200–1700," *Past and Present* 100 (1983): 29–61 and the comment there: "No magisterial reformer included any form of the *Pax* in his communion rite," 57; "Practices of Satisfaction, 1215–1700," in *Studies in Church History* 40, *Revenge, Repentance and Reconciliation,* ed. J. Gregory and Kate Cooper (Bury St. Edmunds: Boydell Press, 2004), 106–5.

18. See Christopher Haigh, "Communion and Community: Exclusion from Communion in Post-Reformation England," *Journal of Ecclesiastical History* 51.4 (2000): 721–40. Grounds for exclusion included ignorance of basic doctrines as well as sin. Canon 26 of the 1604 canons read: "No minister shall in any wise admit to the receiving of the holy communion any of his cure or

flock, which be openly known to live in sin notorious, without repentance; nor any who have ma-
liciously and openly contended with their neighbours, until they be reconciled": *The Anglican
Canons,* ed. Bray, 297. See also the two-part "Homily of the Worthy Receiving and Reverent Esteeming of the Sacrament of the Body and Blood of Christ," in *The Homilies Appointed to Be Read
in Churches* (Brynmill: Preservation Press, 2006), 320–28. Among the avant-garde conformists it is
clear that there is more concern about exclusion from the sacrament than unworthy reception; see
Haigh, 723, and *Visitation Articles and Injunctions of the Early Stuart Church,* ed. Kenneth Fincham
(Church of England Record Society, 1994–98), i. 56, 66–67, 204; ii. 46, 136, 204.

19. This distinction is of course a very vexed one. "Satisfaction" as it develops in the practices after the Fourth Lateran Council is, in Bossy's succinct description: "non-ritual, private, to
the extent that it may not be such as to reveal to the curious what the penitent is satisfying for;
not, in any possible sense, 'equal' to the offence committed; different from restitution where that
is relevant; and performed after absolution, not before it": "Practices of Satisfaction," 107. Restitution concerns one's debts to another person, satisfaction one's debts toward God; see Robert
Alford, "The Figure of Repentance in *Piers Plowman,*" in *Such Werkis to Werche: Essays on Piers
Plowman,* ed. David Miceal F. Vaughan (East Lansing: Colleagues Press, 1993), 14. The relation
between restitution and satisfaction is frequently discussed. Aquinas and Duns Scotus took the
view that it was an essential requisite, a condition of satisfaction, and an act of justice. For a discussion of restitution see H. C. Lea, *A History of Auricular Confession and Indulgences in the Latin
Church,* 3 vols. (London: Swan Sonnenschein, 1896), vol. 2, *Confession and Absolution,* 43ff. See
also Wendy Scase, *Piers Plowman and the New Anti-Clericalism* (Cambridge: Cambridge University Press, 1989), 23–31.

20. In the section on justice in the Secunda Secundae of Thomas Aquinas's *Summa* where
Aquinas cites Ambrose: "It is justice that renders to each one what is his, and claims not another's
property; it disregards its own profit in order to preserve the common equity" (*ST* 2.2.58.11).

21. *ST* 2.2.73.3 in the sed contra: "…Backbiting…is a more grievous sin than theft, but it is
less grievous than murder or adultery."

22. Such a framework is brilliantly diagnosed by Rowan Williams in "The Suspicion of Suspicion: Wittgenstein and Bonhoeffer," in *The Grammar of the Heart: New Essays in Moral Philosophy and Theology,* ed. R. H. Bell (San Francisco: Harper and Row, 1988), 36–53, and his *Lost Icons:
Reflections on Cultural Bereavement* (Edinburgh: T. & T. Clark, 2000).

23. For the vital importance of this moment in *Hamlet,* see John Cox's illuminating comments
in *Seeming Knowledge: Shakespeare and Skeptical Faith* (Waco: Baylor University Press, 2007), 159:
"Only by relying on an audience's belief in the possibility of repentance can Shakespeare clarify
not only Claudius' guilt but the reality of Hamlet's situation as well." This scene is also of central
importance in Ramie Targoff's *Common Prayer: The Language of Public Devotion in Early Modern
England* (Chicago: University of Chicago Press, 2001).

24. In her brilliant book *The Invention of Suspicion: Law and Mimesis in Shakespeare and Renaissance Drama* (Oxford: Oxford University Press, 2007), Lorna Hutson discusses St. German's
complaint that restitution to those wronged was replaced with trentals and obits: "For though
prayers be right expediunt and helthfull to the osule, yet they serve not in all cases to discharge
debtes of restitutions where there is enough to paye them with": "The Debellation of Salem and
Bizance" in *Complete Works of Thomas More,* vol. 10, 345. Hutson reads St. German as subsuming
the functions previously assigned to confession to the common law, now "the guardian of the nation's soul" in matters of restitution. She examines the work of evidence in Shakespearean tragedy
(as well as in Ben Jonson's work) and sees the evidentiary paradigm taking over from the penitential one and being exposed and rejected. If this is the case (and I am persuaded by her excellent argument), then the post-tragic plays return to an exploration of penance again. *The Tempest*
is concerned with the judicial dimensions of the sacrament.

25. Peter Lombard treats restitution in *Sententiae,* 4. Quaestio 15, 2–19.

26. See for example Peter Lombard, *Sententiae,* Book 4, Dist. XV; *Speculum Sacerdotale,* ed. Edward H. Weatherly, *EETS* o.s. 200 (London, 1936), 71; *Jacob's Well,* ed. A. Brandeis, *EETS* o.s. 115 (London: Kegan Paul, 1900), 189. William Lyndwood, *Provinciale,* book 5, title 16, chapter 7, 332–32.

27. The accusation that friars dispensed with the necessity of restitution was a regular component of anti-mendicant complaint. See, for example, the *Memoriale Presbiterorum* where a whole third of the text is devoted to the problem of restitution; Michael Haren, *Sin and Society in Fourteenth Century England: A Study of the Memoriale Presbiterorum* (Oxford: Clarendon Press, 2000).

28. *George Herbert: The Complete English Poems,* ed. John Tobin (Harmondsworth: Penguin, 1991), 212.

29. Ibid., 234.

30. *The First and Second Prayer Books of Edward VI* with an introduction by Rev. Canon J. R. Porter (London: The Prayer Book Society, 1999), 217.

31. Ibid., 383. The language of the feast is also part of the exhortation that might precede communion in the Elizabethan *Book of Common Prayer:* "Ye know how grievous and unkind a thing it is, when a man hath prepared a rich feast, decked his table with all kinds of provision, so that there lacketh nothing but guests to sit down; and yet they which be called without any cause most unthankfully refuse to come": *The Book of Common Prayer,* ed. John Booty (Charlottesville: University of Virginia Press, 2005), 254–55.

32. *First and Second Prayer Books,* 384.

33. See ST.2.2.25.1, and also *ST* 2.2.58.1.ad 6: "Just as love of God includes love of our neighbour, as stated above (Q. 25, A. 1), so too the service of God includes rendering to each his due." See here John Bossy's influential article in which he sees such splittings as evidenced in the way the Decalogue subsumes the seven deadly sins: "Moral Arithmetic: Seven Sins into Ten Commandments," in *Conscience and Casuistry in Early Modern Europe,* ed. Edmund Leites (Cambridge: Cambridge University Press, 1988), 214–34. See also Norman Jones, *The English Reformation: Religion and Cultural Adaptation* (Oxford: Blackwell, 2002), 138ff.

34. *Book of Common Prayer,* ed. Booty, 247.

35. Philip Gorski writes that Calvin, for example, regarded public peccadillos, "which could bring disrepute to the church, more severely than private transgressions, which could not. Indeed, he felt it important that church members avoid even the appearance of sin. Only by remaining blameless and above all reproach could the church fulfill its testimonial function": *The Disciplinary Revolution: Calvinism and the Rise of the State in Early Modern Europe* (Chicago: University of Chicago Press, 2003), 21. See also Alistair Minnis, *Fallible Authors: Chaucer's Pardoner and the Wife of Bath* (Philadelphia: University of Pennsylvania Press, 2008), 16, for the notion of "secret" sins as those about which people were ignorant. One of the major historians of the discipline in Calvin's Geneva has used the language of pollution to describe the church's self-picture, showing how injunctions against adultery ended up incurring the death penalty as they also did in England in 1650: "[They] show us how far the members of this community were willing to go in order to root out all traces of pollution they feared might bring down divine vengeance upon them all": Robert M. Kingdon, *Adultery and Divorce in Calvin's Geneva* (Cambridge: Harvard University Press, 1995), 3.

36. Rowan Williams, "Imagining the Kingdom: Some Questions for Anglican Worship Today," in *The Identity of Anglican Worship,* ed. Kenneth Stevenson and Bryan Spinks (London: Mowbray, 1991), 1.

37. See Alisdair MacIntyre, *Selected Essays,* 2 vols., vol. 2: *Ethics and Politics* (Cambridge: Cambridge University Press, 2006), 146: "charity towards [our neighbour goes beyond, but always includes justice," cited in Terry Eagleton, *Trouble with Strangers: A Study of Ethics* (Oxford: Wiley-Blackwell, 2009), 321.

38. It is worth noting that the most controversial aspect of the Truth and Reconciliation Commission's work was its decision to grant amnesty to those prepared to make a full disclosure of the truth of their crimes. The careful reasoning behind the decision to forgo restitution is discussed by Desmond Tutu in his book *No Future without Forgiveness* (New York: Doubleday, 1999), 30. For a criticism of this view see Wole Soyinka, *The Burden of Memory, the Muse of Forgiveness* (Oxford: Oxford University Press, 1999), 30–31, 36, 80.

39. Aquinas discusses the temporality of restitution in the Quaestio on restitution during a consideration of whether restitution is an aspect of commutative justice: "Besides, that which is past and done with cannot be restored. But justice and injustice are about some actions and undergoing their effects which are transitory and do not last," *ST* 2.2.62.1.

40. *Fasciculus Morum: A Fourteenth Century Preacher's Handbook,* ed. Siegfried Wenzel (University Park: Pennsylvania State University Press, 1989), 189 in Pars III, De Invidia.

41. PP B-text, Coveitise's confession to Repentaunce is in V.196–296, where Coveitise fails to understand the meaning of "restitution." For both Coveitise and "Roberd the Robbere," the injunction "Reddite" (B-text, V. 462) brings the spectre of "wanhope," despair. In the C-text, as Derek Pearsall points out, Robert weeps at the prospect of restitution, not after Sloth's confession, but after Repentaunce's confessing of Coveitise. Coveitise cannot repent, and is not absolved. Coveitise again assails Conscience in Passus XXII when Conscience calls "a leche" who can confess sin, and who will insist on "redde quod debe" (Give back what you owe). But Conscience is subverted, and the Barn of Unity which is the church is destroyed. For the importance of restitution in *Piers Plowman* C-Text, see VI. 1; VI. 308; XVI. 25–38; XIX. 291. I am in disagreement with Robert Adams's argument that in the confession scene "the emphasis falls not on the objective ritual of penance but on the psychological reality of repentance": "Langland's Theology," in *A Companion to Piers Plowman,* ed. John A. Alford (Berkeley: University of California Press, 1988), p. 101. This is the kind of splitting alien to Langland's poem; see Aers, *Sanctifying Signs.*

42. George Eliot, *Adam Bede* (London: Penguin, 1985), 313. It might be worth commenting here that making amends has become inter-personal. *Adam Bede* situates Hetty Sorrel's seduction in the context of a failed confession scene in which Arthur Donnithorne has found himself unable to come clean to his priest, a priest who is also a friend and one who perhaps too ardently respects his social position. This is part of George Eliot's fascinating and consistent examination of clerical life and the fortunes of forgiveness in a secularizing context. *Daniel Deronda* pursues similar themes: "It is hard to say how much we could forgive ourselves if we were secure from judgment by an other whose opinion is the breathing medium of all our joy—who brings to us with close pressure and immediate sequence that judgment of the Invisible and Universal which self-flattery and the world's tolerance would easily melt and disperse. In this way our brother might be in the stead of God to us, and his opinion which has pierced even to the joints and marrow, may be our virtue in the making": George Eliot, *Daniel Deronda* (Harmondsworth: Penguin, 1967), 833. For an insightful contemplation of Shakespeare's influence on George Eliot, see Marianne Novy, *Engaging with Shakespeare: Responses of George Eliot and Other Women Novelists* (Athens: University of Georgia Press, 1994).

43. There is clearly a reflection in the play about the impossibility of absolutely new beginnings.

44. See part 1 for "the vanishing of the human" and the problems around agency addressed there.

45. Stephen Orgel, *The Illusion of Power: Political Theater in the English Renaissance* (Berkeley: University of California Press, 1975), 45–49. See especially David Lindley, "Music, Masque, and Meaning in *The Tempest,*" in *The Court Masque,* ed. Lindley (Manchester: Manchester University Press, 1984), 47–59, and his further comments in the introduction to his edition of *The Tempest* (Cambridge: Cambridge University Press, 2002), 13.

46. The involuntary nature of forgetting is explored in fascinating ways in Avishai Margalit, *The Ethics of Memory* (Cambridge: Harvard University Press, 2002), 183–209.

47. See W. James Booth, *Communities of Memory: On Witness, Identity, and Justice* (Ithaca: Cornell University Press, 2006), 70, and 169 on the problems liberal modernity has with the involuntary character of the presence of the past.

48. Anne Barton, *Ben Jonson, Dramatist* (Cambridge: Cambridge University Press, 1984), 32–33.

49. For Prospero and Ovid's Medea from Golding's translation of Ovid's *Metamorphoses* 7.197–209, see Jonathan Bate, *Shakespeare and Ovid* (Oxford: Clarendon Press, 1993). For Virgil and *The Tempest* see Hamilton, *Virgil and The Tempest*.

50. *Shakespeare in Production: The Tempest*, ed. Christine Dymkowski (Cambridge: Cambridge University Press, 2000), 49.

51. Cavell, *The Claim of Reason,* 372. For a helpful commentary on this passage, from which I have benefitted, see Ludger H. Viefhues-Bailey, *Beyond the Philosopher's Fear: A Cavellian Reading of Gender, Origin, and Religion in Modern Skepticism* (London: Ashgate, 2007), 74.

52. Cavell, *The Claim of Reason,* 377.

53. Prospero is thus related to Shakespeare's other private linguist—Leontes, and behind him, King Lear. See part 1 and chapter 4 on *Pericles* for Shakespeare's analysis of the attempts to secure meaning and intelligibility outside of the human conditions of meaning and intelligibility. This is what Shakespeare sees as tragedy, ensuring isolation, lostness, and emptiness. Shakespeare, as I have been arguing, is Wittgensteinian.

54. Simon Palfrey, *Doing Shakespeare* (Padstow: Thomson, 2000), 49, though I cannot agree that the island is a "mental space."

55. Explored in "The Avoidance of Love" in *The Cavell Reader,* ed. Stephen Mulhall (Malden: Blackwell, 1996), 143–155.

56. Ibid., 333. Cavell explores the question: how do we put ourselves in another's presence? "By revealing ourselves, by allowing ourselves to be seen. When we do not, when we keep ourselves in the dark, the consequence is that we convert him into a character and make the world a stage for him."

57. This tendency is patiently and relentlessly dismantled by Gordon McMullan in *Shakespeare and the Idea of Late Writing: Authorship in the Proximity of Death* (Cambridge: Cambridge University Press, 2007).

58. See *Philosophical Investigations,* Remark 241: "what is true or false is what human beings *say;* and it is in their *language* that human beings agree. This is agreement not in opinions but in forms of life." For superb commentary on this passage, see Cavell, *The Claim of Reason,* 30, 32, 35, and for "agreement in judgments" see 31–32, 35–36, 118. For the difference between agreeing in and not on language, see Sandra Laugier, "Wittgenstein and Cavell: Anthropology, Skepticism, and Politics," in *The Claims to Community: Essays on Stanley Cavell and Political Philosophy,* ed. Andre Norris (Stanford: Stanford University Press, 2006).

BIBLIOGRAPHY

Adams, Robert. "Langland's Theology." In *A Companion to Piers Plowman*, ed. John A. Alford, 87–116. Berkeley: University of California Press, 1988.

Adelman, Janet. "Bed Tricks: On Marriage as the End of Comedy in *All's Well That Ends Well* and *Measure for Measure*." In *Shakespeare's Personality*, ed. Norman N. Holland, Sidney Homan, and Bernard J. Paris, 151–74. Berkeley: University of California Press, 1989.

Aers, David. *Salvation and Sin: Augustine, Langland, and Fourteenth-Century Theology.* Notre Dame: University of Notre Dame Press, 2009.

———. *Sanctifying Signs: Making Christian Tradition in Late Medieval England.* Notre Dame: University of Notre Dame Press, 2004.

Aers, David, and Sarah Beckwith. "The Eucharist." In *Cultural Reformations: Medieval and Renaissance in Literary History*, Oxford Twenty-First Century Approaches to Literature, vol. 2, ed. Brian Cummings and James Simpson. Oxford: Oxford University Press, 2010.

Affeldt, Steven. "The Ground of Mutuality: Criteria, Judgment, and Intelligibility." *European Journal of Philosophy* 6.1 (1998): 1–31.

Alford, John A. "The Figure of Repentance in Piers Plowman." In *Such Werkis to Werche: Essays on Piers Plowman*, ed. Michael Vaughan, 3–28. East Lansing: Colleagues Press, 1993.

Altieri, Charles. *The Particulars of Rapture: An Aesthetics of the Affects.* Ithaca: Cornell University Press, 2003.

Altman, Joel. "'Vile Participation': The Amplification of Violence in the Theater of Henry V." *Shakespeare Quarterly* 42 (1991): 1–32.

Andrewes, Lancelot. *Ninety Six Sermons by the Right Honourable and Reverend Father in God, Lancelot Andrewes, Sometime Bishop of Winchester.* Vol. 5. Oxford: John Henry Parker, 1843; New York: AMS Press, 1967.

——. *Selected Sermons and Letters.* Ed. Peter McCullough. Oxford: Oxford University Press, 2005.

Anspach, Mark Rogin. *A charge de revanche: Figures élémentaires de la réciprocité.* Paris: Seuil, 2002.

Arendt, Hannah. *The Human Condition.* Chicago: University of Chicago Press, 1958.

Augustine of Hippo. *Confessions.* Trans. Henry Chadwick. Oxford: Oxford University Press, 1991.

Austin, J. L. *How to Do Things with Words.* 2nd ed. Ed. J. O. Urmson and Marina Sbisa. Cambridge: Harvard University Press, 1975.

——. *Philosophical Papers.* 3rd ed. Ed. J. O. Urmson and G. J. Warnock. Oxford: Oxford University Press, 1979.

Bacon, Francis. *Letters and Life of Francis Bacon.* Vol. 1. Ed. James Spedding. London: Longmans, Green, 1890.

Bale, John. *The Complete Plays of John Bale.* 2 vols. Ed. Peter Happé. Woodbridge, Suffolk: D. S. Brewer, 1985–86.

Barber, C. L. *Creating Elizabethan Tragedy: The Theater of Marlowe and Kyd.* Ed. Richard Wheeler. Chicago: University of Chicago Press, 1988.

——. "'Thou that beget'st him that did thee beget': Transformation in *Pericles* and *The Winter's Tale.*" *Shakespeare Survey* 22 (1969): 59–67.

Barkan, Leonard. *The Gods Made Flesh: Metamorphosis and the Pursuit of Paganism.* New Haven: Yale University Press, 1986.

Bartlett, Robert. *Trial by Fire and Water: The Medieval Judicial Ordeal.* Oxford: Clarendon Press, 1986.

Barton, Anne. Introduction to *Measure for Measure,* by William Shakespeare. In *The Riverside Shakespeare,* 2nd ed., ed. G. Blakemore Evans and J. J. M. Tobin, 579–83. Boston: Houghton Mifflin, 1996.

Bate, Jonathan. *Shakespeare and Ovid.* Oxford: Clarendon Press, 1993.

Beaumont, Francis. *The Knight of the Burning Pestle.* Ed. Sheldon P. Zitner. Manchester: Manchester University Press, 2004.

Beckerman, Bernard. *Shakespeare at the Globe 1599–1609.* New York: Macmillan, 1962.

Beckwith, Sarah. Introduction. In *Premodern Shakespeare,* ed. James Simpson and Sarah Beckwith. *JMEMS* 40.1 (2010): 1–5.

——. "The Play of Voice: Acknowledgment, Knowledge, and Self-Knowledge in *Measure for Measure.*" In *Spectacle and Public Performance in the Late Middle Ages and the Renaissance,* ed. Robert E. Stillman, 121–44. Leiden: Brill, 2006.

——. *Signifying God: Social Act and Symbolic Relation in The York Corpus Christi Play.* Chicago: University of Chicago Press, 2001.

Becon, Thomas. *The Early Works of Thomas Becon.* Ed. John Ayre. Cambridge: The University Press, 1843.

——. *The Catechism of Thomas Becon With Other Pieces Written by Him in the Reign of King Edward the Sixth,* Ed. John Ayre for the Parker Society. Cambridge: The University Press, 1844.

Benson, Larry D., general ed. *The Riverside Chaucer.* 3rd ed. Boston: Houghton Mifflin, 1987.

Benson, Sean. *Shakespearean Resurrection: The Art of Almost Raising the Dead.* Pittsburgh: Duquesne University Press, 2009.

Berger, Harry. *Making Trifles of Terrors: Redistributing Complicities in Shakespeare.* Stanford: Stanford University Press, 1997.

Biel, Gabriel. *Collectorium circa quattuor libros Sententiarum, Libri quarti pars prima.* Ed. Wilfridus Werbeck and Udo Hofmann. Tübingen: J. C. B. Mohr, 1975.

Bishop, T. G. *Shakespeare and the Theater of Wonder.* Cambridge: Cambridge University Press, 1996.

——. "Shakespeare's Theatre Games." *JMEMS* 40.1 (2010): 65–88.

Boitani, Piero. *The Bible and Its Rewritings.* Oxford: Oxford University Press, 1999.

Booth, W. James. *Communities of Memory: On Witness, Identity, and Justice.* Ithaca: Cornell University Press, 2006.

Booty, John, ed. *The Book of Common Prayer 1559.* Charlottesville: University Press of Virginia, 2005.

Bossy, John. "Blood and Baptism: Kinship, Community and Christianity in Western Europe from the Fourteenth to the Seventeenth Centuries." In *Studies in Church History,* vol. 10. Ed. D. Baker (1973): 129–43.

——. *Christianity in the West 1400–1700.* Oxford: Oxford University Press, 1985.

——. "The Mass as a Social Institution 1200–1700." *Past and Present* 100 (1983): 29–61.

——. "Moral Arithmetic: Seven Sins into Ten Commandments." In *Conscience and Casuistry in Early Modern Europe,* ed. Edmund Leites, 214–34. Cambridge: Cambridge University Press, 1988.

——. *Peace in the Post-Reformation.* Cambridge: Cambridge University Press, 1998.

——. "Practices of Satisfaction, 1215–1700." In *Retribution, Repentance, and Reconciliation: Papers Read at the 2002 Summer Meeting and 2003 Winter Meeting of the Ecclesiastical History Society,* 106–18. Woodbridge, Suffolk: Boydell Press, 2004.

Boulton, J. P. "The Limits of Formal Religion: The Administration of Holy Communion in Late Elizabethan and Early Stuart London." *London Journal* 10.2 (1984): 135–54.

Boyle, Leonard E. "The Fourth Lateran Council and the Manuals of Popular Theology." In *The Popular Literature of Medieval England,* ed. Thomas J. Heffernan, 30–43. Knoxville: University of Tennessee Press, 1985.

——. *Pastoral Care, Clerical Education and Canon Law, 1200–1400.* London: Varorium Reprints, 1981.

Branch, Lori. *Rituals of Spontaneity: Sentiment and Secularism from Free Prayer to Wordsworth.* Waco, TX: Baylor University Press, 2006.

Brandeis, A., ed. *Jacob's Well.* EETS o.s. 115. London: Kegan Paul, 1900.

Bray, Gerald, ed. *The Anglican Canons, 1529–1947.* Woodbridge, Suffolk: Boydell Press, 1998.

——, ed. *Documents of the English Reformation, 1526–1701.* Cambridge: James Clarke, 1994, rpt. 2004.

———, ed. *Tudor Church Reform: The Henrician Canons of 1535 and the Reformatio Legum Ecclesiasticarum.* Woodbridge, Suffolk: Boydell Press, 2000.

Brigden, Susan. *London and the Reformation.* Oxford: Clarendon Press, 1989.

Brook, Peter. *Bodywork: Objects of Desire in Modern Narrative.* Cambridge: Harvard University Press, 1993.

Brundage, James A. *Medieval Canon Law.* New York: Longman, 1995.

Bullough, Geoffrey, ed. *Narrative and Dramatic Sources of Shakespeare.* Vol. 6. London: Routledge and Kegan Paul, 1966.

Bullough, Geoffrey, and Martin Butler, eds. *Cymbeline.* Cambridge: Cambridge University Press, 2005.

Calvin, John. *Institutes of the Christian Religion.* 2 vols. Trans. Ford Lewis Battles. Ed. John T. McNeill. Notre Dame, IN: Ave Maria Press, 1960.

Carlson, Eric Josef. *Marriage and the English Reformation.* Oxford: Wiley-Blackwell, 1994.

Casagrande, Carla, and Silvana Vecchio. *I peccati della lingua ed etica della parola nella cultura médiévale.* Rome: Istituo della Encliclopedia Italiana, 1987.

Cavanaugh, William. *Torture and Eucharist: Theology, Politics, and the Body of Christ.* Oxford: Wiley-Blackwell, 1998.

Cave, Terence. *Recognitions: A Study in Poetics.* Oxford: Oxford University Press, 1988.

Cavell, Stanley. *The Claim of Reason: Wittgenstein, Skepticism, Morality, and Tragedy.* 1979. 2nd ed. New York: Oxford University Press, 1999.

———. *Conditions Handsome and Unhandsome: The Constitution of Emersonian Perfectionism.* Chicago: University of Chicago Press, 1990.

———. *Disowning Knowledge in Seven Plays of Shakespeare.* 1987. 2nd ed. Cambridge: Cambridge University Press, 2003.

———. Foreword to *The Scandal of the Speaking Body: Don Juan with J. L. Austin, or Seduction in Two Languages,* by Shoshana Felman, xi–xxi. Stanford: Stanford University Press, 2003.

———. *In Quest of the Ordinary: Lines of Skepticism and Romanticism.* Chicago: University of Chicago Press, 1988.

———. *Must We Mean What We Say?* 2nd ed. Cambridge: Cambridge University Press, 2002.

———. *Philosophy the Day after Tomorrow.* Cambridge: Harvard University Press, 2005.

———. *A Pitch of Philosophy: Autobiographical Exercises.* Cambridge: Harvard University Press, 1996.

———. *The Pursuits of Happiness: The Hollywood Comedy of Remarriage.* Cambridge: Harvard University Press, 1981.

Coetzee, J. M. "Confession and Double Thoughts: Tolstoy, Dostoevsky, and Rousseau." *Comparative Literature* 37 (1985): 193–232.

Coleman, David. *Drama and the Sacraments in Sixteenth Century England: Indelible Characters.* Houndmills: Palgrave, 2007.

Collinson, Patrick. "Shepherds, Sheepdogs, and Hirelings: The Pastoral Ministry in Post-Reformation England." In *The Ministry: Clerical and Lay: Papers Read at the 1988 Summer Meeting and the 1989 Winter Meeting of the Ecclesiastical History Soci-*

ety, Studies in Church History 26, ed. W. Sheils and Diana Wood, 185–220. Oxford: Blackwell, 1989.

———. *From Cranmer to Sancroft.* London: M.P.G. Books, 2006.

Como, David. *Blown by the Spirit: Puritanism and the Emergence of an Antinomian Underground in Pre–Civil War England.* Stanford: Stanford University Press, 2004.

Cooper, Helen. *The English Romance in Time: Transforming Motifs from Geoffrey of Monmouth to the Death of Shakespeare.* Oxford: Oxford University Press, 2004.

———. "'This worthy olde writer': *Pericles* and Other Gowers, 1592–1640." In *A Companion to Gower,* ed. Sian Echard, 99–113. Cambridge: D. S. Brewer, 2004.

Cox, John D. *Seeing Knowledge: Shakespeare and Skeptical Faith.* Waco, TX: Baylor University Press, 2007.

———. "Was Shakespeare a Christian, and If So, What Kind of Christian Was He?" *Christianity and Literature* 55.4 (2006): 539–66.

Cranmer, Thomas. *The Remains of Thomas Cranmer, Archbishop of Canterbury.* 4 vols. Oxford: The University Press, 1833.

Crary, Alice. *Beyond Moral Judgment.* Cambridge: Harvard University Press, 2007.

Craun, Edwin D. *Lies, Slander, and Obscenity in Medieval English Literature: Pastoral Rhetoric and the Deviant Speaker.* Cambridge: Cambridge University Press, 1997.

Cressy, David. *Birth, Marriage, and Death: Ritual, Religion, and the Life-Cycle in Tudor and Stuart England.* Oxford: Oxford University Press, 1997.

Cummings, Brian. *The Literary Culture of the Reformation: Grammar and Grace.* Oxford: Oxford University Press, 2002.

Davlin, Mary Clemente, O.P. "'Kynde Knowing' as a Middle English Equivalent for 'Wisdom' in *Piers Plowman* B." *Medium Aevum* (1981): 5–17.

Dawson, Anthony, and Paul Yachnin. *The Culture of Playgoing in Shakespeare's London: A Collaborative Debate.* Cambridge: Cambridge University Press, 2001.

Denery, Dallas G. *Seeing and Being Seen in the Later Medieval World: Optics, Theology and Religious Life.* Cambridge: Cambridge University Press, 2005.

Descartes, René. *Philosophical Writings.* 2 vols. Vol. 1. Trans. J. Cotingham, R. Stoothoff, and D. Murdoch. Cambridge: Cambridge University Press, 1985.

Diehl, Huston. *Staging Reform, Reforming the Stage: Protestantism and Popular Theater in Early Modern England.* Ithaca: Cornell University Press, 1997.

Doniger, Wendy. *The Bedtrick: Tales of Sex and Masquerade.* Chicago: University of Chicago Press, 2000.

Drury, T. W. *Confession and Absolution: The Teaching of the Church of England as Interpreted and Illustrated by the Writings of the Reformers of the Sixteenth Century.* London: Chas. J. Thynne, 1903.

Drury, T. W., and Mark Eccles, eds. *The Macro Plays.* EETS. 262. Oxford: Oxford University Press, 1969.

Eagleton, Terry. *Trouble with Strangers: A Study of Ethics.* Oxford: Wiley-Blackwell, 2009.

Edwards, Philip. "Shakespeare's Romances: 1900–1957." *Shakespeare Survey* 11 (1958): 1–18.

Eldridge, Richard. *Leading a Human Life: Wittgenstein, Intentionality, and Romanticism.* Chicago: University of Chicago Press, 1997.

Eliot, George. *Adam Bede.* London: Penguin, 1985.

———. *Daniel Deronda.* Harmondsworth: Penguin, 1967.

———. *Middlemarch.* Oxford: Oxford University Press, 1996.

Elton, Geoffrey. *Policy and Police: The Enforcement of the Reformation in the Age of Thomas Cromwell.* Cambridge: Cambridge University Press, 1972.

Elton, William. *King Lear and the Gods.* San Marino: Huntington Library, 1966.

Emmison, F. G. *Elizabethan Life: Morals & the Church Courts, Mainly from Essex Archidiaconal Records. Essex Record Office Publications.* No. 63. Vol. 2. Colchester: Benham, 1973.

Ewbank, Inga-Stina. "'My Name is Marina': The Language of Recognition." In *Shakespeare's Styles: Essays in Honour of Kenneth Muir,* ed. Philip Edwards, Inga-Stina Ewbank, and G. K. Hunter, 111–30. Cambridge: Cambridge University Press, 2004.

Farber, Liana. *An Anatomy of Trade in Medieval Writing: Value, Consent, and Community.* Ithaca: Cornell University Press, 2006.

Ferrell, Lori Anne. *Government by Polemic: James I, the King's Preachers, and the Rhetorics of Conformity, 1603–1625.* Stanford: Stanford University Press, 1998.

Fincham, Kenneth, ed. *Visitation Articles and Injunctions of the Early Stuart Church.* Church of England Record Society. Woodbridge, Suffolk: Boydell Press, 1994–98.

Fincham, Kenneth, and Nicholas Tyacke. *Altars Restored: The Changing Face of English Religious Worship 1547–c.1700.* Oxford: Oxford University Press, 2007.

Fincham, Kenneth, and Roger Warren, eds. *Pericles.* Oxford: Oxford University Press, 2003.

The First and Second Prayer Books of Edward VI. Garlick Hill, London: The Prayer Book Society, 1999.

Fleming, Richard. *First Word Philosophy: Wittgenstein-Austin-Cavell, Writings on Ordinary Language Philosophy.* Lewisburg: Bucknell University Press, 2004.

Flesch, William. *Generosity and the Limits of Authority: Shakespeare, Herbert, Milton.* Ithaca: Cornell University Press, 1992.

"The Forgiveness Project." http://www.theforgivenessproject.com/ (accessed August 31, 2009).

Forsyth, Robert Stanley. *The Relation of Shirley's Plays to the Elizabethan Drama.* New York: Columbia University Press, 1914.

Fowler, Elizabeth. "Chaucer's Hard Cases." In *Medieval Crime and Social Control,* ed. Barbara Hanawalt and David Wallace, 24–42. Minneapolis: University of Minnesota Press, 1999.

———. *Literary Character: The Human Figure in Early English Writing.* Ithaca: Cornell University Press, 2003.

———. "Towards a History of Performativity: Sacrament, Social Contract, and *The Merchant of Venice.*" In *Shakespeare and the Middle Ages,* ed. John Watkins and Curtis Perry, 68–77. Oxford: Oxford University Press, 2009.

Frere, Walter Howard. *Puritan Manifestoes: A Study in the Origins of Puritan Revolt.* London: S.P.C.K, 1954.

Friedman, Michael D. *The World Must Be Peopled: Shakespeare's Comedies of Forgiveness.* Cranbury, NJ: Associated University Presses, 2002.

Gaita, Raimond. *A Common Humanity: Thinking about Love and Truth and Justice.* London: Routledge, 1998.

———. *Good and Evil: An Absolute Conception.* 2nd ed. New York: St. Martin's Press, 1991.

Gallagher, Lowell. *Medusa's Gaze: Casuistry and Conscience in the Renaissance.* Stanford: Stanford University Press, 1991.

Gascoigne, Thomas. *Myroure of Oure Ladye. EETS* e.s. 19. Ed. J. H. Blunt. London: Kegan, Paul, Trench, Trubner, 1989.

Geneva Bible: A Facsimile of the 1560 Edition, with an introduction by Lloyd Berry. Madison: University of Wisconsin Press, 1969.

Gerson, Jean. *Oeuvres complètes.* Ed. P. Glorieux. 10 vols. Paris: Desclée, 1960–.

Goering, Joseph. "The Internal Forum and the Literature of Penance and Confession." In *History of Medieval Canon Law,* ed. W. Hartmann and K. Pennington, 1–75. Washington, DC: Catholic University Press of America, 2001.

Gorski, Philip. *The Disciplinary Revolution: Calvinism and the Rise of the State in Early Modern Europe.* Chicago: University of Chicago Press, 2003.

Gould, Timothy. *Hearing Things: Voice and Method in the Writing of Stanley Cavell.* Chicago: University of Chicago Press, 1998.

———. "The Unhappy Performative." In *Performativity and Performance,* ed. Andrew Parker and Eve Kosofsky Sedgwick, 19–44. New York: Routledge, 1995.

Gower, John. *Confessio Amantis.* 3 vols. Ed. Russell A. Peck. Kalamazoo, MI: Medieval Institute Publications, Western Michigan University, 2000–04.

Graham, Kenneth. "George Herbert and the Discipline of History." *JMEMS* 31.2 (2001): 349–78.

Graham, Kenneth J. E., and Philip E. Collington. *Shakespeare and Religious Change.* Houndmills: Palgrave Macmillan, 2009.

Greenblatt, Stephen. *Hamlet in Purgatory.* Princeton: Princeton University Press, 2001.

———. "The Mousetrap." In *Practicing New Historicism,* ed. Catherine Gallagher and Stephen Greenblatt, 136–62. Chicago: University of Chicago Press, 2000.

———. "Shakespeare and the Exorcists." In *Shakespearean Negotiations,* 94–128. Berkeley: University of California Press, 1988.

Greenham, Richard. *"Practical Divinity": The Works and Life of Revd. Richard Greenham.* Ed. Kenneth L. Parker and Eric J. Carlson. Aldershot: Ashgate, 1998.

Greer, Rowan A. *Christian Life and Christian Hope: Raids on the Inarticulate.* New York: Crossroad, 2001.

Griffiths, John, ed. *The Homilies Appointed to Be Read in Churches.* Revised by Ian Robinson. Bishopstone, Hertfortshire: Brynmill Press, 2006.

Grindal, Edmund. *The Remains of Edmund Grindal.* Cambridge: The University Press, 1843.

Haigh, Christopher. "Communion and Community: Exclusion from Communion in Post-Reformation England." *Journal of Ecclesiastical History* 51.4 (2000): 721–40.

———. *The Plain Man's Pathway to Heaven: Kinds of Christianity in Post-Reformation England, 1570–1640.* Oxford: Oxford University Press, 2007.

Halpern, Richard. "Intimate Histories: Stanley Cavell on, and as, King Lear." Unpublished paper.

Hamilton, Donna. *Virgil and The Tempest: The Politics of Imitation.* Columbus: Ohio State University Press, 1990.

Hamm, Berndt. *The Reformation of Faith in the Context of Late Medieval Theology and Piety: Essays by Berndt Hamm.* Leiden: Brill, 2004.

Haren, Michael. *Sin and Society in Fourteenth Century England: A Study of the Memoriale Presbiterorum.* Oxford: Clarendon Press, 2000.

Hauerwas, Stanley. *Performing the Faith: Bonhoeffer and the Practice of Nonviolence.* Grand Rapids, MI: Brazos Press, 2004.

Hayne, Victoria. "Performing Social Practice: The Example of *Measure for Measure.*" *Shakespeare Quarterly* 44.1 (Spring 1993): 1–29.

Helmholz, R. H. *Roman Canon Law in Reformation England.* Cambridge: Cambridge University Press, 1990.

———. *The Spirit of the Classical Canon Law.* Athens: University of Georgia Press, 1996.

Herbert, George. *George Herbert: The Complete English Poems.* Ed. John Tobin. London: Penguin, 1991.

Herdt, Jennifer. *Putting on Virtue: The Legacy of the Splendid Vices.* Chicago: University of Chicago Press, 2006.

Herold, Niels. "Movers and Losers: *Shakespeare in Charge* and *Shakespeare Behind Bars.*" In *Native Shakespeares: Indigenous Appropriations on a Global Stage,* ed. Craig Dionne and Parmita Kapadia, 153–72. Aldershot: Ashgate, 2008.

Hillman, David. *Shakespeare's Entrails: Belief, Skepticism, and the Interior of the Body.* Basingstoke: Palgrave Macmillan, 2007.

Hirschfeld, Heather. "'And he hath enough': The Penitential Economies of *The Merchant of Venice.*" *JMEMS* 40.1 (Winter 2010): 89–117.

Hirst, David. *The Tempest.* Houndmills, Basingstoke: Macmillan, 1984.

Hooker, Richard. *Of the Laws of Ecclesiastical Polity: Books VI, VII, VIII.* Ed. Peter Stanwood. Cambridge: Harvard University Press, 1981.

Houlbrooke, Ralph. *Death, Religion and the Family in England, 1480–1750.* Oxford: Oxford University Press, 1998.

Hugh of St. Victor. *On the Sacraments of the Christian Faith.* Cambridge, MA: Medieval Academy of America, 1951.

Hunter, Robert Grams. *Shakespeare and the Comedy of Forgiveness.* New York: Columbia University Press, 1965.

Hutson, Lorna. *The Invention of Suspicion: Law and Mimesis in Shakespeare and Renaissance Drama.* Oxford: Oxford University Press, 2007.

Hyde, Lewis. *The Gift: How the Creative Spirit Transforms the World.* Edinburgh: Canongate, 2006.

James, Heather. *Shakespeare's Troy: Drama, Politics, and the Translation of Empire.* Cambridge: Cambridge University Press, 1997.

James I. *The Political Works of James I.* Ed. Charles Howard McIlwain. Cambridge: Harvard University Press, 1918.

Jennings, Margaret. "From Demon to Tutivillus." *Studies in Philology* 74.5 (1977): 1–95.

Jewel, John. *The Works of John Jewel, Bishop of Salisbury.* 4 vols. Ed. John Ayre for the Parker Society. Cambridge: Cambridge University Press, 1845–50.

———. *The Works of John Jewell.* 8 vols. Ed. Richard William Jelf. Oxford: Oxford University Press, 1848.

Jones, David Martin. *Conscience and Allegiance in Seventeenth Century England: The Political Significance of Oaths and Engagements.* Rochester: University of Rochester Press, 1999.

Jones, Norman. *The English Reformation: Religion and Cultural Adaptation.* Oxford: Blackwell, 2002.

Jupin, Arvin H., ed. *A Contextual Study and Modern Spelling Edition of Mucedorus.* New York: Garland, 1987.

Kantorowicz, Ernst Hartwig. *The King's Two Bodies: A Study in Medieval Political Theology.* Princeton: Princeton University Press, 1957.

Kearney, Richard. "Spectres of *Hamlet.*" In *Spiritual Shakespeares,* ed. Ewan Fernie, 157–85. London: Routledge, 2005.

Kermode, Frank. *Shakespeare's Language.* London: Allen Lane, 2000.

Kerr, Fergus. *Theology after Wittgenstein.* Melksham: Cromwell Press, 1997.

———. *Work on Oneself: Wittgenstein's Philosophical Psychology.* Arlington, VA: Institute for the Psychological Sciences Press, 2008.

Kerrigan, John. *Revenge Tragedy: Aeschylus to Armageddon.* Oxford: Oxford University Press, 1996.

Kingdon, Robert M. *Adultery and Divorce in Calvin's Geneva.* Cambridge: Harvard University Press, 1995.

Kipling, Gordon. *Enter the King: Theatre, Liturgy, and Ritual in the Medieval Civic Triumph.* Oxford: Clarendon Press, 1998.

Knapp, Jeffrey. *Shakespeare's Tribe: Church, Nation, and Theater in Renaissance England.* Chicago: University of Chicago Press, 2002.

Krog, Antjie. *Country of My Skull: Guilt, Sorrow, and the Limits of Forgiveness in the New South Africa.* New York: Random House, 1998.

Kurath, Hans, ed. *Middle English Dictionary.* Ann Arbor: University of Michigan Press, 1952–2001.

Lake, Peter. *The Anti-Christ's Lewd Hat: Protestants, Papists, and Players in Post-Reformation England.* New Haven: Yale University Press, 2002.

———. *The Box-maker's Revenge: "Orthodoxy," "Heterodoxy," and the Politics of the Parish in Early Stuart London.* Stanford: Stanford University Press, 2001.

———. "Lancelot Andrewes, John Buckeridge, and Avant-Garde Conformity at the Court of James I." In *The Mental World of the Jacobean Court,* ed. Linda Peck, 113–33. Cambridge: Cambridge University Press, 2005.

———. "Religious Identities in Shakespeare's England." In *A Companion to Shakespeare,* ed, David Scott Kastan, 57–84. Oxford: Blackwell, 1999.

Landgraf, Artur. *Dogmengeschichte der Frühscholastik.* Regensburg: Pustet, 1952.

Laugier, Sandra. "Wittgenstein and Cavell: Anthropology, Skepticism, and Politics." In *The Claim to Community: Essays on Stanley Cavell and Political Philosophy,* ed. Andrew Norris, 19–37. Stanford: Stanford University Press, 2006.

Lea, H. C. *A History of Auricular Confession and Indulgences in the Latin Church.* 3 vols. London: Swan Sonnenschein, 1896.

Leites, Edmund, ed. *Conscience and Casuistry in Early Modern Europe.* Cambridge: Cambridge University Press, 1988.

Lindley, David. "Music, Masque, and Meaning in *The Tempest.*" In *The Court Masque,* ed. David Lindley, 47–59. Manchester: Manchester University Press, 1984.

Lipton, Emma. *Affections of the Mind: The Politics of Sacramental Marriage in Late Medieval English Literature*. Notre Dame: University of Notre Dame Press, 2007.

Logan, F. D. *Excommunication and the Secular Arm in Medieval England*. Toronto: Institute for Medieval Studies, 1968.

Lubac, Henri de. *The Christian Faith: An Essay on the Apostle's Creed*. San Francisco: Ignatius Press, 1986.

Lumiansky, R. M., and David Mills, eds. *The Chester Mystery Cycle*, 2 vols., vol. 1. *EETS* s.s. 3. Oxford: Oxford University Press, 1974.

Lupton, Julia Reinhard. *Citizen-Saints: Shakespeare and Political Theology*. Chicago: University of Chicago Press, 2005.

Luther, Martin. *Ninety Five Theses or Disputations on the Power and Efficacy of Indulgences*. In *Luther's Works*, vol. 31. Ed. Harold J. Grimm. Philadelphia: Muhlenberg Press, 1957.

———. *The Sermon on the Mount and The Magnificat*. In *Luther's Works*, vol. 21. Ed. and trans. Jaroslav Pelikan. St. Louis: Concordia University Press, 1956.

———. *D. Martin Luthers Werke: Kritische Gesamtausgabe*. 127 vols. Weimar: H. Böhlau, 1883–2009.

Luther, Martin, and John Calvin. *Luther and Calvin: On Secular Authority*. Ed. Harro Höpfl. Cambridge: Cambridge University Press, 1991.

Luther, Martin, and Desiderius Erasmus. *Luther and Erasmus: Free Will and Salvation*. Ed. E. Gordon Rupp and Philip S. Watson. Philadelphia: Westminster Press, 1969.

Lyndwood, William. *Provinciale seu constitutiones angliae*. Oxford, 1679: rpt. Hants, 1968.

MacCulloch, Diarmaid. *The Reformation*. New York: Viking, 2003.

———. *Thomas Cranmer: A Life*. New Haven: Yale University Press, 1996.

Macy, Gary. *The Hidden History of Women's Ordination*. Oxford: Oxford University Press, 2008.

Mannyng, Robert. *Handlyng Synne*. Ed. Frederick J. Furnivall. *EETS* o.s. 119. London: K. Paul, Trench, Trübner, 1901.

Margalit, Avishai. *The Ethics of Memory*. Cambridge: Cambridge University Press, 2002.

Marliangeas, B. D. *Clés pour une théologie du ministère*. Paris: Editions Beauchesne, 1978.

Marsh, Christopher. "'Common Prayer' in England 1560–1640: The View from the Pew." *Past and Present* 171 (2001): 66–94.

Marston, John. *The Fawn*. Lincoln: University of Nebraska Press, 1965.

———. *The Malcontent*. Ed. M. L. Wine. Lincoln: University of Nebraska Press, 1965.

Marston, John, and William Maskell, eds. *Monumenta Ritualia Ecclesiae Anglicanae*. 3 vols. Oxford: Clarendon Press, 1882.

Maus, Katherine Eisaman. *Inwardness and Theater in the English Renaissance*. Chicago: University of Chicago Press, 1995.

McCarthy, Conor. *Marriage in Medieval England: Law, Literature, and Practice*. Woodbridge, Suffolk: Boydell Press, 2004.

McGrath, Alister E. *Iustitia Dei: A History of the Christian Doctrine of Justification*. Cambridge: Cambridge University Press, 1986.

McIntosh, Marjorie Keniston. *Controlling Misbehaviour in England 1370–1600*. Cambridge: Cambridge University Press, 1998.

McMullan, Gordon. *Shakespeare and the Idea of Late Writing: Authorship in the Proximity of Death.* Cambridge: Cambridge University Press, 2008.

McSheffrey, Shannon. *Marriage, Sex, and Civic Culture in Late Medieval London.* Philadelphia: University of Pennsylvania Press, 2006.

Michaud-Quantin, Pierre. *Sommes de casuistique et manuels de confession au moyen âge (XII–XVI siècles.* Louvain: Analecta Mediaevalia Namurcensia, 1962.

Middleton, Thomas. *Thomas Middleton: The Collected Works.* Ed. Gary Taylor and John Lavagnino. Oxford: Clarendon Press, 2007.

Milbank, John. *Being Reconciled: Ontology and Pardon.* London: Routledge, 2003.

Minnis, Alastair. *Fallible Authors: Chaucer's Pardoner and the Wife of Bath.* Philadelphia: University of Pennsylvania Press, 2008.

Miola, Robert, ed. *Early Modern Catholicism: An Anthology of Primary Sources.* Oxford: Oxford University Press, 2007.

Mirk, John. *Instructions for Parish Priests.* Ed. Gillis Kristensson. Lund: CWK Gleerup, 1974.

Moi, Toril. *What Is a Woman? and Other Essays.* Oxford: Oxford University Press, 1999.

Montrose, Louis. *The Purpose of Playing: Shakespeare and the Cultural Politics of Elizabethan Theatre.* Chicago: University of Chicago Press, 1996.

Moran, Richard. "The Expression of Feeling in Imagination." *Philosophical Review* 101 (1994): 75–106.

More, Thomas. *A Dialogue Concerning Heresies.* Ed. T.M.C. Lawler, Germain Marc'hadour, and Richard Marius. *The Complete Works of Thomas More,* vol. 6, pt. 1–2. New Haven: Yale University Press, 1981.

Muir, Edward. *Ritual in Early Modern Europe.* Cambridge: Cambridge University Press, 1997.

Mullaney, Steven. "'All That Monarchs Do': The Obscured Stages of Authority in Pericles." In *The Place of the Stage,* reprinted in *Pericles: Critical Essays,* ed. David Skeele, 168–83. New York: Garland, 2000.

Myers, David. *"Poor Sinning Folk": Confession and Conscience in Counter-Reformation Germany.* Ithaca: Cornell University Press, 1996.

Nashe, Thomas. *The Unfortunate Traveller and Other Works.* Ed. J. B. Steane. Harmondsworth: Penguin, 1972, rpt. 1982.

Neill, Michael. *Issues of Death: Mortality and Identity in English Renaissance Tragedy.* Oxford: Oxford University Press, 1997.

———. "'The Language of the Heart': Confession, Metaphor, and Grace in J. M.Coetzee's *Age of Iron.*" In *New Windows on a Woman's World: Scholarly Writing in Honour of Jocelyn Harris,* ed. Colin Gibson and Lisa Marr, 515–43. Dunedin: University of Otago English Department, 2005.

———. "Remembrance and Revenge: *Hamlet, Macbeth* and *The Tempest.*" In *Jonson and Shakespeare,* ed. Ian Donaldson, 33–66. London and Canberra: Macmillan/ HRC, 1983.

Norris, Andrew, ed. *The Claims to Community: Essays on Stanley Cavell and Political Philosophy.* Stanford: Stanford University Press, 2006.

North, Marcy L. *The Anonymous Renaissance: Cultures of Discretion in Tudor-Stuart England.* Chicago: University of Chicago Press, 2003.

Novy, Marianne. *Engaging With Shakespeare: Responses of George Eliot and Other Women Writers.* Athens: University of Georgia Press, 1994.

———. *Love's Argument: Gender Relations in Shakespeare.* Chapel Hill: University of North Carolina Press, 1984.

———. *Reading Adoption: Family and Difference in Fiction and Drama.* Ann Arbor: University of Michigan, 2009.

Oberman, Heiko. "Facientibus quod in se est non denegat gratiam: Robert Holcot O.P., and the Beginnings of Luther's Theology." *Harvard Theological Review* 55 (1962): 317–42.

———. *Luther: Between God and the Devil.* Trans. Eileen Walliser-Schwarzbart. New York: Doubleday, 1989.

Orgel, Stephen. *The Illusion of Power: Political Theater in the English Renaissance.* Berkeley: University of California Press, 1975.

Osborne, Kenan B. *Reconciliation and Justification: The Sacrament and Its Theology.* New York: Paulist Press, 1990.

Palfrey, Simon. *Doing Shakespeare.* Padstow: Thomson, 2000.

Palmer, Lee Wandell. *The Eucharist in the Reformation: Incarnation and Liturgy.* Cambridge: Cambridge University Press, 2006.

Parker, Patricia. *Inescapable Romance: Studies in the Poetics of a Mode.* Princeton: Princeton University Press, 1979.

Paulson, Julie. "A Theater of the Soul's Interior: Contemplative Literature and Penitential Education in the Morality Play *Wisdom.*" *JMEMS* 38.2 (2008): 253–83.

Pearsall, Derek, ed. *Piers Plowman by William Langland: A New Annotated Edition of the C-Text.* Exeter: University of Exeter Press, 2008.

Pelikan, Jaroslav. *The Reformation of the Church, 1300–1700.* Chicago: University of Chicago Press, 1984.

Peter Lombard, *Sententiae in IV Libris Distinctae.* Ed. Ignatius Brady. 3rd ed. 2 vols. Grottaferrata: Editiones Collegii S. Bonaventura ad Claras Aquas, 1971 and 1981.

Porter, H. C. *Reformation and Reaction in Tudor Cambridge.* Cambridge: Cambridge University Press, 1958.

Questier, Michael. *Conversion, Politics, and Religion in England 1580–1625.* Cambridge: Cambridge University Press, 1996.

———. "Loyalty, Religion, and State Power in Early Modern England: English Romanism and the Jacobean Oath of Allegiance." *The Historical Journal* 40.2 (1997): 311–29.

Rappaport, Roy. *Ritual and Religion in the Making of Humanity.* Cambridge: Cambridge University Press, 1999.

Reinhard, Wolfgang. "Zwang zur Konfessionalisierung? Prologemena zu einer Theorie des konsessionellen Zeitalters." In *Zeitschrift für historische Forschung* 10 (1983): 257–77.

Rhu, Lawrence F. *Stanley Cavell's American Dream: Shakespeare, Philosophy, and Hollywood Movies.* New York: Fordham University Press, 2006.

Ricoeur, Paul. *The Course of Recognition.* Trans. David Pellauer. Cambridge: Harvard University Press, 2005.

Ridley, Nicholas. *The Works of Nicholas Ridley.* Ed. Rev. Henry Christmas. Cambridge: The University Press, 1941.

Robbins, William. "Romance, Exemplum, and the Subject of the *Confessio Amantis.*" *Studies in the Age of Chaucer* 19 (1997): 157–81.

Rogers, D. M., ed. *A Confutation of a Booke.* English Recusant Literature 1558–1640, vol. 310. Ilkley, Yorkshire: Scolar Press, 1976.

Rosendale, Timothy. *Liturgy and Literature in the Making of Protestant England.* Cambridge: Cambridge University Press, 2007.

Scase, Wendy. *Piers Plowman and the New Anti-Clericalism.* Cambridge: Cambridge University Press, 1989.

Schalwyck, David. *Speech and Performance in Shakespeare's Sonnets and Plays.* Cambridge: Cambridge University Press, 2002.

———. "Shakespeare's Speech." *JMEMS* 40.2 (Spring 2010): 373–400.

Schanzer, E. "The Marriage Contracts in *Measure for Measure.*" *Shakespeare Survey* 13 (1960): 81–89.

Schilling, Heinz. *Die Konfessionkonflict und Staatsbildung.* Gütersloh: Gütersloher Verlagshauser, 1981.

Schmidt, A.V.C., ed. *The Vision of Piers Plowman: A Critical Edition of the B-Text.* London: J. M. Dent, 1978.

Schroeder, H. J., ed. *Disciplinary Decrees of the General Councils: Text, Translation, and Commentary.* St. Louis: B. Herder, 1937.

Schwartz, Regina. *Sacramental Poetics at the Dawn of Secularism: When God Left the World.* Stanford: Stanford University Press, 2008.

Shaffern, Robert W. *The Penitent's Treasury: Indulgences in Latin Christendom, 1175–1375.* Scranton: University of Scranton Press, 2007.

Shagan, Ethan. "The English Inquisition: Constitutional Conflict and Ecclesiastical Law in the 1590s." *The Historical Journal* 47.3 (2004): 541–65.

Shakespeare, William. *The Norton Shakespeare.* Ed. Stephen Greenblatt. New York: W. W. Norton, 1997.

———. *The Riverside Shakespeare,* 2nd ed. Ed. David Bevington. Boston: Houghton Mifflin, 1997.

Shakespeare Behind Bars. DVD. Directed by Hank Rogerson. Los Angeles: Shout Factory, 2006.

Sharpe, James. "Last Dying Speeches: Religion, Ideology, and Public Execution in Seventeenth Century England." *Past and Present* 107 (1985): 144–67.

Shuger, Deborah. *Censorship and Cultural Sensibility: The Regulation of Language in Tudor-Stuart England.* Philadelphia: University of Pennsylvania Press, 2006.

———. "The Reformation of Penance." In *The Huntington Library Quarterly* 71.4 (2008): 557–71.

Simpson, James. "Diachronic History and the Shortcomings of Medieval Studies." In *Reading the Medieval in Early Modern England,* ed. David Matthews and Gordon McMullan, 17–30. Cambridge: Cambridge University Press, 2007.

———. *Piers Plowman: An Introduction.* 2nd ed. Exeter: University of Exeter Press, 2007.

Skinner, Quentin. *The Foundations of Modern Political Thought.* 3 vols. Vol. 2, *The Age of Reformation.* Cambridge: Cambridge University Press, 1978.

Smith, Wilfred Cantwell. *Believing: A Historical Perspective.* Oxford: One World, 1977.

Sokol, B. J. *Art and Illusion in The Winter's Tale*. Manchester: Manchester University Press, 1994.

Soyinka, Wole. *The Burden of Memory, the Muse of Forgiveness*. Oxford: Oxford University Press, 1999.

Speed Hill, W., ed. *The Folger Library Edition of the Works of Richard Hooker*. 7 vols. Cambridge: Harvard University Press, 1977–98.

Spenser, Edmund. *The Fairie Queene*. Ed. A. C. Hamilton. Padstow: Longman, 2001.

Spykman, Gordon J. *Attrition and Contrition at the Council of Trent*. Kampen: J. H. Kok, 1955.

Stachniewski, John. *The Persecutory Imagination: English Puritanism and the Literature of Religious Despair*. Oxford: Oxford University Press, 1991.

Steinmetz, David. *Luther in Context*. Grand Rapids, MI: Baker Academic, 2002.

——. "Reformation and Grace." In *Grace upon Grace: Essays in Honor of Thomas A. Langford,* ed. Robert K. Johnston, L. Gregory Jones, and Jonathan R. Wilson. Nashville: Abingdon Press, 1999.

Stevens, Martin, and A. C. Cawley, eds. *The Towneley Plays,* 2 vols. *EETS* s.s. 13. Oxford: Oxford University Press, 1994.

Szittya, Penn. *The Anti-Fraternal Tradition in Medieval Literature*. Cambridge: Cambridge University Press, 1989.

Tanner, Tony. *Adultery in the Novel: Contract and Transgression*. Baltimore: Johns Hopkins University Press, 1979.

Targoff, Ramie. *Common Prayer: The Language of Public Devotion in Early Modern England*. Chicago: University of Chicago Press, 2001.

Tavormina, Teresa. *Kindly Similitude: Marriage and Family in Piers Plowman*. Cambridge: D. S. Brewer, 1995.

Taylor, Gary, and Michael Warren, eds. *The Division of the Kingdoms: Shakespeare's Two Versions of King Lear*. Oxford: Clarendon Press, 1983.

Taylor, Gary, and Stanley Wells. *William Shakespeare: A Textual Companion*. New York: W. W. Norton, 1997.

Thomas Aquinas. *Summa Theologica*. Complete English edition. 5 vols. Trans. and ed. the English Dominican Province. Notre Dame, IN.: Ave Maria Press, 1984.

——. *Summa Theologiae*. 61 vols. Ed. Thomas Gilbey and T. C. O'Brien. London: Blackfriars, 1964–1973.

Tierney, Brian. "Canon Law and Institutions." In *Proceedings of the Seventh International Congress of Medieval Canon Law,* ed. Peter Lineham, 49–69. Vatican City: Bibliotheca Apostolica Vatican, 1988.

Todd, Margo. *The Culture of Protestantism in Early Modern Scotland*. New Haven: Yale University Press, 2002.

Tutu, Desmond. *No Future without Forgiveness*. New York: Doubleday, 1999.

Tyndale, William. *An Answer to Thomas More's Dialogue in Works of the English and Scottish Reformers*. Vol. 3. Ed. Thomas Russell. London: Ebenezer Palmer, 1828.

——. *The Obedience of a Christian Man*. Ed. David Daniell. London: Penguin, 2000.

Vallance, Edward. *Revolutionary England and the National Covenant: State Oaths, Protestantism and the Political Nation 1553–1682*. Woodbridge, Suffolk: Boydell Press, 2005.

Viefhues-Bailey, Ludger H. *Beyond the Philosopher's Fear: A Cavellian Reading of Gender, Origin, and Religion in Modern Skepticism*. London: Ashgate, 2007.

Weatherly, Edward, ed. *Speculum Sacerdotale. EETS* o.s. 200. London: Oxford University Press, 1936.

Weigel, Luther A. *The New Testament Octapla: Early English Versions of the New Testament in the Tyndale–King James Tradition*. Edinburgh: Thomas Nelson, 1946.

Wenzel, Siegfried, ed. *Fasciculus Morum: A Fourteenth Century Preacher's Handbook*. University Park: Pennsylvania State University Press, 1989.

Wetzel, James. "Wittgenstein's Augustine: The Inauguration of the Later Philosophy." *Polygraph: An International Journal of Culture and Politics* 19.20 (2008): 129–47.

Wheeler, Richard. "Acknowledging Shakespeare: Cavell and the Claim of the Human." In *The Senses of Stanley Cavell*, ed. Richard Fleming and Michael Payne, 132–60. Lewisburg, PA: Bucknell University Press, 1989.

Whitgift, John. *The Works of John Whitgift*. 3 vols. Ed. for the Parker Society by Rev. John Ayre. Cambridge: Cambridge University Press, 1853.

Williams, Rowan. "Imagining the Kingdom: Some Questions for Anglican Worship Today." In *The Identity of Anglican Worship*, ed. Kenneth Stevenson and Bryan Spinks, 1–13. London: Mowbray, 1991.

———. *Lost Icons: Reflections on Cultural Bereavement*. Edinburgh: T. & T. Clark, 2000.

———. *Resurrection: Interpreting the Easter Gospel*. Harrisburg, PA: Morehouse, 1982.

———. "The Suspicion of Suspicion: Wittgenstein and Bonhoeffer." In *The Grammar of the Heart: New Essays in Moral Philosophy and Theology*, ed. R. H. Bell, 36–53. San Francisco: Harper and Row, 1988.

Wiltenburg, Mary. "Shakespeare Behind Bars: Acting with Conviction." *Christian Science Monitor*. http://www.csmonitor.com/specials/shakespeare/index.html (accessed 8 September 2009).

Witte, John. *Law and Protestantism: The Legal Teachings of the Lutheran Reformation*. Cambridge: Cambridge University Press, 2002.

Wittgenstein, Ludwig. *On Certainty*. Ed. G.E.M. Anscombe and G. H. von Wright. New York: Harper and Row, 1969.

———. *Philosophical Investigations*. 2nd ed. Ed. G.E.M. Anscombe. Oxford: Blackwell, 1958.

Womack, Peter. *English Renaissance Drama*. Oxford: Blackwell, 2006.

Yates, Julian. *Error, Misuse, Failure: Object Lessons from the English Renaissance*. Minneapolis: University of Minnesota Press, 2002).

Zeeman, Nicolette. *Piers Plowman and the Medieval Discourse of Desire*. Cambridge: Cambridge University Press, 2006.

INDEX

CPSIA information can be obtained at www.ICGtesting.com
Printed in the USA
BVOW08s1757100813

328213BV00004B/40/P